THE GUILD™

A SOURCEBOOK OF AMERICAN CRAFT ARTISTS

Kraus Sikes Inc.
New York, New York

Published by:
Kraus Sikes Inc.

Chairman of the Board:
William M. Kraus

President:
Toni Fountain Sikes

Director of Information Services:
Gina Roose

Production Associate:
Gretchen Bailey Wohlgemuth

Office Manager:
Kevin O'Connor

Assistant to Production:
Lynne Reynolds

Sales Representatives:
Christilyn Biek
Catharine Hiersoux
Daniel Mack
Susan L. McLeod
Sylvia Haimoff White

Production Consultant:
Fiona L'Estrange

Book Design:
Waldbillig and Besteman, Inc.

Typesetting:
U.S. Lithograph, typographers

Color Separation, Printing and Binding:
Dai Nippon Printing Co. Ltd., Tokyo, Japan

TABLE OF CONTENTS

Introduction

One year ago we introduced THE GUILD as a new concept in the marketing of the crafts. Its purpose was to connect craft artists to designers and architects in an organized and efficient way.

In a world where dreams seldom come true, it has been gratifying to watch as design professionals have become aware of the possibilities, the alternatives provided by the crafts field. Indeed, we can now say with assurance and pride that the dream is a reality. THE GUILD is working. It works for the artists, the interior designers, the architects—for anyone and everyone who is in or interested in the crafts.

And so we proudly present THE GUILD 1987.

This new edition is bigger—the work of 319 artists is on display here. This new edition is better—the quality and sophistication of the photographs speak for themselves. And this new edition has more sections which are both better organized and more useful to design professionals.

The sections in the front of THE GUILD are devoted to objects. The middle sections are filled with larger interior items. And the back of the book consists of new sections which display work that is integral to the structure of a building.

The work in this book is created by a select group of artists. They deal as professionals with professionals. Not only do they provide designers and architects with a multiple of skills in a variety of media, but each artist is also a designer in his or her own right, adept at finding beautiful and functional solutions to design problems. Many also invite collaborations on design projects. All do individual commissions and work with designers and architects in the creation of interior or exterior spaces.

The work in this book is beautiful, stimulating, artistically gratifying. It delights the eye and pleases the senses. It is not for everyone, but it is for everyone who has a passion for excellence.

And it is a pleasure to report that the people who have that passion are finding THE GUILD an essential tool with which to discover the world of the crafts. Open the book...enter...and enjoy.

William M. Kraus
Toni Fountain Sikes

LIGHTING

Harry Anderson

6805 N. 12th Street
Philadelphia, PA 19126
(215) 548-8074

Harry Anderson is an artists who makes lamp assemblages. He combines found objects, neon, and blown glass to create one of a kind sculptures that often suggest a human form. The "Stickman Series" are running or standing figures. They are whimsical in form as well as in the relationship of materials. In "Dyna" garden hose is used along with glass, iron and brass to imply the gesture of a posed dancer.

"Running With a Bright Idea" is the title of a recent solo exhibition at The Gallery of Applied Arts in New York City. He has also exhibited at the Red Studio in New York, Functional Art, in Los Angeles, Helander Gallery in Palm Beach, Florida and at Henri, Washington, D.C. Anderson also does much commission work and custom designed lighting installations.

Curtis and Suzan Benzlé

Benzle Porcelain Co.
6100 Hayden Run Road
Hilliard, OH 43026
(614) 876-5237

Illumination as accessory

Quality transluscent porcelain captures light and shadow to define space. Individually designed in consideration of your color and size specifications. Ideal for conference areas, offices, in home and any interior environment where ambient lighting supports or replaces natural light.

Created by Curtis and Suzan Benzle. The Benzles have been honored with representation in such distinctive collections as the Smithsonian Institution, Museo Internazionale Delle Ceramiche, Italy; Cleveland Museum of Art and the Illinois State Museum. Work by the Benzles has been featured in more than twenty national and international publications, including American Craft, Metropolitan Home and Craft-Arts, Australia.

Fashioned for long life in translucent porcelain; framed in aluminum; plexiglass core. Please allow three weeks for delivery of in-stock items; custom work delivery varies by project.

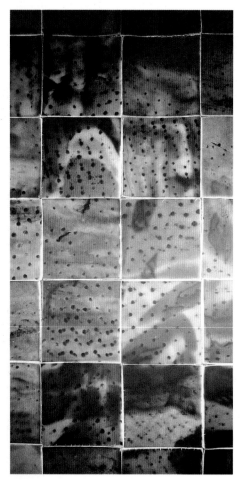

Anthony Beverly

Woodenworks
P.O. Box 229
Stephentown, NY 12168
(518) 733-6095

Anthony Beverly designs and produces furniture in a variety of exotic and domestic hardwoods.

The lamp shown is zebrawood, purple heart and madrone burl with a spun aluminum globe and 500 watt halogen fixture.

18″ × 18″ × 76″ 1,200.00

Noel F. Hilliard
Janene A. Hilliard

Lamps By Hilliard
886 'A' Street
Arcata, CA 95521
(707) 822-4361

Represented to the design trade by
KNEEDLER-FAUCHERE; Los Angeles, San Francisco, Denver, Seattle.

Heat formed glass, cast bronze, and innovative ideas set Hilliard Lamps apart.

The twisted glass louvers shown here in the Wall Fan and Umbrella Floor Lamp represent only one of their many unusual and exciting new ideas.

(top) Wall Fan; Ceramic base, color variations available. Small 14" wide, 12" height, 8" deep. Medium 20" wide, 10" height, 10" deep. (Pictured) Large 27" wide, 13" height, 12" deep.
(bottom) Umbrella Floor Lamp, solid cast bronze base, three-way/lighted floor section, 22" diameter, 60" height.

Ray King

603 S. 10th Street
Philadelphia, PA 19147-1917
(215) 627-5112

Site-specific sculptures in metals, glass, and light—suspended and wall-mounted—for interior and exterior sites. Chandeliers, sconces, lamps, and lighting. Stained glass windows.

(left) <u>Constellation</u> - Cluster of color anodized aluminum forms, some inset with crystal prisms or lenses, suspended in multistory space (40'h × 32'w × 25'd). Exhibition, Royal Institute of British Architects, London, 1986.

(top) <u>U.F.O. Chandelier</u> - Gray body, red fins, turquoise and yellow trim in anodized aluminum with etched optical glass fins and ring (1'-6"h × 4'0"w × 6'-0"d). 1986

(bottom) <u>Jenkintown Station</u> - Cone chandeliers in gold anodized aluminum inset with crystal lenses and concentric ½" laminated glass rings (7'-2" diam. × 3'h). Window in etched and leaded stained glass, steel frame (5'-7"h × 9'6"w). Pyramid lamps in gold and turquoise anodized aluminum; slumped and etched glass shade (18" sq. × 13"h). 1986.

Dennis Luedeman

1673 8th Street
Oakland, CA 94607
(415) 835-5109

Hatley Martin Gallery
41 Powell Street
San Francisco, CA 94102
(415) 392-1015

Dennis Luedeman creates unique, one-of-a-kind and limited edition sculpture, furniture, and lamps. Each piece is made by the artist, signed, dated, and/or numbered. He has exhibited in museums, galleries, and academic institutions across the country. His recent shows in San Francisco have received excellent reviews in the San Francisco Chronicle.

"Space Lamp," 36" × 18" dia., forged and fabricated steel, glass

Floor Lamps, 8' × 18" × 18", fabricated steel, glass shade
Coffee Table, 3' × 4' × 17", forged and fabricated steel, glass top

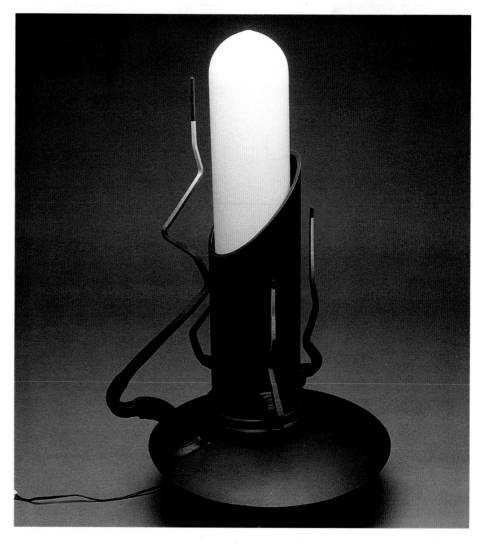

Mark McDonnell

Architectural Glass & Lighting
12 Rhode Island Avenue
Providence, RI 02906
(401) 331-2958

McDonnell designs and fabricates both utopian and site-specific lighting devices. Materials currently used are glass, marble, granite, gold leaf, spun metal and wood with acrylic enamel paint. Lamps are equipped with incandescent or quartz halogen sockets. Lamps are available in pairs and small editions, and are priced in the $3,000 to $6,000 range.

McDonnell's work is collected internationally and can be seen in the Musée des Arts Décoratifs, Paris; The Corning Museum of Glass, New York; Haaretz Museum, Tel Aviv. He has been published in Vogue, Art in America, American Craft and in various books on lighting. He has also received numerous grants, awards and commissions.

Torch lamp 70"H; Wall sconces 37"H; Table lamp 27"H.

Rick Melby

Architectural Arts
1812 N. 15th Street
Tampa, FL 33605
(813) 248-1899

Rick Melby has been designing and fabricating leaded glass for ten years. He currently specializes in unique lighting and light sculpture, both decorative and functional. Distinctive in design, they incorporate etched, hand-blown, textured, and opalescent glass to create engaging optical effects from all sides. One-of-a-kind pieces and limited editions are available.

Melby's work includes etched and leaded glass for all architectural applications. He emphasizes original design and quality craftsmanship, seeking to satisfy the aesthetic and functional requirements of each commission. High quality glass, divers metals, and an intensive attention to detail combine synergetically to offer the discerning client a visually stimulating alternative in handcrafted glasswork.

Call or write for more information.

(top) 13"H × 13"L × 5"W
(bottom) 17"H × 12"L × 4"W

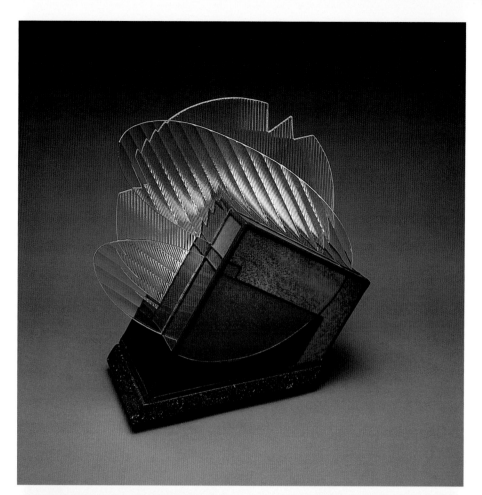

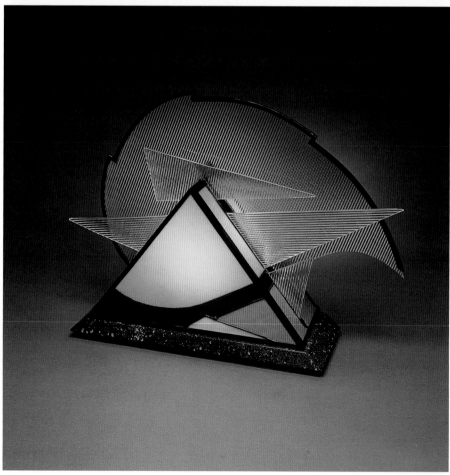

Benjamin Moore

Benjamin Moore Inc.
1213 South King Street
Seattle, WA 98144
(206) 329-8607

Benjamin Moore Inc. is a design studio and production factory specializing in hand-blown glass for contemporary architectural settings. This unique production situation provides architects and designers with a domestic source for specialty lighting and decorative objects. Collaborating with designers, Moore creates custom lighting fixtures suitable for hotels, restaurants, and corporate settings. Production lines of decorative vessels are also manufactured and wholesaled to fine department stores. Finally, Moore's innovative design approach finds expression in one-of-a-kind pieces which are exhibited in galleries throughout the United States.

(top) Alabaster Hornet, pendant lighting fixture (15"H × 15"Dia.) Commissioned for 'Lola' restaurant, New York City. Collection of Corning Museum of Glass.
(bottom right) Interior Fold Series, exhibition platter (27"Dia) and vase (8½"H × 14" Dia.)
(bottom left) Crystal Column Series (max. 18" H × 7"W). Selected for the 1986 Corning new glass review.

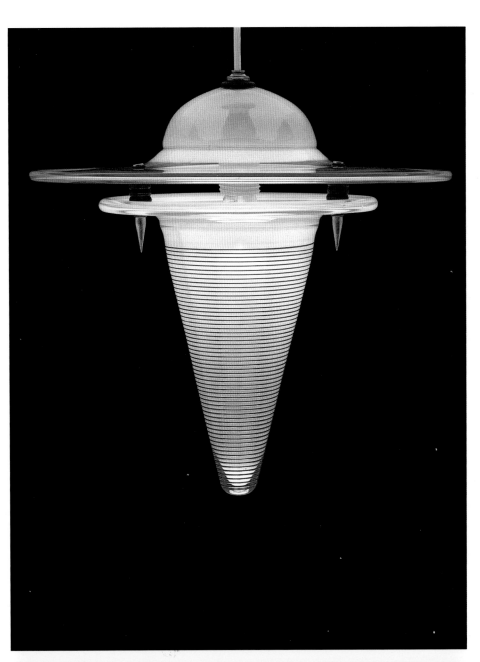

Dennis Laine Peabody

84 Barker Street
Hartford, CT 06114
(203) 525-8811

Dennis's work reflects innovative and contemporary ideas. Diverse elements from regular geometric patterns to spontaneous organic forms are evident in both lamp shade and stained glass panel designs. Light rendering materials such as minerals and prisms are often incorporated into works. Windows include both installed and portable hanging panels.

One-of-a-kind works are produced in limited amounts while interactive design and color selection will be arranged for production pieces. Please call or write for further information.

(top left) 30" × 42" "SEASCAPE" Free-hanging panel
(top right) 24" dia. shade in pinks from above
(bottom) 3 shades - 12 panel braid design - wide torch table lamp (smooth edge) - narrow torch table lamp (scalloped edge)

Pinkwater Glass

RD10 Church Hill Rd.
Carmel, NY 10512
(914) 225-1057

Lisa Schwartz and Kurt Swanson established Pinkwater Glass after receiving their masters degrees in 3-D design and glass in 1983. Working collaboratively, they combined both of their senses of design, humor and skills to create glasswork that is truly original.

Schwartz and Swanson specialize in high quality production pieces, one-of-a-kind sculptural pieces and innovative lighting and lamps.

Pinkwater Glass is not limited to blown glass; many pieces incorporate cast glass techniques and mixed media.

Schwartz and Swanson's work has been shown nationally and has been recently featured in many publications including the "Home Section" of the New York Times, and Metropolitan Home magazine.

Pinkwater Glass accepts both orders for their production line and one-of-a-kind commission pieces.

Brochure available upon request.

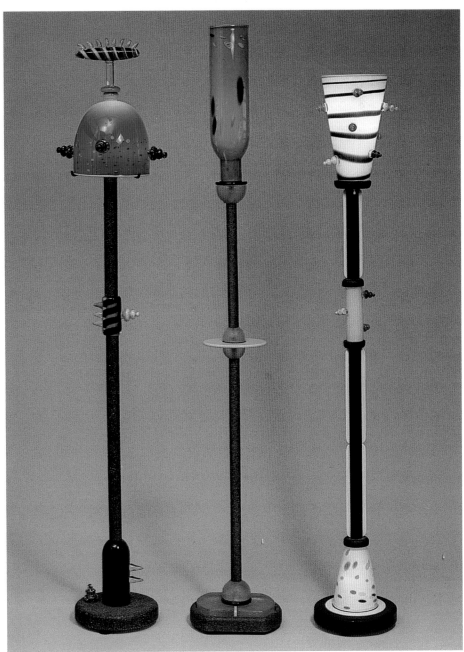

Roger Roberge

Box 31
Topsham, VT 05076
(802) 439-5734

Roger Roberge specializes in functional porcelain and stoneware with calm, natural elegant designs. The examples shown can be ordered as a table lamp or vase. Each piece is made individually in sizes to your specification. Pairs must be ordered at the same time. A variety of functional kitchen and table ware is also available. Brochure on request.

(top right) Lamp with underglaze design on porcelain, the shade is painted textile dye on cotton and has been Scotch Guarded. Total height: 18"
(top left) Stoneware vase, height: 9½"
(bottom) Porcelain with incised designs under pale blue or pale green glaze. Tallest shown height: 13"

James Thomas

Thomas Sculpture Studio
1237 East Main Street
Rochester, NY 14609

Thomas creates beautiful interior light sculptures that radiate atmospheric light and color. These finely crafted constructions in acrylic plastic, flourescent light and color emphasize the sensuality of organic growth and the logic of geometric order. The transparency of material and form and the subtle use of color enable the sculptures to blend harmoniously with varied interior environments both residential and corporate.

The artist produces a variety of concepts, including wall reliefs, pedestal supported works and free standing sculptures. Individual sculptures are available but the artist would accept moderately scaled commissions designed for specific environments. A slide folio is available upon request.

(right) "Rising Ambience" 14¼" D. × 38"H.
(bottom) " Column of Blue Silence" 12" D. × 36"H.

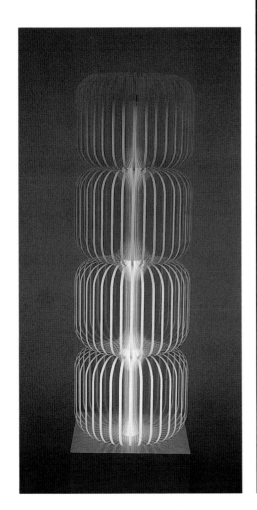

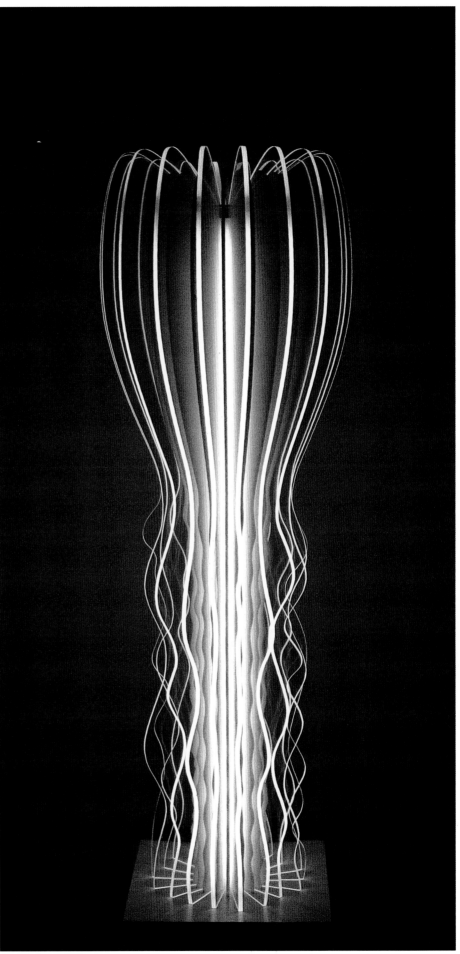

VESSELS AND BASKETS

Lynne Alexander

1719 Trosper Road
Greensboro, NC 27405
(919) 288-3017

Lynne Alexander creates one-of-a-kind and limited edition porcelains. Her forms are noted for their sculpted edges, simplicity, and elegance. Each piece is wheel-thrown and glazed in a range of neutrals and soft pastels including rose, apricot, blue, and turquoise. Shapes include large vases, jars, bowls, and platters and are suitable for both residential and corporate interiors.

The artist's award-winning work has been exhibited nationally and is represented in numerous private and corporate collections, including Arthur Andersen & Co., NCNB National Bank, Philip Morris Inc., and R.J. Reynolds Industries. Inquiries and commissions are welcomed. Resumé, list of private collections, and price list are available upon request.

(top right) vase, 13"H × 10"W
(bottom) vases, approx. 7" × 13"H
(bottom right) platter, 18" in diameter

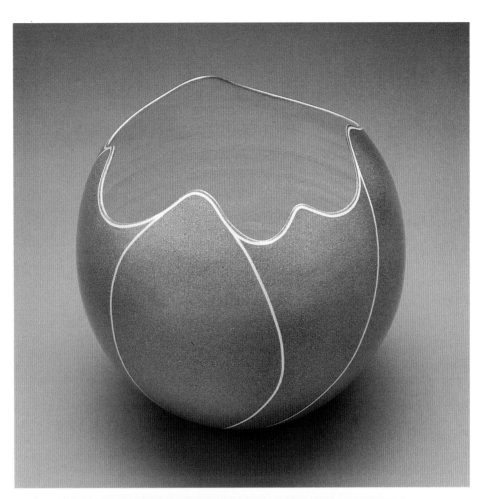

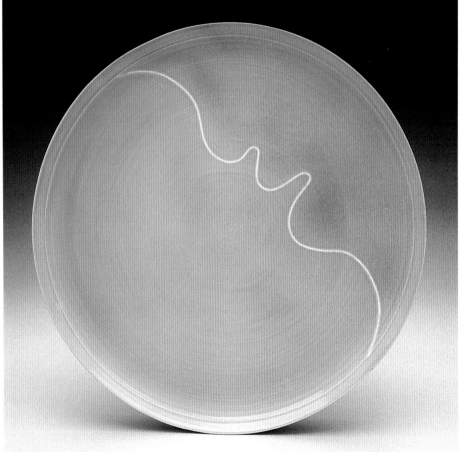

Wesley Anderegg

4242 N. 19th Place
Phoenix, AZ 85016
(602) 274-7682

Wesley Anderegg has been perfecting his Raku firing process for the past five years. Through this process he achieves the unique coloration distinctive to each piece. His pieces have been exhibited across the country at national juried craft fairs and galleries. Additional information available upon request.

(top) Cut Bowl 9" x 14"
(bottom) Raku Vessel 12" × 12"

Michael Bailot

P.O. Box 31007
Santa Barbara, CA 93130
(805) 964-2735

I produce one of a kind sculptural basket forms in a wide variety of natural plant fibers, with careful attention to detail, construction, and durability. My work encompasses a broad range of original design concepts, employs a complete color palette, and is in a scale from table top pieces to larger architectural works.

My baskets are shown nationally in major fiber exhibitions and in many fine galleries and have received a number of awards.

I am primarily interested in creating commissioned pieces.

(top) "Pathway to Wigigi" Date Palm, inflorescens, dyed and laminated hardwood. 8"D x 38" H
(bottom) "Telluride!": Dyed palm inflorescens, peppergrass, lichen, broomcorn, sisel. 10" × 14".

Steven Branfman

The Potters Shop
Lasell Jr. College (studio in Carter Hall)
1844 Commonwealth Avenue
Newton, MA. 02166
(617) 965-3959

Steven works in the Raku technique producing one-of-a-kind wheel-thrown pieces. His vessels display carved and textured surfaces with multi-layers of glaze including gold, silver and copper lusters as well as subtle tones of brown, grey and black. Steve's pieces range in size from small shapes to floor pieces over 35" high and 24" in diameter.

Since receiving his Masters with honors from Rhode Island School of Design, Steven has had over 50 select solo and group shows and has appeared in American Craft, The Crafts Report, Folio, Ceramics Monthly and The Boston Globe among others. His work is in collections across the U.S.

Commissions and special orders are welcome. A variety of work is available from inventory.

(Top, left to right) Lamp 13"H w/o shade, Urn 18"Hx14"D, Bowl 12"Hx16"D
(Bottom left) Bowl 11"Hx16"D
(Bottom right) Vase 31"Hx12"D

Robert E. Carlson & Marilee Hall

Primus Studio
RR2 Box 138N
Princeton, WI 54968
(414) 295-6032

Carlson and Hall have collaborated for nine years to produce fine art pottery, sculptural forms, wall constructions and major architectural pieces.

With clay as a base material, the works are raku fired. They receive post-firing embellishment, or are otherwise combined with, nonceramic materials, including 23K gold leaf; inks; enamel, acrylic and latex paints; pastels; Prismacolor pencils; metal screens and acrylics.

Their work is available from designers, showrooms and galleries throughout the U.S. Inquiries and commissions are welcomed. Resumé and slides depicting additional work are available upon request.

(top) "A Man and a Woman," 27" × 27" (bottom, left to right) MV Vessel, 9" dia × 14" ht; # One Vessel, 14" dia × 26" ht; Tulip Form, 9" dia × 14" ht

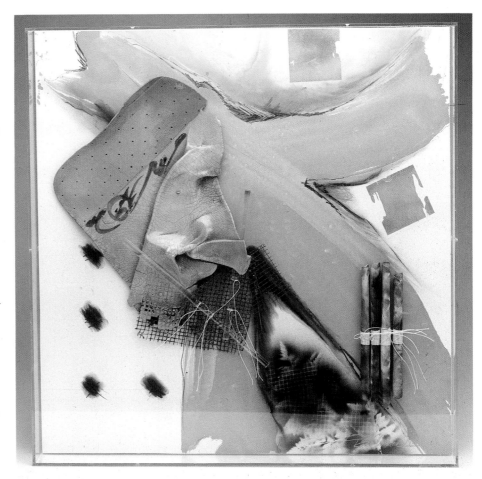

Kathleen Cerveny

Cervenova Studios
7714 St. Clair Avenue
Cleveland, OH 44103
(216) 881-2353

Kathleen Cerveny is a ceramic artist whose work has been exhibited widely throughout the United States.

Her vessels reflect an oriental aesthetic. Sawdust-fired stoneware vessels are classically shaped, handbuilt forms with subtle surface decoration. Covered vessels are bound with natural fibers. Ms. Cerveny's AI-ZAN (love of mountains) series are meditative works, incorporating found objects, stones and water.

Recent major exhibitions: CERAMICS BY SEVEN, a two year traveling exhibition of seven Ohio ceramic artists, chosen by Doug Heller. Exhibition was sponsored by Ohio Designer/Craftsmen and the Ohio Foundation on the Arts.

CERVENOVA (Cher' ve no' va) is the old world, feminine form of Ms. Cerveny's surname. In translation—the color red.

Jean Cohen

6104 Eastcliff Dr.
Baltimore, MD 21209
(301) 367-0488

Jean Cohen has been designing and producing porcelain pieces professionally for 8 years. The work is traditional in nature with special attention to simplification of form.

The pieces are large wheel-thrown porcelain with cut edges and applied designs. They are spray-glazed and gas fired to 2300° making them completely waterproof and functional. The bowls average 5"Hx14"W, the plates average 3"Hx16"W and the vases average 10"Hx5"W. Other forms are also available as well as other colors. The retail prices range from $30 to $150.

Some of the galleries currently featuring her work are the American Hand in Washington, D.C. and Incorporated Gallery in New York. She has also been juried into the ACC Craft Fair in Baltimore for the past six years and the Washington Craft Show for the past three years.

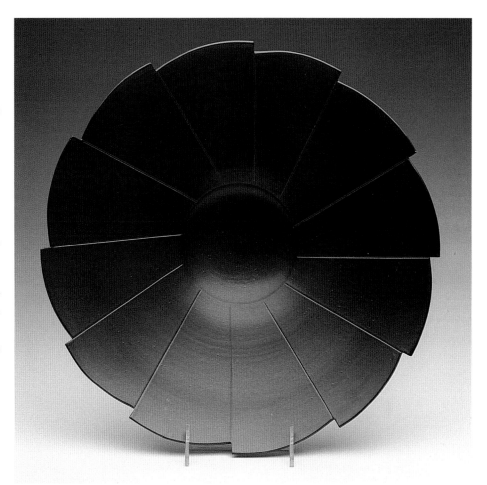

Brian Dougan

Small Axe Productions
RR #2 Box 8
Hope Valley, RI 02832
(401) 596-6241

Educated in architecture, Brian Dougan has been producing fine crafts since 1980. His baskets are primarily made of newspapers and personally harvested native vines and plants. Colors originate from advertisments, comics and various newspaper supplements. Each piece is dealt with individually, becoming a suprisingly strong, functional, one-of-a-kind basket. Handle size and shape, color and texture of newsprint, depth, width, and height is therefore different on each finished basket. Additional techniques, applications and materials, both natural and synthetic, are also used depending on desired results.

More information and prices are available upon request.

(top) detail of multicolored newspaper basket.
(bottom) predominantly pink newspaper and bittersweet vine basket. 16" diameter.

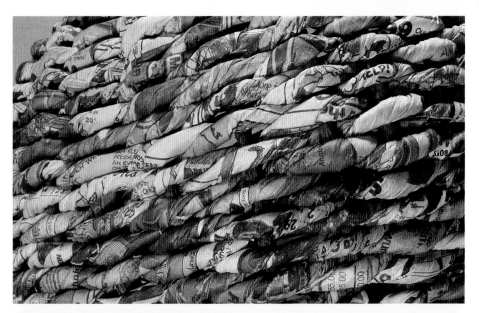

Maggie Furman

1013 Poplar Hill Road
Baltimore, MD 21210
(301) 433-3595

Maggie Furman hand builds large decorative pots in low-fire clay. Their unique surface patterns result from the use of stained clay bodies and a coil-building technique that "weaves" the clay into the desired form. They are then burnished, fired and waxed to a shiny patina. Many different shapes and color combinations can be created, as well as sizes, ranging from 8 inches high to 25 inches high. These one-of-a- kind pieces start at $100 wholesale.

Maggie has an MFA in Ceramics from George Washington University, Washington, D.C., and has been professionally involved in ceramics for ten years.

Galleries currently showing Maggie's work are Gallery 500, Philadelphia; Opus II, New York City; Kornbluth Gallery, Fairlawn, New Jersey; Carlin, Ltd., Design Center, Washington, D.C., and Mirage Collectable, Miami.

Also in the collections of The National Museum for Women in the Arts, Washington, D.C.; and CIGNA Corporation, Philadelphia, Pa.

Anne Goldman

1972 Meadow Road
Walnut Creek, CA 94595
(415) 935-4165

Working with high fired ceramics, Anne Goldman carves deep textures into her vessels. The unique surfaces and powerful forms are inspired by nature, making her work suitable for indoor and outdoor locations.

Her pieces are either one-of-a-kind or limited editions and can be used in residential and corporate installations. Artwork can be custom-designed to fit a specific space.

Ms. Goldman's work is displayed in galleries, interior design showrooms and private collections throughout the United States. She has had numerous one-woman museum exhibits, and has participated in many national juried and invitational shows.

(left) Sea Erosion Vessel, 30"H × 12"D
(right) Coastal Rock Vessel, 33"H × 12"D

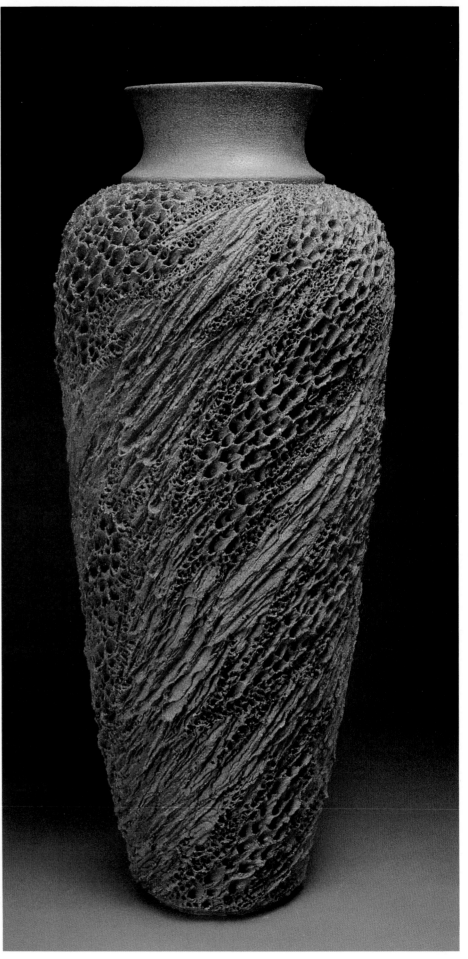

Anne Goldman
1972 Meadow Road
Walnut Creek, CA 94595
(415) 935-4165

(top left) Tree Bark Planter, 16″ × 17″W
(top right) Tide Pool Vessel, 10″H × 17″D
(bottom) Left-Pitted Rock, 9″H × 16″D
right Carved Porcelain, 10″H × 17″D

Ilena Grayson

Represented by
Conway Art Consultants and Gallery
1501 Mountain Road NW
Albuquerque, NM 87104
(505) 843-6931

A contemporary southwestern style is exemplified in these vessel-oriented sculptural forms. Using few tools and primitive construction techniques, they are handbuilt from slabs and coils of a red earthenware clay. The organic shapes evolve during construction, reflecting the influence of gourds and rock formations; the surface is burnished to a smooth satin finish. Each piece is fired at a low temperature, giving maximum strength, but remaining porous enough to accept the carbon from the smoke firing which "paints" the surface with ghostly clouds. The final decorative step is the application of metal leafing after which the surface is sealed. Slight variations in each piece should be expected due to the handcrafted nature of the work. These vessls complement both commercial and residential environments. A portfolio is available upon request.

Hedgerow Fiberworks

Brent Brown/Dave Davis
P.O. Box 20542
Crest, CA 92021
(619) 579-0773

Honeysuckle, willow and palm inflorescence are combined to create the sculptural basketry of Hedgerow Fiberworks.

Gestural forms, rough in texture yet finely executed, these elemental sculptures are designed with structural integrity and durability in mind. A preservative is applied for added protection.

Although one-of-a-kind work is emphasized, a few production pieces are available. Pieces may be custom designed for private, corporate and architectural settings.

A photo set of 10-12 currently available pieces can be sent when $10.00 is received with initial inquiry. The $10.00 will be deducted from the first order.

(top right) "Arch,", 20″ × 18″ × 8″, $80.00 (retail)
(top left) Coil work, $65.00 - $300.00 (retail)
(bottom left) "Santa Fe", 46″ × 30″ × 10″
(bottom right) "Untitled", 24″ × 28″ × 20″

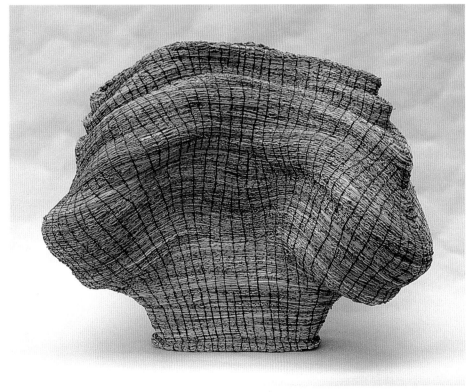

Catharine Hiersoux

437 Colusa Avenue
Berkeley, CA 94707
(415) 524-8005

Fine contemporary porcelain

These pieces represent a range of porcelain work including large plates, bowls and classical vase forms

Catherine Hiersoux has exhibited nationally and is represented in major collections including: The Renwick Gallery, Smithsonian Institution, American Craft Museum, Everson Museum, The White House, Washington, D.C.

(top) Porcelain Plate 18" diam.
Collection American Craft Museum
(bottom) "New Beginnings" porcelain bowl 16" diam.

Mark Hines

Mark Hines Company
724 N. Lake Street
Burbank, CA 91502
(818) 845-9251
(800) 423-3622

Mark Hines is an artist specializing in design and limited production of ceramic art featuring a variety of wheelthrown and sculpted forms (some as large as 48 in.).

Mark is best known for his glaze finishes which include celadon, dry matte, gold luster, primitive pit fire, and RAKU which is pictured below. In this 16th century Japanese glazing technique, each piece is fired individually to a bright yellow temperature and removed with tongs; then placed in a can of leaves where the unpredictable combination of smoke, fire and air make the copper in the glaze react in such colorful ways.

Mark Hines ceramics have been featured in numerous galleries and expositions, used on movie and TV shows and available thru Bloomingdales.

Tom Krueger

3289 Bay Settlement Road
Green Bay, WI 54301
(414) 468-5134

Krueger strives to bring out the natural "beauty" of clay in a simple form. The artist creates panoramas of his environments, finding inspiration in an eclectic range of experiences and ideas. He incorporates both geometric and organic images in a consistent landscape theme.

His lowfire salt process has evolved from various firing techniques, resulting in the striking array of soft, yet deep, pastel colors and images displayed in his present work.

Krueger's work is available in contemporary galleries and selected art fairs throughout the U.S. Studio visits by appointment.

(top) Landscape Vase, 12"H × 14"W
(bottom) Landscape Vase, 18"H × 16"W

Washington Ledesma

Tranquil Hands
Box 101 Star Route
Milanville, PA 18443
(717) 729-7577

Washington Ledesma's work in clay is known for its unique technique and designs that transcend time with mesmerizing colorful animals and human creatures which touch our oneness with nature. Every work is one of a kind. Underglazes, sgraffito and clear glazes encompass the surface treatment of terracotta clay wheel thrown or handbuilt tiles, sculptures and large vases. Special commissions accepted.

(top) Rectangular Platter. 21" × 17" Earthenware clay. Underglazes, sgraffito and clear glaze.
(bottom) Vase. 29"H × 10"W Earthenware clay underglazes and sgraffito

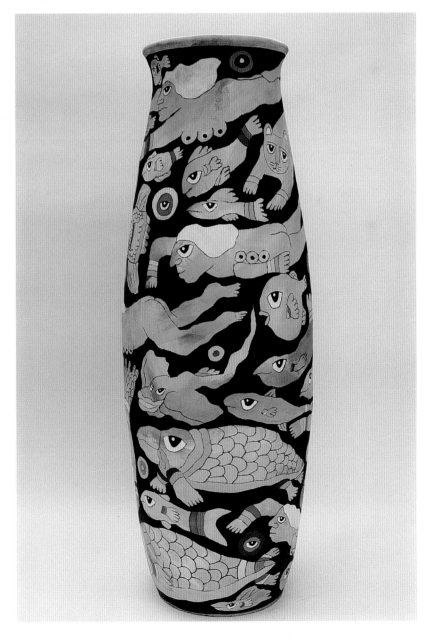

Susan Levin

Ceramic Vessels
512 Kings Highway W.
Haddonfield, NJ 08033
(609) 428-4583

Susan Levin's work returns stoneware to its most basic and enduring elements. Whatever the final form, these pieces reflect the timeless structure of the earth, as well as the rhythm of life inherent in all of us. Each piece is made with a specific theme. Size depends on interpretation and function.

Each vessel is placed on a pedestal to provide initial visual impact, with further personal consideration as to the visual height and lighting required for display. Pieces can be commissioned or chosen from an existing portfolio.

(top) "Black Orpheus" Total height 21½" × 20½" × 20¾" w/ pedestal
(bottom) "Octopus Vessel" Total height 32"h w/pedestal 19" d.

Susan Livingston

241 23rd Avenue N
St. Petersburg, FL 33704
(813) 898-2746

Susan Livingston has been working with coil/handbuilt clay for twelve years. She has an M.F.A. in painting and is self taught in clay. Her work exhibits strong classical form and contemporary imagery. The technique of using different kinds of stoneware clays together has been her signature. The introduction of colored clays and more recently, slips, are exhibited in these works.

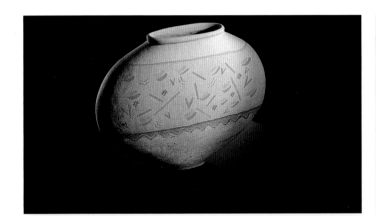

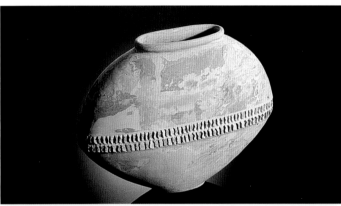

Gary McCloy

Gary McCloy Ceramic Design
2630 Hollyridge Drive
Hollywood, CA 90068
(213) 467-6844

Gary McCloy has been professionally involved in designing and making ceramic vessels for more than twenty years. His specialty is a richly glazed surface, set off by a simple, classically-inspired shape. Each vessel may go through as many as fifteen separate firings of underglaze, slip, glaze, overglaze, luster and enamel to capture all the best elements of each. All work is hand thrown on the potters wheel; each is one-of-a-kind, signed and copyrighted.

McCloy specializes in custom vessels for residential and commercial interiors. A few recent commissions have included vessels for major hotels in Singapore, Melbourne, Hong Kong, Tokyo, Honolulu, San Francisco, Los Angeles, Tucson, Las Vegas, Chicago, Atlantic City.

His ceramics have been shown in Architectural Digest, Metropolitan Home, Interior Design, Design Specifier, Better Homes and Gardens, Los Angeles, and Home Magazines.

(top) Hat Jar, Multiple firings 16W x 18H
(bottom) Hat Jar, Multiple firings 16W x 18H

Carol McFarlan

P.O. Box 692
Mednales, New Mexico 87548
(505)685-4331

Wheel thrown porcelain clay vessels, individually decorated or sculpted. Vases, covered containers, bowls and platters and either surface decorated with abstract designs (as shown), using a combination of colored clay slips, sgraffito and glazes; or they are altered by paddling to create asymmetry, and cut to show the interior. Slap pieces are sometimes added to suggest handles. Glazes are in earth tones, blue/greens or black. The platters pictured here are 16" in diameter and can be made 22" in diameter. Portfolio available upon request.

Greg Miller

Fine Clay
5668 Monches Road
Colgate, WI 53017
(414) 628-2261

Specializing in large decorative vessels and sculptural forms, Greg employs a wide variety of techniques.

Shown here are examples of Miller's sagger-fired earthenware. The vessel forms are air brushed with terra sigilatta and individually fired in clay saggers.

Greg's work has been featured in national and international shows and can be viewed in numerous corporate settings and fine homes around the country.

Grouping, left to right: amphora; 14" Diam. × 24" H; cradled covered jar, 8" Diam. × 18" H.; handled jar, 8" Diam. × 18" H; round jar, 13" Diam., urn; 14" Diam. × 24" H. Technique; terra sigilatta on earthenware, saggerfired.

(bottom) Standing amphora, 14 ½ Diam. × 35" H. Technique; Terra sigilatta on earthenware, sagger-fired.

Kathleen O'Brien

1014 Dorothea Drive
Raleigh, NC 27603
(919) 828-9919

Kathleen O'Brien's vessels are made with porcelain which has been hand mixed and colored with ceramic pigments. This technique gives the work an unusual depth of color and composition. The designs may go all the way through the piece or may be inlaid or pressed into the surface. These vessels are done in small limited editions and start at $140. Portfolios are available for viewing by request.

(top) "Chlorine Stripes", design similar on reverse, 9½ inches on square plate.

(bottom) "Chards", surface is inlaid and reverse is white, 10 inches in diameter plate.

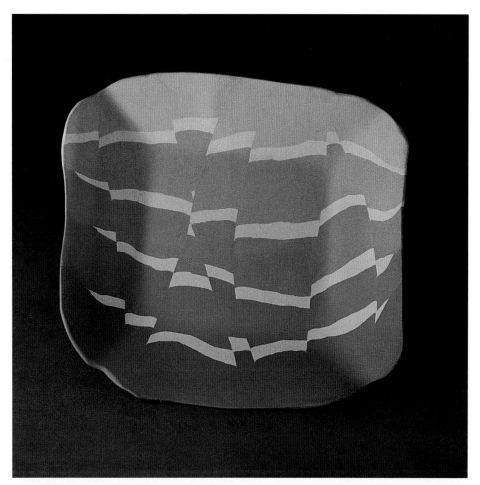

Mollie Poupeney

Cave Canon Design
21 Francisca Drive
Moraga, CA 94556
(415) 376-3401

Mollie Poupeney's burnished coilbuilt pottery reflects 30 years of excitement, experience and excellence. She presents a variety of elegant, colored forms constructed by coiling and polishing with a stone several times before firing. Finger marks and the subtle impressions of the polishing stone give each earthenware piece its distinctive character. Firemarkings dramatize the tradition of ancient low-fire pottery that inspires her work. Her articles on the primitive process have appeared in Ceramic Monthly. Her work is included in many private and corporate collections in the United States and Near East.

Studio visits and commissions welcomed.

(left) Shell Pink 10½" × 6½"
Red 10" × 10½"
(right)
Fireburned Black 10½" × 9"
Seafoam Blue 11" × 6"
Leatherbound Jar 12" × 10"
(bottom) Meditation Bowl 7" × 6"
Red and Grey 15" × 15"
Effigy 11" × 7"
Reconstructed Red 10½" × 11"

Richard Schneider

Represented by
Sylvia Ullman American Crafts Gallery
13010 Woodland Avenue
Cleveland, OH 44120
(216) 231-2008

Richard uses universal symbols inspired by such past civilizations as the Egyptians, Greeks, Africans, and American Indians. For this reason, he chooses to work in terra cotta clay, incorporating warm, bright colors. Each piece is unique and hand made, specifically designed to compliment both residential and corporate settings.

His body of work encompasses diptychs, triptychs and other multiple series for the wall, as well as vessel forms that may incorporate handles and legs. Shapes range both horizontally and vertically and also in scale from small to very large.

Exhibits: Utah Museum of Fine Art, Butler Museum of American Art, National Gallery shows. Publications: Ceramics Monthly , Sept. 1976, Oct. 1982, Feb. 1986.

Commissions invited; slides available.

(top) "Carnival Basket", terra cotta, 28" h × 8" d × 8" w
(bottom) Four Plates (prepared for wall terra cotta clay, 20" di. × 3"-5" dp.

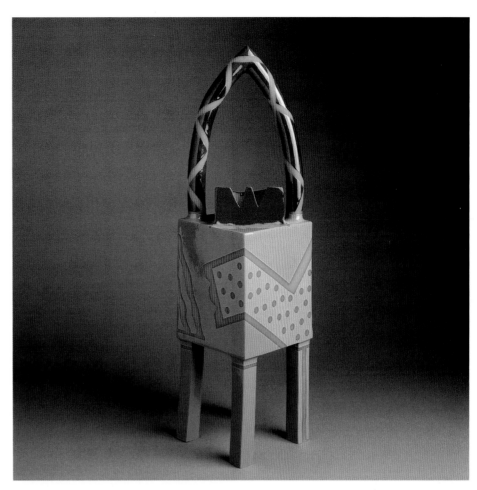

SCULPTURAL OBJECTS

Peter Bramhall

Box 163,
Bridgewater Center Road
Bridgewater, VT 05034
(802) 672-5141

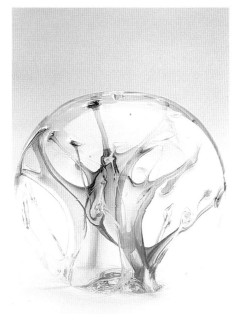

Known for his glass sculpture, "INTERIORS", (below) Peter Bramhall is one of the few glass artists working large. He creates both functional and non-functional pieces 9" × 30" hwd in size. Suitable for corporate buildings, traditional and contemporary homes, work is available in color and size ranges to meet the needs of your client. "Perhaps the most exciting object was a resolutely non-functional piece of glass by Peter Bramhall. A globular form about a foot in diameter, it is a marvelously complex and serene work, which has to be termed sculpture, filled with richly interpenetrating forms. Such a work of art would only be possible in glass." The New York Times Dec. 14, 1980

(top left) "Interior" on pedestal: FOR DRAMATIC NIGHT EFFECT LIGHTED! and in groups at different heights.
(top right) "Springtime Interior"
(bottom) "New Summer Evening Interior", 18"H

Rehumanization

I think it is a fair statement that the most important input to the design of a space for living or working is made by the accountants. If the accountants do not say a living or working space can rent or sell profitably, the builders will not undertake its construction.

In putting together a budget that will assure profitability, very often the first values to be eliminated are the esthetic ones. Mass production materials and techniques are employed in the new building because they afford the best "value," i.e., lowest cost per square foot, and the new building must compete with existing structures and those yet to come.

The result is cliche sterility which denies human input and comfortable human occupancy.

If major architectural elements cannot be employed to evidence human creativity—and therefore human interest—in the creation of people-spaces, the economics then relegate these elements to smaller inclusions: a portal rather than a full facade; a woven tapestry rather than a hand-loomed floor covering; an impressive reception desk instead of a beautifully paneled reception room.

Unfortunately, when one seeks these objects in the marketplace, one quickly finds that the same economies of material, efficiencies of manufacture and competitive climate have robbed most of these smaller objects of their character, design and individuality, just as in the case of the building.

The blessing is that most craftsmen can't afford, or won't tolerate, accountants. As a result, they go on producing beautiful or unique objects driven by the need to create. I've heard the same said of painters and sculptors: "If you do not absolutely have to paint (or sculpt or pot), don't."

Generally, handcrafted objects offer a better link between viewer and maker than a painting. A painting says "Don't touch me." Most paintings are static, placed within a frame, two-dimensional objects in a three-dimensional world. Most frequently, handcrafted objects carry evidence of being handled, and invite touch. A piece of pottery with texture suggests you can delight senses other than your eye: I have watched very young children try to taste the bright color of objects at hand. A handwoven coverlet or pillow is to be stroked and enjoyed tactilely as well as visually. A glass object plays with the light around it, becoming part of a total three-dimensional environment, and visually reorients a small piece of that environment.

Crafted objects enter into space with us and become very accessible parts of our world, things with which we can communicate because they invite communication. They were born as efforts of one human mind and hand to reach another.

As we all suffer the effects of greater space-compression and visual sterility, the crafts have an increasingly important role to play in helping to make our world more pleasantly habitable. The problem is bringing these creators of beautiful things together with the professionals who recognize the need for their art and have the professional training to use them skillfully. Craftsmen work, of necessity, where space is cheap. Market centers, by definition, are in expensive places.

Attempting to bridge this gap, there has been established a beautiful block-long marketplace for the work of over 200 craftspeople, showing thousands of selected objects and selling them every business day of the year. You can buy the objects they make or communicate with an artist about making the object you need. Recognizing that marketing is communication, the not-for-profit National Craft Showroom in New York is testing the feasibility of making handcrafted solutions available to problem-solvers. After two years of quiet existence, it appears to be working.

Norbert N. Nelson
Director, National Craft Showroom
New York, New York

Thomas Buechner III

Vitrix Hot Glass Studio
77 West Market Street
Corning, NY 14830
(607) 936-8707

Sensuous forms in glass by Thomas S.
Buechner III. From $300 to $1,000.
Shown here: Blown glass sculpture, 12″ × 20″.

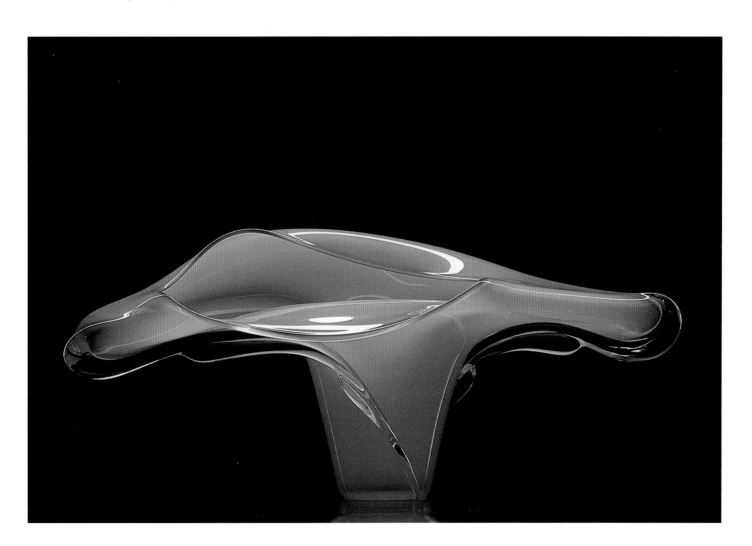

Kerry Feldman

Fineline Studios
4228¾ Glencoe Avenue
Venice, CA 90292
(213) 827-8692

Imbued with a keen sensitivity from the classical to the whimsical, Kerry Feldman creates decorative, functional and sculptural works in glass and mixed-media. Pieces are executed with a range of techniques including blowing, casting, fabrication and fusing of glass. Commissions for specific forms and projects are welcomed.

(top) Amphora, 18"h, Bowl, 7"h × 10"d, Vessel, 12"h
(bottom left) Plate, 18"d
(bottom right) Sculpture, 30"h

Jim Foster

10315 North County Road 15
Fort Collins, CO 80524
(303) 568-7768

Individual wall sculpture and large-scale installations in bronze, porcelain, aluminum. Rich color palette employs metallic lustres, patinae, ceramic stains. Integral mounting supports provide secure, immediate installation on existing walls. Dimensions variable from 20" to 60". Commissions require four to six weeks. Limited, on-hand inventory.

Installations: University of Colorado, Boulder.-Pontifical College Library, Columbus, Ohio. AT&T, Denver. Burroughs Corp., Lombard, Illinois.
Gallery representation around the U.S.

(top) Cast Bronze Sculpture, 24 inches.
(bottom) Cast Bronze Sculpture, 30 inches.

Giles Gilson

The Gilson Studio
766 Albany Street
Schenectady, New York 12307
(518) 370-1677

Mr. Gilson has been making industrial models and prototypes for many years. He designs and creates objects for industrial ads, corporate awards, and is a consulting artist and technician.

Mr. Gilson works with whatever material he feels will serve the object. He favors wood in combination with various metals, plastics, and lacquers. His designs are unique, leaning toward a contemporary feel, with classical overtones. His art is part of major collections, including the Metropolitan Museum, NYC. He has written articles, received awards, and his work has been published in books and magazines.

(right) "Graphic Reversal", 13" × 7". Iridescent lacquered wood, hand-turned aluminum, black acrylic inlay in aluminum.
(bottom left) "Black Ribbon Vase", 10" × 8". Iridescent lacquers over wood.

Opposite Page (top left and right) "Untitled Wall-Cabinet," 25" high. Three shelves, pearlescent lacquer and exotic woods. Detail: interior.
(bottom) "Feathered Container", 14" × 8" × 6". Exotic wood iridescent lacquers, stainless steel.

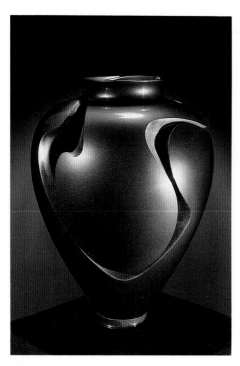

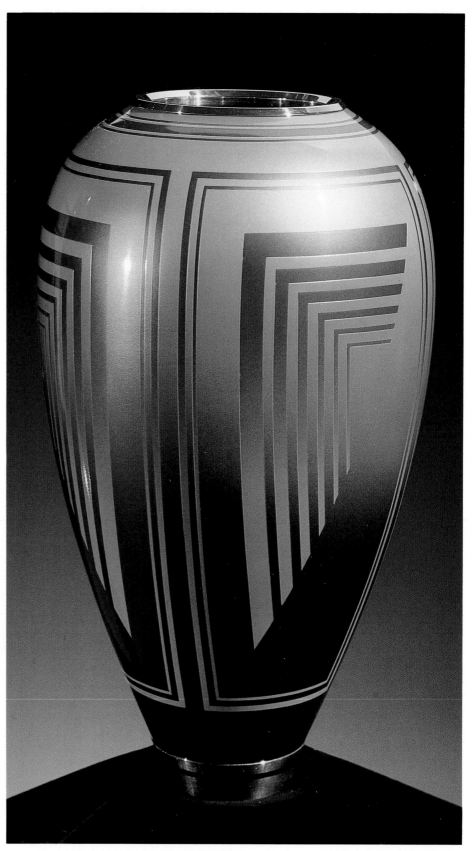

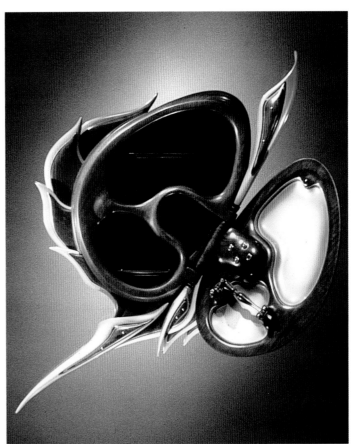

David Mark Goldhagen

Goldhagen Studios
Rt. 1 Box 277
Hayesville, NC 28904
(704) 389-8847

David specializes in blown glass vessels and sculptural forms. The vessels have two motifs: an abstract ribbon pattern in pastels, cobalt blue, and burgundy and a realisitic floral depiction of orchids. The colors are layered in the clear glass, creating an intriguing dimensional quality.

The sculptural forms capture a fluid twisting motion, standing upright (as pictured) and reclined, forming an arch of transparent colors.

The works pictured here are in limited editions: the florals are one-of-a-kind and are priced at between $200 and $600. Limited editions of large and small vases, perfume bottles and paperweights range from $30 to $300.

David has studied at Tulane, Penland and Pilchuk. Collections include Disney World, Arvida, R.J. Reynolds, and Coca Cola Executive Gift Commissions.

(left) "Cross drawing vase." cobalt, 20"H × 10"W × 4"W
(right) "Column Twist Series," 24"H × 5"W × 5"D

Brochure available.

58

Russell Kagan

6900 Sconfinato Drive
Hartford, WI 53027
(414) 966-3370

Kagan is internationally known for his technical and aesthetic excellence in clay. He creates large, classically shaped vessels. Inspired by raku, a centuries-old Japanese method of firing, the artist produces colorful, velvet-like surfaces. The decorative forms, installed singularly or in a group, can be enclosed in plexiglass boxes if desired. Kagan's work is included and enjoyed in important private, corporate and museum collections in the United States, Europe, Canada, South America, the Near East and Far East.

Brochure available upon request.

(top) "Amphora" clay/raku, 38"H x 16"W, wrapped in leather installed on plexiglass pedestal. Collection of Wisconsin Electric Power Company.
(bottom) "Amphora III", clay/raku, 36"H x 56"W, wrapped in leather.

Steven Maslach

44 Industrial Way
Greenbrae, CA 94904
(415) 924-2310

Steven Maslach has been working in glass for 17 years. He is represented in many private and public collections including The Corning Museum of Glass, The Smithsonian, The White House, The High Museum of Art, and the Oakland Museum.

His most recent work utilizes both blown and polished glass which has been cut, faceted and laminated with various optical lenses. The pieces are highly kinetic, as they change color depending upon the angle of light and the position of the viewer.

The artworks shown are vessel forms, though Maslach's work is wide ranging. Commissions have included chandeliers for the Hotel Utah in Salt Lake City and cast glass tiles for the City of San Francisco. The current work is graceful and distinctive, in sizes to 18″ diameter.

Rick and Janet Nicholson

Nicholson Blown Glass
5555 Bell Road
Auburn, CA 95603
(916) 823-1631

Nicholson Blown Glass is a two person studio where the emphasis is on creativity and innovation over production.

Each piece is a free hand expression of the excitement and risk taking only found in the small, experimental glassblowing studio. The piece shown is attached hot to a cast foot and finished as one, allowing the piece to float and retain balance.

Other work involves vase and bowl forms along with limited edition, constructed sculptural pieces.

A slide portfolio and price list are available upon request.

Form on cast foot, 9"H × 9½ " W

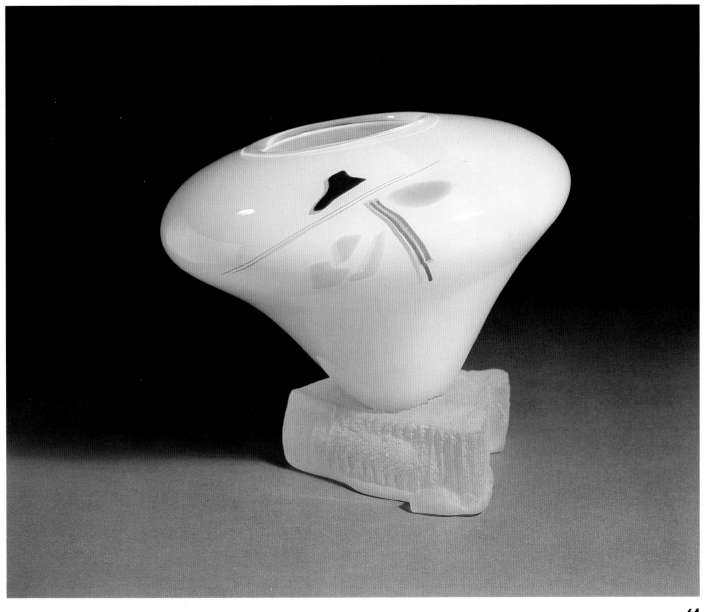

Rick and Janet Nicholson

Peter M. Petrochko

370 Quaker Farms Road
Oxford, CT 06483
(203) 888-9835

My work in wood crafts is an outgrowth of studying both Architecture, and Fine Arts. I create pieces which range from geometrically patterned band saw bowls, to more natural bowls which are hand carved from a single log.

While some of these bowls are utilitarian, most are one of a kind display pieces in which I explore relationships in form, pattern, texture, and natural colors, while using native and exotic woods. Bowls of varying shapes and sizes are possible.

Currently, I am represented by over 20 galleries nationwide. Collections include; The Museum of Fine Arts, Boston; Marshall Fields, Chicago; and numerous private collections, U.S.A., Japan and Europe.

Awards: Recipient, "Creativity Award", Washington Craft Show 1985.

(left) Bubinga, wenge, walnut, poplar, ebonized poplar, mahogany, purpleheart, shedua, padouk 13"H × 12"W × 18"L
(right) Ziricote, padouk 12"H × 12"W × 18"L

Jeffrey Seaton

Seaton Wood Design
5 Orange Avenue #D
Goleta, CA 93117
(805) 964-5352

For over a decade Jeffrey Seaton has been designing one-of-a-kind decorative accent containers. These containers, concentrically cut from a solid block of exotic hardwood, are lined with suede leather and polished to a satin luster. Works featuring natural textured surfaces are available in American Desert Ironwood and five western burlwoods. Elliptical monoliths in sets of three are available in five exotic hardwoods or individually commissioned. Works are included in the permanent collection of the Museum of Modern Art, New York City and are currently on display in selected galleries throughout the United States.

Color brochure and prices available on request.

(top left) American Desert Ironwood, 14" × 8" × 10"
(bottom left) Elliptical Monoliths, set of three in macassar ebony, 9½" × 5½ " × 2½", 5½" × 4" × 1½", 3' × 3" × 1"
(right) Elliptical Monoliths, set of three in cocobolo rosewood, 11½" × 6" × 2½", 8" × 4½" × 1½", 5" × 3½" × 1"

Josh Simpson

Josh Simpson Contemporary Glass
Frank Williams Road
Shelburne Falls, MA 01370
(413) 625-6145

Josh Simpson's work is in the permanent collection of the Corning Museum of Glass and has been exhibited in numerous galleries and museums, including the Smithsonian's Renwick and Cooper Hewitt Museums, the Victoria and Albert Museum in London, and the Metropolitan Museum of Art in New York.

(top) "Tecktite", 8"H, Handblown iridescent silver interior, black meteorite glass exterior.
(bottom) "Tecktite" 16" L.

Shaun Fabian Weisbach

2377 San Jose Avenue
San Francisco, CA 94112
(415) 585-5652

Glass artist and craftsman Shaun Weisbach presenting his work in the Guild for his second year is adding a new dimension to his earlier plate forms. In this new series of "Landscape Vessels" Weisbach has been inspired by dramatic landscapes such as the wheat fields of the Midwest as well as vibrant colors reminiscent of the Southwest.

This versatile California artist is a graduate of the California College of Arts and Crafts and is a member of the Bay Area Studio Art Glass group known as BASAG.

Weisbach has shown in major gallery and museum shows throughout the United States, his work is included in numerous public and private collections. Commissions include: IBM, The Marriot Hotels, The Regent Hotel, Washington, DC. Inquiries and commissions are invited.

(top left) "Landscape in Black, Grey & White" is 16" × 4".
(top right) "Desert Landscape" (detail).
(bottom) Group Shot, left to right - "Desert Cactus" is 16" × 4", "Desert Landscape" is 16" × 4", "Summer Wheat" is 16" × 4".

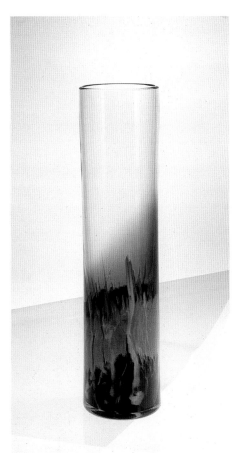

SCULPTURE

Deborah Banyas

Black River Studios
181 Forest Street
Oberlin, OH 44074
(216) 774-8319

Deborah Banyas creates textile sculptures that take the shape of animals in anthropomorphic, witty situations. Relief or freestanding pieces can be made with or without furniture for use in lobbies, windows, advertising graphics, corporate and personal collections. Sketches and color work-ups for a specific site can be made, and the artist is willing to work on projects involving elaborate environments. Examples of some creatures available: goat, bird, dog, fish, snake, fox, ram, cat. Slide or print portfolio is available.

(top) "Leopard With Walking Blackfish," 31" × 40" × 26" appliquéd, embroidered, stitched, stuffed cotton

(bottom) "Love Birds," 22" × 36" × 21".

William N. Baran-Mickle

Meditari Studio
1237 East Main Street, 3rd Floor
Rochester, NY 14609
(716) 288-8320

Baran-Mickle has been working in metals, exhibiting in national competitions and invitationals since 1978. For the last four years he has concentrated on creating one-of-a-kind sculpture, sculptural-vessels and wall pieces. Most works are created by hand and hammer, fabricated from sheets of brass, copper and nickel-silver. Other materials are used as needed: paper, wood, glass, stone, etc.

Imagery usually deals with landscapes: from a sense of realism with land and relationships, to the abstractions of senses and thoughts.

Work is done as series/progressions or as individual statements. Each is signed and dated.

(top left) Detail of "High Tides"
(top right) "Misguided Wishes" Triptych: Peony/Freesia/Chicory
20" × 16" × 10"', mixed metals, wood, stone, paint.
(bottom) "High Tides" 27" × 21" × 12"
brass, copper, nickel, wood

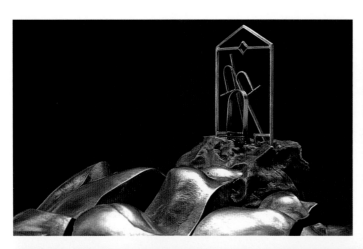

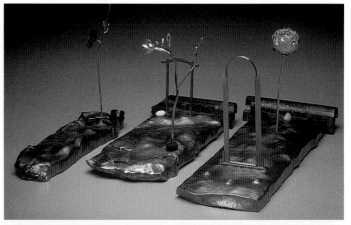

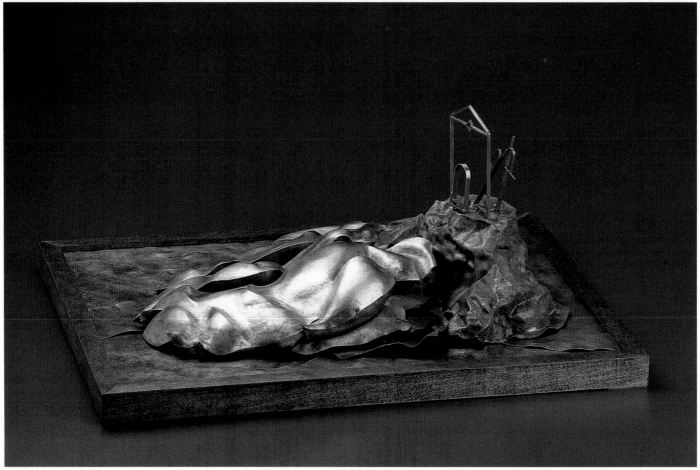

Margaret Barnaby

Winter: P.O. Box 950
Canal Street Station
New York, NY 10013
(212) 226-5955

Summer: Box 190, Bean Road, RDI
Center Harbor, NH 03226
(603) 253-4255

Inspired by insects and sea life, Margaret Barnaby makes one-of-a-kind sculptures, vessels, wall reliefs and lighting fixtures. She studied chasing and repoussé at Reed and Barton in Taunton, Massachusetts, and combines these techniques with hollow-forming, mokumé-gané and married metals. Materials include copper, brass and sterling silver, with accents of glass and semiprecious stones.

(top) "Katydid," brass, ammonia fume patina, 19" tall
(bottom) "Bedbug," sterling silver, copper, incandescent light, 22" across

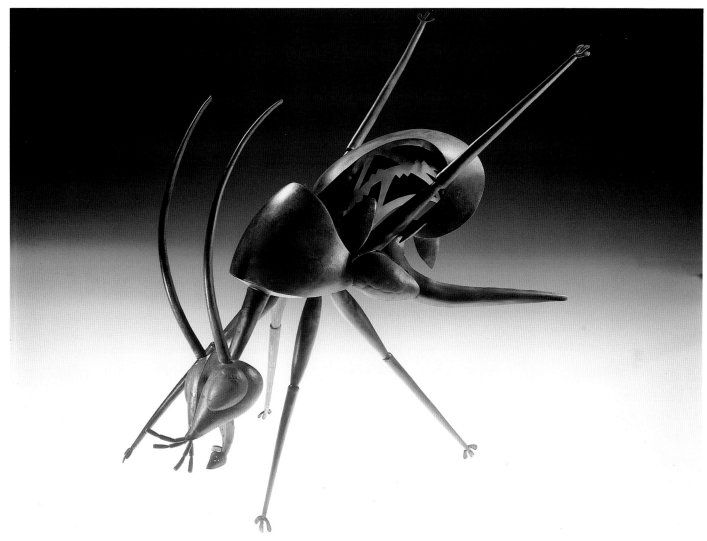

Sandra Christine Q. Bergér

Quintal Unlimited
100 El Camino Real, #202
Burlingame, CA 94010
(415) 348-0310

Distinctive glass sculpture for architectural installations and delicate, interior accents are designed with precision by Bergér. Modular construction facilitates shipping, handling, and installation.

The "Kinetic Vessel Sculptures" (top right and left), ranging from 10" diameter to 34" height, can be rearranged into a variety of compositions. This interactive quality inspires creativity and engages a collector to become involved with a work.

On a larger scale, "Syncopation" (below) 47"W × 44"H is a sleek, reflective black wall sculpture. Incorporating glass, acrylic, wood, and steel, industrial adhesive technology was integral to the assembly.

Bergér's corporate, commercial, and residential commissions also include window and entrance treatments.

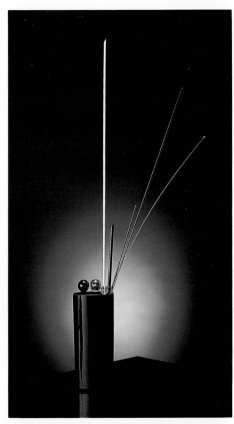

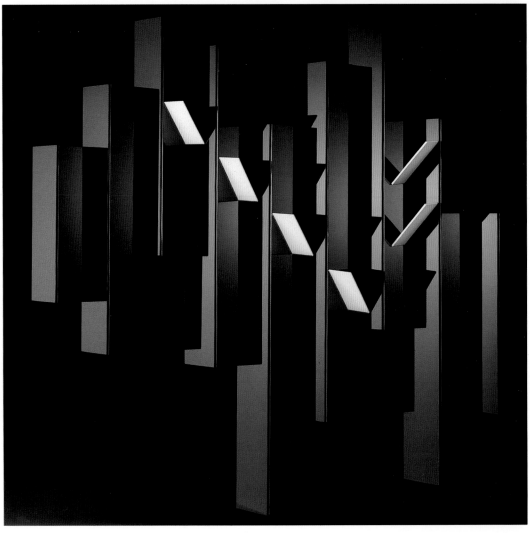

Jeanette Bernhard

Studio: Shapes 'n Forms
6808 N. 17th Place
Phoenix, AZ 85016
(602) 264-9145

One-of-a-kind stoneware sculpture built in sections; suitable for indoor or outdoor sites.

The outdoor sculpture takes on a quality from the natural growth of the surroundings.

Prices determined by material involved; allow 3 months for average delivery, F.O.B. Phoenix, Arizona

(right) 4' tall × 15" circumference. Buff colored body/red iron oxide top 3 sections

(left) Red stoneware; 20" × 8" × 4" 2 sections

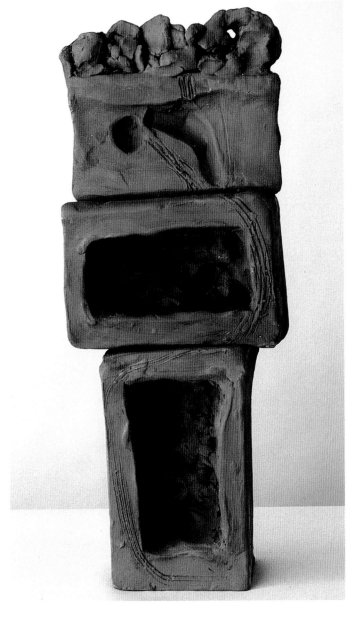

Peter Bramhall

Box 163,
Bridgewater Center Road
Bridgewater, VT 05034
(802) 672-5141

Suitable for indoor and outdoor settings, Peter Bramhall's sculptures can accommodate a wide range of size and scale to fit spatial and esthetic requirements. When quoted recently on his work, he said, "The imagery grows from a continuing study of nature, human relationships and their conflicts, and African sculpture." Currently devoting half his year to the development of glass and half to bronze, Mr. Bramhall is also proficient in materials such as aluminum, steel, and wood. Since receiving his degree from the Cleveland Institute of Art, he has spent the last fifteen years working at his studio in Vermont.

"Tempest II", cast bronze, 27" × 16" × 22" ©1983, one of sixteen pieces available.

Kathleen Cerveny

Cervenova Studios
7714 St. Clair Avenue
Cleveland, OH 44103
(216) 881-2353

Ms. Cerveny's most recent commission (pictured here) is ST. VINCENT STELE, an 11½ ft. tall freestanding sculpture for the lobby of St. Vincent Charity Hospital Medical Office Building in Cleveland. Developer: Howley and Company, Cleveland, Ohio.

Brochure available upon request.

CERVENOVA (Cher' ve no' va) is the old world, feminine form of Ms. Cerveny's surname. In translation—the color red.

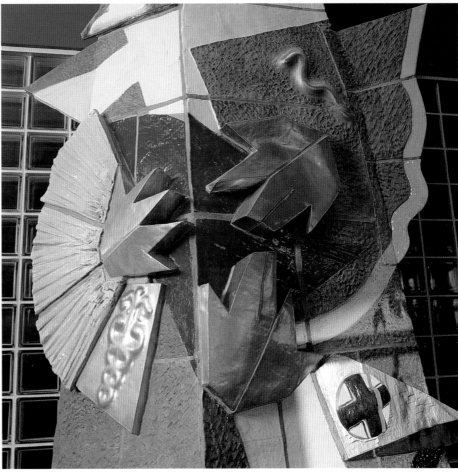

The Heirlooms of Tomorrow

Remember when the word "crafts" used to mean rustic brown pots, quilts and crude chairs?

Today American craftsmen have grown so in sophistication that American crafts are the most diverse, most refined, and perhaps even the most fashion-conscious in the world. Craftsmen are well aware of not only creative work in their own media, but are increasingly cognizant of what's going on in painting, in graphic art, advertising, industrial design and in fashion.

Yet, despite their ability to borrow from other disciplines, other cultures and the past, our craftsmen imbue their objects with a great deal of originality...maybe because we haven't a single, pervasive 'old craft' tradition in this country that permits such wide-ranging creativity in American crafts today.

We are also beginning to see artist-craftsmen move easily from one medium to another, guided only by their artistic impulse to decide the most appropriate materials and techniques to fulfill their ideas.

I truly believe that the fine quality of handmade objects today will make their owners cherish them and pass them on to future generations. They are the heirlooms of tomorrow!

Lloyd E. Herman

Lloyd E. Herman
Independent Curator
Founding Director, Renwick Gallery
Arlington, Virginia

Jonathan J. Clowes

J. Clowes Woodworking
RFD 3 Box 306
Waldoboro, Maine 04572
(207) 832-5191

Jonathan Clowes designs and builds mobiles to enhance corporate and residential spaces. His work reflects a love for the sea and sailing in fluid lines and rhythms. The mobiles' elegant compositions incorporate subtle tensions and balances, making them appear to float in air. The sculptural elements themselves are created in boldly shaped hardwoods with handwrought metal connections. The mobiles are designed for particular spaces and priced accordingly.

"Haiku for Nancy" is a commissioned work designed to add excitement and artistry to an entryway stairwell of a modern home. This mobile moves through an 8' diameter space and is 5' high. It is composed of laminated ash elements with copper fittings. "Haiku for Nancy" won a place in "Makers '86." Clowes' work has been juried into 5 national shows and can be seen in several galleries.

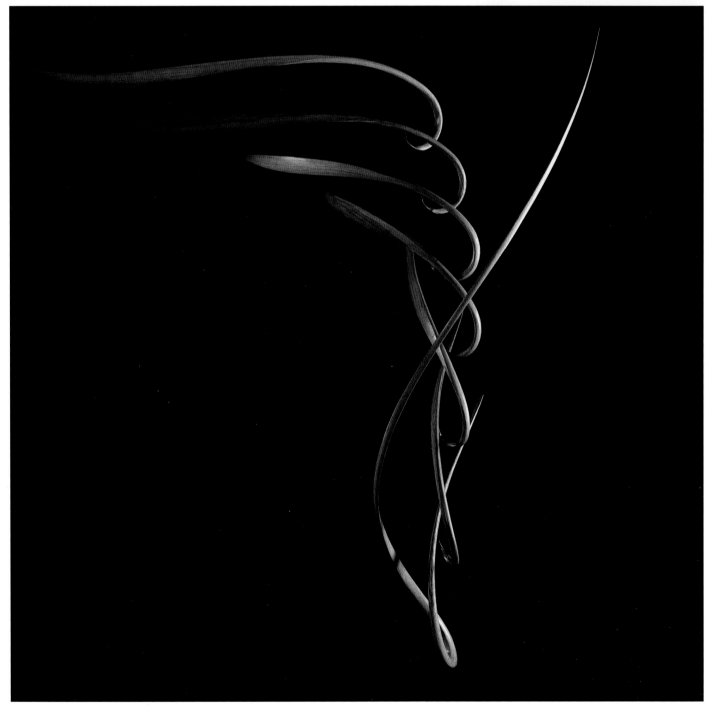

Mary Costantini

Bottega 565 Inc.
100 Broadway
Jersey City, NJ 07306
(201) 333-6366

Costantini is a sculptor whose work has been recognized as having an "omnificient presence". Commissions include liturgical, commercial, and residential installations. Mediums vary from the traditional to polyurethane and thermoplastics.

The sculpture shown is designed in clay, cast in fiberglass with a ceramic tile surface. Found furniture is also an inspiration to the tile treatment.

Specialization lies in designing works that are environmentally compatible, from the 150 foot dragon in Shun Lee Restaurant, New York City, to relief work for a private residence.

Costantini, educated in Italy, apprenticed in Pietrasanta, holds an M.A. in sculpture. Presently directing Bottega 565 Inc., (established in 1980), she teaches and lectures actively in the metropolitan area.

"Liberta"—5' × 2'4" ceramic tile
cabinet—26" × 17" ceramic tile

Don Drumm

Don Drumm Studios and Gallery
437 Crouse Street
Akron, OH 44311
(216) 253-6268

Drumm is both a Sculptor and Designer/Craftsman. He maintains his own aluminum foundry, where he produces an emense variety of work. Here he creates his "one of a kind" sculpture, a group of limited edition sculptures, and an evergrowing selection of functional craft objects.

Environmental art is his other love. His architectural sculpture and crafts are known and owned world wide.

(bottom) "Sky Notch"; 20' High; all weathering steel
(top left) Cocktail table; aluminum
(top left) Limited edition sculpture; 18" High; aluminum

Brochures available on the Architectural work, small sculpture, or the craft lines. Please specify.

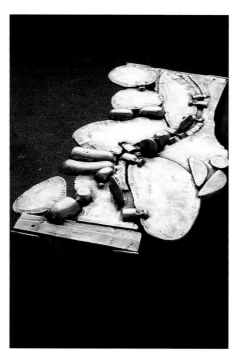

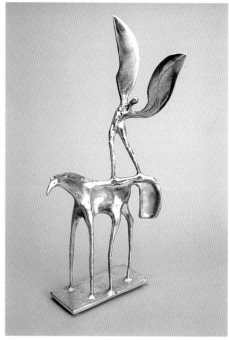

Bill Farrell

831 Mapleton
Oak Park, IL 60302
(312) 524-9732

I build freestanding clay sculpture that bring together existing elements in the architecture. My clay formula is designed to work in indoor and outdoor applications, decorative or structural.

(top right) "Water Spill", 7' High × 14' Long, clay, steel, concrete, 1986
(bottom right and detail) "Obsession Collection", 4' × 4 × 16', ceramic and wire, 1986

Barbara Grygutis

273 North Main Avenue
Tucson, AZ 85701
(602) 622-5214

"Barbara Grygutis, a ceramics sculptor gaining a reputation for spare, monumental pieces that speak the tones and rhythms of the desert." New York Times and International Herald Tribune

REDROCK, Radisson Suites Hotel, 1986

REDROCK stands in the courtyard of the four-hundred room Radisson Suites Hotel, an agora of nearly 30,000 square feet. Surrounding it are the wings of guest rooms, five stories high. A man-made canyon, with REDROCK a focal point of contradictory character: monumental yet intimate.

They are ceramic blocks, some low and squat; some stacked into tall, tapering or leaning monoliths. Three rise from a shallow pool of water; four others hang around nearby, like silent spectators. Each has an individual personality, and in concert they form a pleasantly erratic crowd, a suite of seven monoliths.

"REDROCK is user-friendly sculpture. It asks to be wandered through, touched, and sat upon." Tucson Citizen

SCULPTURE THAT CREATES SPECIAL PLACES

James R. Harmon

31 Second Avenue
New York, NY 10003
(212) 228-1297

James Harmon is an internationally exhibited artist. His primary focus is in the medium of glass. Previous works in light and neon installed at Art Park, Lewiston, N.Y.; Danceateria, New York City; Heller Gallery, New York City; Hellen Drutt Gallery, Philadelphia, Penn.; and "The Becker Window," Philadelphia, Penn.

His work revolves around a theme of "subliminal symbolisms" that are randomly compacted in a particular space, causing the viewer to refer to his or her own set of symbols or memories, subconscious or conscious. This in turn evokes a feeling of complex didactic experience as the viewer "reads" the piece.

Vera Lightstone

347 West 39th Street
Loft 7 West
New York, NY 10018
(212) 947-6879

"We needed a wall piece that would enhance the image of our law firm. Her sculpture is just what we were looking for — elegant and intriguing."
Joseph Gulmi, Attorney, New York City

This sculpture incorporates a unique, easily assembled system which can be wall mounted or free standing. The work retains its high quality both indoors and outdoors and is especially effective mounted over a reflecting pool.

The surface pictured is textured unglazed stoneware. Surfaces can also be colored with oxide, glaze or acrylic. Each work is one-of-a-kind, signed and copyrighted. Prices range from $300 to $600 per linear foot.

The artist, whose work is shown in museums and galleries nationwide, welcomes site-specific commissions.

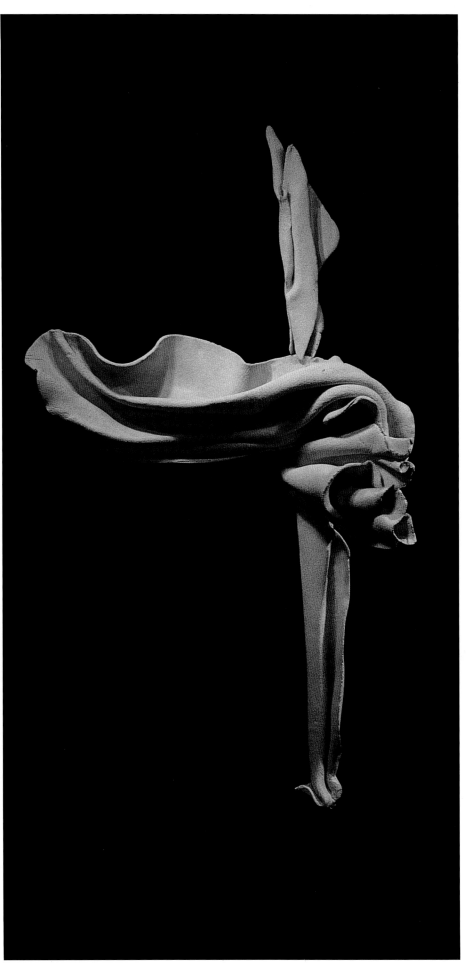

Rob MacConnell

White Crane Studios
37 Ethel Avenue
Mill Valley, CA 94941
(415) 383-0945

MacConnell's large sculptural works have a timeless quality created by his handbuilding techniques and firing processes. Softly smoked in raku firings, the semi-matte, textured surfaces are highlighted with centuries-old calligraphy and further enhanced with subtle shadows produced from leaves and pine needles. Sizes are approximate with color variations within each piece. Suitable for indoor and outdoor (mild climate) installations.

Collaborations with his wife, Rosemary Ishii MacConnell, employ various combinations of contrasting surface textures: the translucent and reflective qualities of paper, clay, fused glass and at times, with the added dimension of neon.

(top) 42″ × 33″H, "Middle Passage", Raku, paper and argon
(bottom) Temple Stones, approx. 18″H to 7′H, 10% non-refundable down

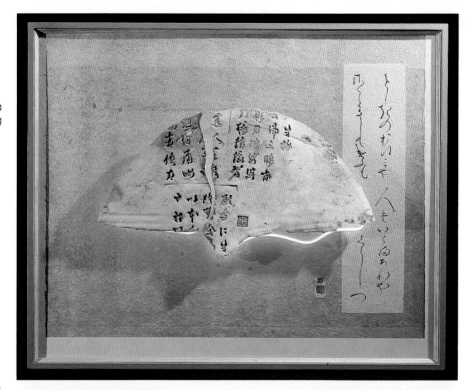

Tom Neugebauer

Box 8990 Sawkill Road
Milford, PA 18337
(717) 296-6901

Forms that breathe, stretch, expand, and dance.
Movement of form in space, the motion of Spirit in growth.
Clay and Steel: Feminine and Masculine.
Interaction and opposition, a dialogue within us and between us.
Earth-born materials, transformed by fire, symbol of the inner life.

Imprints of fire upon the raw clay surface.
Primal images...
To express my search for Unity,
To celebrate my discoveries.

Widely exhibited and collected in both corporate and residential settings, Tom's work is produced as one-of-a-kind and limited-edition series, in addition to site-specific commissions. Primarily designed for interior placement, outdoor adaptations are available.
Tom is also known for his Raku and Pit-Fired vessels and wall plates.
Additional information and brochure available upon request.

(top left) "Lifedance II". Pit-smoked clay/brushed steel. 44"H × 24" diam.
(bottom left) "The Harvester/Chac Mool". Pit-smoked clay. Iron and ochre slips. 34"H × 16"W × 16"D.
(right) "In the Beginning...". Textured, polished steel and pit-smoked clay. 7'4"H × 4'2"W × 2'D.

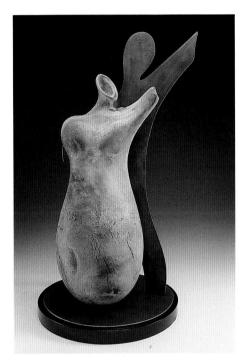

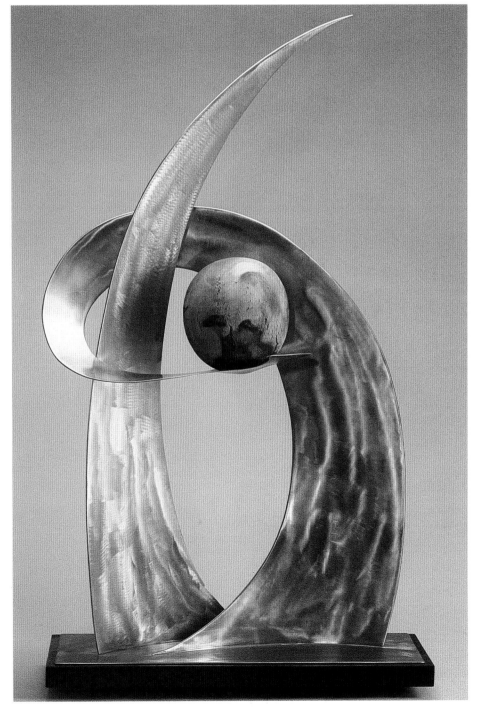

Gene Olson

The Mettle Works
756 Curfew Street
St. Paul, MN 55114
(612) 647-1635

Gene Olson and his studio company, the Mettle Works, have produced major works for SITE Architects, artists Stuart Nielsen, Philip Larson and others. Among his clients are: General Mills, First Banks, BEST Products, Medtronics, Dayton/Hudson, and Hennepin Center for the Arts.

"I find working with other artists can be stimulating. I greatly enjoy the sort of mutual professional growth that can develop in these collaborations and look forward to each new opportunity. If Mr. Nielsen's or Ms. Wilson's work should interest you or your clients, I would be glad to assist."

(top) "Flying Lady", Cast bronze door handle by Chris Wilson, Mettle Works artist. Size: 9" × 4½" × 3".

(bottom) "Untitled", by Stuart Nielsen, and Mettle Works staff. Size: 35' × 10' × 24'h. Commissioned by I.C. System, Inc. Vadnais Heights, Minnesota.

Gene Olson

The Mettle Works
756 Curfew Street
St. Paul, MN 55114
(612) 647-1635

Olson's award winning cast/welded/woven sculptures are durable pieces made of bronze, aluminum and/or steel. They can conform to curved surfaces and are suitable for both interior and exterior applications.

"In 1979, while contemplating a tapestry, it occurred to me that I could stress and define a fabric with metal rods. They were 'plastic' and could leave the surface, undulate and return to the order of the weave; yet, they remained durable, weldable, workable, capable of a multitude of patina and form."

(top left) "Seltzer", woven bronze and copper with brushed steel by Gene Olson. Size: 12" × 24"
(top right) Detail, woven bronze and copper
(bottom) "Untitled", woven aluminum by Gene Olson. Size: 44" × 66"

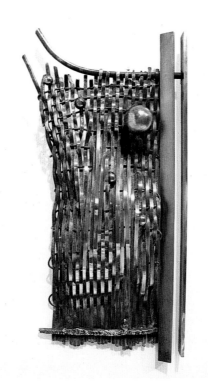

J. R. Reed

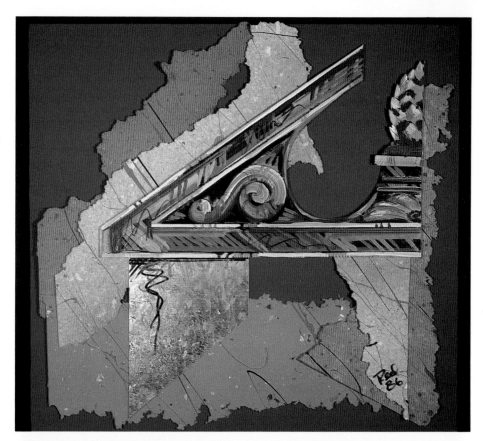

AQL Fine Art
209 N. Harbor Blvd.
Fullerton, CA 92632
(714) 870-6471

Works of handmade paper, mixed media
and neon; two dimensional wall hangings
and three dimensional free-standing pieces
in any size. Works on paper include mono-
prints, prisma pencil drawings and chine
collage.

Major commissions and collections include:
Smithsonian Institution, Crocker National
Bank, Security Pacific National Bank, Hilton
Sydney Hotel, et. al.

Curriculum Vitae and additional information
provided upon request.

(top) "Classic Moments: Split Impediment,"
handmade paper, shaped and painted
plexiglass, and metal. 29" × 31"
(bottom) "Crystal Garnet," handmade
paper, acrylic and neon. 24" × 24" × 40"

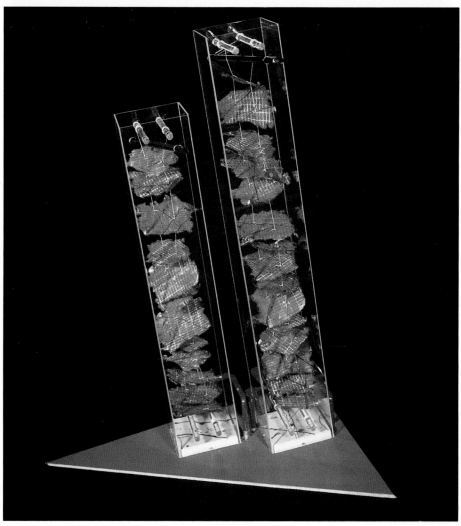

Timothy Rose

Timothy Rose Mobiles
340 Industrial Center Building
Sausalito, CA 94965
(415) 332-9604

Timothy Rose has been creating and realizing mobile sculptures for more than 20 years. He has a degree in anthropology and has lived and exhibited in Europe. He presently works in Marin County, California.

The pieces shown here are from his current "Surprise" series of mobiles. They are highly colored, asymetrically balanced, and evocative of a 'surprise' in the viewer. All are constructed of wire, wood, metal and paint and can be replicated on various scales to suit the location.

Brochure and resumé available upon request.

(top left) "Green Cloud" Surprise Mobile, approx 42" high
(top right) "Starry Crescent" Surprise Mobile, approx. 36" high
(bottom) "Spring Garden Carousel" Surprise Mobile, approx. 36" diam.

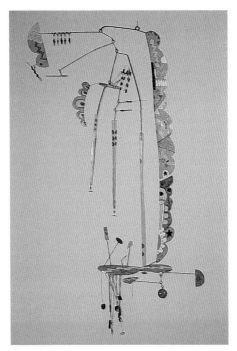

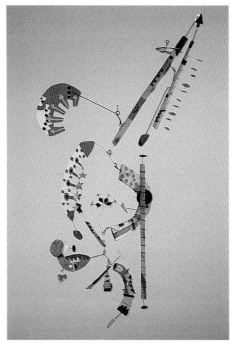

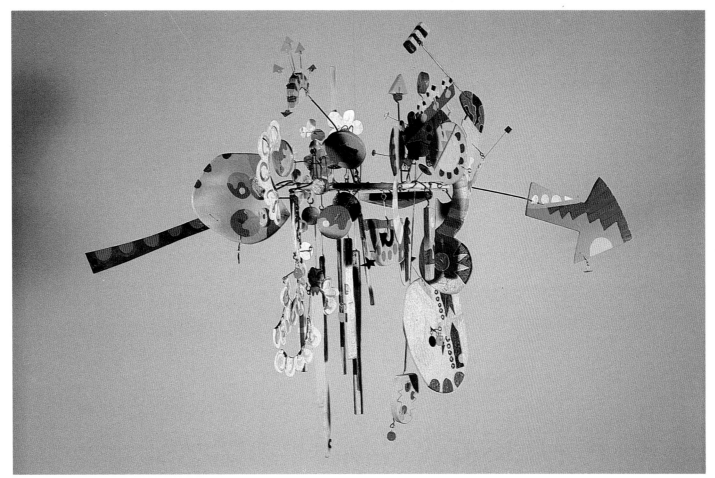

Katherine L. Ross

3157 South Archer
Chicago, IL 60608
(312) 376-0131

Commissions sought for site-specific and architecturally specific sculpture, tile work, and fountains. Intimate to large scale, interior and exterior. The primary material is ceramic.

"Corridor of the Antipodes"
12 × 40 × 6 ft.
Ceramic, Steel

Kurt and Marsha Runstadler

Runstadler Studios, Inc.
4625 Ravenwood Avenue
Sacramento, CA 95821
(916) 488-4400

Kurt and Marsha Runstadler specialize in three dimensional glass and metal sculptures. These pieces ranges from pedestal and table top sizes to large scale free standing or wall mounted major architectural installations. Using primarily laminated plate glass and combinations of brass, copper, or stainless steel, they offer a wide array of designs for the modern home, office, or corporate situation. The Runstadlers offer a series of limited edition sculptures or they will accept private commissions. Slides of the limited edition works are available at a nominal charge upon request.

The Runstadlers have been working in glass for twelve years and currently exhibit with museums and galleries around the country. Collections include Saks Fifth Avenue, Sheraton, Hilton, McDonalds Corporation, etc.

Pictured are sculptures from the limited edition series.

(top) "Crosspointe" 18"h x 18"w x 4"d
(bottom) "Coquille" 18"h x 17"w x 4"d

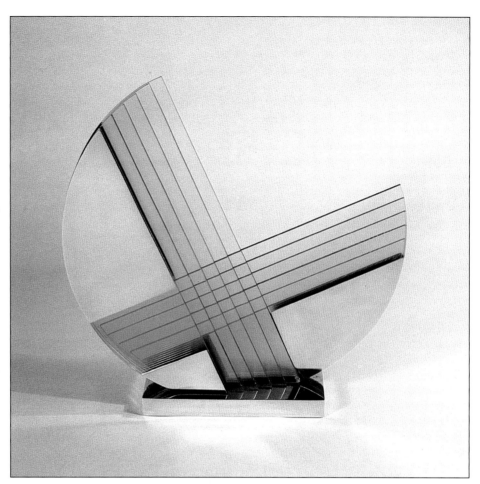

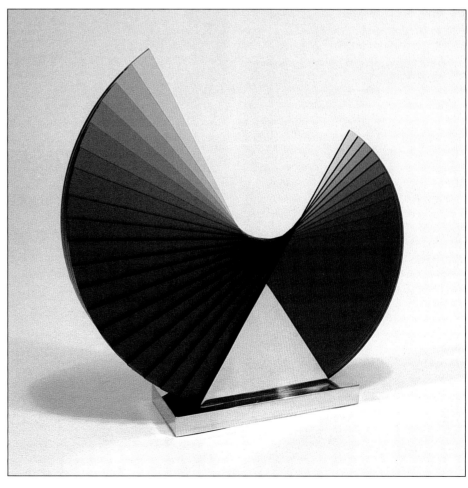

Chris and Pat Shatsby

Silvercreek Bronze
213 North Main
Lewisburg, Ohio 45338
(513) 962-4102
The National Craft Showroom (New York City)

Exquisite cast bronze vessels, small sculpture, and decorative accessories for any setting. Simply the best hand-crafted bronze articles available. Anywhere. Commissions accepted. Please write for a free catalog.

Albert Strausman

59 West 9th Street
New York, NY 10011
(212) 260-8524

Mr. Strausman collects intriguing artifacts of our past; machine parts, ornaments from factory, farm, railroad, ships and architecture. He transforms these treasures into compelling sculpture, timeless expressions that embody the mystery of another time and place.

"Grand Street", (left) a free standing sculpture measuring 89", is named for the artist's impression of that Manhattan street. Its clocklike presence is an abstract expression of a clock that could stand there. "2AG2", (right) another floor piece, measures 53 ½". A metal plate on one of its found pieces reading "2AG2" became an appropriate title for its robotlike posture.

The sculptures range in size from 15" to 90" and also include wall, mantlepiece, tabletop and shelf pieces.

David Trezise

2901 Pheasant Branch Road
Middleton, WI 53562
(608) 836-1390

David Trezise's hand-carved stone sculptures are both original and traditional in nature. The figurative images he carves demonstrate a thorough knowledge of the various materials he uses. Although Trezise works in marble, his preferred material is Indiana limestone (a highly consistent and durable stone which has, for decades, been a favorite of architects, stone masons and sculptors alike). Trezise's work can be commissioned for both indoor and outdoor settings. Slides and prices are available upon request.

(top): Oracle (Size: Height 16" × Width 16"; Material: White Alabama Marble with a Green Vermont Marble base)
(bottom) Spirit Grouping (Sizes range from height 18" - 24"; Materials: Indiana limestone)

FURNITURE AND CABINETRY

Amy Anthony

36 Saint Paul Street
Room 102
Rochester, NY 14604
(716) 232-6536

Amy Anthony portrays subtle optical illusions in her designs which are mainly constructed of aluminum, stainless steel, and slate. She encaptures a type of sensual, yet bold movement which entices the viewer. The two photographs display her distinctive designs and craftsmanship.

Any custom designs and special orders are welcome. Please allow eight to ten weeks for delivery.

(top) Coffee Table, 17½" × 30" × 30", aluminum and slate
(bottom) Coat Rack, 5'6" × 7" round, aluminum, installed at the Cat Doctor's, Rochester, New York

Dale Broholm

Box 653
Jamaica Plains, MA 02130
(617) 524-0072

Working from one-of-a-kind and limited production format, Dale Broholm has been
designing/making wooden furniture for the
past seven years. Combining traditional
woodworking techniques with both contemporary and historically based design elements, his work can be found in private,
corporate and museum collections
nationwide.

After receiving a BFA in Wooden Furniture
Design and Construction from the Program
in Artisanry, Boston University, he established
his studio in the greater Boston area.

His work is of the highest quality. Built with the
integrity and exacting craftsmanship
demanded by work of this nature. When collaborating with designers and architects he
strives to create exactly what the client has
proposed, thus bringing to life the client's
idea.

A representative portfolio is available upon
request.

(top) Kitchen view, private residence
chairs, cabinetry, counter surfaces 1985
(bottom) "High Boy" cabinet 1984
Curly birch, ebony, leather

Jack Brubaker and Susan Showalter

Jack Brubaker Blacksmith
R.R. #2, Box 102A
Nashville, IN 47448
(812) 988-7830

Fine contemporary furniture and decorative accessories designed by Jack Brubaker and Susan Showalter

Our hand forged metalwork with natural oxide surfaces (the pinks and purples of copper, the yellows and browns of brass and the greys and blacks of steel) are inherently beautiful and durable. Very little maintenance is required.

Shown in major national and international exhibitions throughout the United States and Europe, our work includes interior functional pieces and sculpture. Our production shop with several blacksmiths and apprentices also accepts large architectural commissions.

Catalog Available

(top) "Floor Sculpture #3," hand forged solid brass and cooper, 57" tall (other styles, sizes and metals available)
(bottom) "Table," hand forged steel and brass, glass, 48" long × 26" wide × 18" tall (other styles, sizes and metals available)

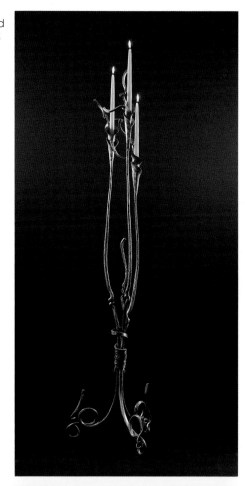

Robin Carley

Carley, Wood Associates
651 West Doty Street
Madison, WI 53703
(608) 257-4226

Carley, Wood Associates was created specifically to build architectural designs of custom executive furniture. Most of our work is conference tables, desks, credenzas, reception areas and built-in cabinetry. We use many materials, including stainless steel, brass, bronze, marbles, leather and glass to coordinate with wood and provide a total package for any custom project.

We have built furniture for clients from coast to coast and can supply individual pieces or entire office suites. We can also include detailed shop drawings, custom or standard finishes, shipping and installation with any project.

Member of Wisconsin A.W.I.

(bottom) 22' long × 7' wide oval conference table, black walnut, double wenge inlay, reverse diamond matched veneer pattern. Designer: Robin Carley. Client: American Family Insurance National Headquarters.

(top left) (Detail of tabletop and buffet)

(bottom) 108″ long × 44″ wide bird's-eye maple dining room table. Padauk bent-wood laminate base, wenge and padauk inlay and details.

(top) 84″ long × 26″ deep buffet to match table. Designer: Robin Carley. Client: Private Residence

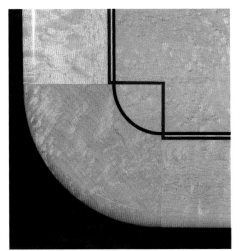

Stephen Laurence Casey

Casey Designs
5560 Fairview Place
Agoura Hills, CA 91301
(818) 886-1872

Producing original furniture and sculpture in the Los Angeles area since 1977. Specializing in wood design and fabrication and also combining lacquers, plastic laminate, metals, mylar and a variety of other materials.

Casey Designs' services and products include: furniture, cabinets and case goods, entertainment centers, design and fabrication, commissions, limited production, one-of-a-kind originals and collaborative design projects.

(top) Entertainment Center
84"L × 84"H × 24"W, White oak, white stain/lacquer finish. Custom made to fit customer criteria.
(bottom) Coopered Chest 36"L × 18"H × 18"W Imbua, Koa, rosewood. Limited edition of 6

Jonathan Cohen

Jonathan Cohen Fine Woodworking
3410 Woodland Park Ave. N.
Seattle, Wash. 98103
(206) 632-2141

B.A. Graphic Design Cornell Univ.; studied Furniture Making in Denmark; Apprenticed in Seattle; set up own shop in 1979; has since received national recognition, and shows in New York, Boston, Cleveland, Tempe, Portland, and Seattle; owner/member of N.W. gallery of fine woodworking.

Will accept commissions to build for designers/architects, or design and build directly with client.

"It seems to me that designing and building one-of-a-kind furniture is in no small way an intimate process involving myself and my client."

Works primarily in exotic woods such as bubinga, imbuya, rosewood, and ebony. Much use of curved lines; some hand-planed, others bent-laminated.

"I strive to impart a graceful, yet muscular, elegance to my pieces".

Publications: American Crafts Magazine, Fine Woodworking Magazine

Tiger Desk, (with four secret compartments), bubinga and E.I. rosewood.
Hauberg Wing Table; imbuya and ebony. Both designs copyrighted.

John Dodd

1237 East Main Street
Rochester, NY 14609
(716) 482-7233

John Dodd has maintained a professional furniture design studio for the past eight years. He is also affiliated with the School of American Craftsman as both a graduate and lecturer.

Unique limited editions are created on a commissioned and speculative basis.

Slides and brochure are available upon request for a nominal fee.

Cylindrical Compliment
Editions One & Two
Five center-hung drawers for small collectible items.
12" diameter, 48" high

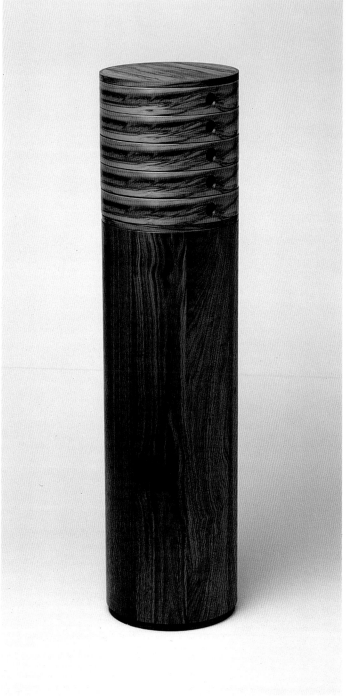

Kenneth Ray Fisher

455 Carroll Street
Brooklyn, NY 11215
(718) 875-3799

The strength of Ken's work relies on the use of contrasting woods, size and craftsmanship combined with a juxtaposition of the organic and structural. Illustrated are representations of flowering and structural elements derived from his intense interest in plant life and structural steel forms. This effective merging of contrasting forms is one of several distinctive characteristics of Ken's powerful and innovative designs in wood.

The artistic forms are conceived, designed and produced to work in the environment and space they will occupy.

Ken has a B.S. in Life Science (Biology) from The University of Southern Indiana and an M.F.A. in furniture design from The Rhode Island School of Design. His work has been on exhibit in numerous museums and galleries and has been featured in art and design publications.

Fred Gemmell

Gemmell and Associates
2051 Commercial St.
San Diego, CA 92113
(619) 232-2874

New materials. New Colors. New possibilities. Designed furniture utilizing light, hardwoods, acrylics, Italian veneers, metal and stone. Noteworthy finishes, pure designs, impeccable quality. Custom and limited production.

AZTECH DESK exploits the elegance of Norwegian gray granite and the optical clarity of acrylic.

LUMINOS LOW TABLE presents indirect light concealed in a rosewood form which supports glass and plexiglass cross planes.

Showroom: San Diego, CA.

Anthony Giachetti

Furniture Designer/Maker
P.O. Box 504
East Boothbay, Maine 04544
(207) 633-3740

Anthony Giachetti makes one-of-a-kind furniture for residential and office use. Special-function cabinets, such as the ones illustrated here, are of great interest to the artist. Graceful curved forms are achieved through the use of form-laminating techniques. Woods of exceptional color and figure are employed in combination to articulate forms and illuminate the surface. Mr. Giachetti has maintained a studio in East Boothbay, Maine, since 1974. Photos and prices available upon request.

(top left, top right) Jewelry Chest-on-Stand, twenty-eight drawers velvet lined; Rosewoods, Australian Lacewood, 60"H × 25"W × 15"D.

(bottom) Display Cabinet-on-Stand, lighted interior of Swiss Pearwood, cabinet and stand rosewoods, doors of curly mahogany with pearwood inlay. 60"H × 25"W × 15"D.

Peter Handler

Peter Handler Studio
2400 W. Westmoreland St.
Philadelphia, PA 19128
(215) 483-4100

Peter Handler designs and produces custom and limited production anodized aluminum and glass furniture for the home and office. Using high strength clear adhesives to join metal and glass, he creates furniture which is eminently functional, yet aesthetically and structurally minimal. Working with an excellent commercial anodizer, Handler produces a broad range of colors, frequently developing new ones to meet his clients' needs. Anodized aluminum, with its vibrant color spectrum, has a hard permanent surface that is highly scratch and stain resistant, requiring little care. Portfolio and aluminum color samples are available on request.

(top left) Coffee table, anodized aluminum and glass, 40" × 40" × 15"
Side tables, anodized aluminum, 15" × 30" × 17½"
Torchère quartz halogen, anodized aluminum, 8" × 10" × 72"
(bottom left) Pair of side tables. Graphics by Barbara Satterfield. Each table 12" × 24" × 17½". Tables, room dividers, and wall pieces with "painted" anodized aluminum graphics are commissionable.

Peter Handler

Peter Handler Studio
2400 W. Westmoreland St.
Philadelphia, PA 19128
(215) 483-4100

(bottom) Dining table, anodized aluminum
and glass, 29" × 60" diameter.

Jeffrey Harris

Designer/Woodworker
1663 11th Street
Sarasota, FL 33577
(813) 365-3669

Utilizing a wide variety of hardwoods and finishes, Jeffrey Harris and co-worker Jim Hubert have been building one of a kind fine furniture for residential, executive, and liturgical clients since 1975. He works closely with designers and architects from conception to installation. All work is done by commission.

As interior designers we appreciate Jeffrey's quality and understanding of design that adds the edge of perfection we need to produce a fine interior...
Victor Appel, ASID
Design Integrity, Inc.
Sarasota, Florida

Major commissions include:
Corporate offices of South Hopkins Coal Co. (pictured above. Oak with white-wash finish, walnut inlay)
Saint Gregory's Catholic Church, Miami
Epiphany Catholic Church, Venice

Highland Woodworks, Inc.

Bruce MacPhail
Box 22
South Strafford, VT 05070
(802) 785-4364

Bruce has been hand-building his own designs for fifteen years. He is a juried member of the League of New Hampshire Craftsmen, the Society of Arts and Crafts (Boston) and the Vermont State Craft Centers. He employs a clean, timeless line and traditional joinery, and each piece is meticulously finished and signed and numbered.

Most work is of oil-finished New England hardwoods like cherry and maple (including bird's-eye and curly), although any wood is available. Custom work can also be done in marble, slate or granite, alone or in combination with wood or metal.

Production and custom designs include fixed or extension dining tables which feature geared slides and in-table leaf storage, desks, laminated side-chairs in a variety of seatings, beds and more. Design service and brochure are available.

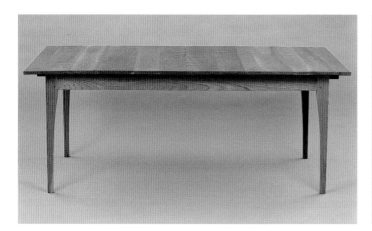

Jeff Kellar

P.O. Box 4770
Portland, ME 04112
(207) 773-6269

My work has appeared in American Craft, The New York Times Magazine, Interior Design and Industrial Design. Awards include the Daphne Award for occasional seating.

(top left) Detail of a tall cabinet, number two in the Ariel Series, a series of pieces the focus of which is interior space and sense of place. 65" × 34" × 22", East Indian rosewood, pearwood, gold leaf, palladium leaf, blown glass, rose quartz.
(top right) Plus Chair (lounge chair) 24" × 24" × 30 1/2 ", teak, cotton tape, foam.

(bottom) writing table 28" × 54" × 29", quilted mahogany, ebony. Plus Chair (desk/dining chair) 21" × 21" × 29 1/2 ", quilted mahogany, cotton tape, foam.

Please contact me for more information.

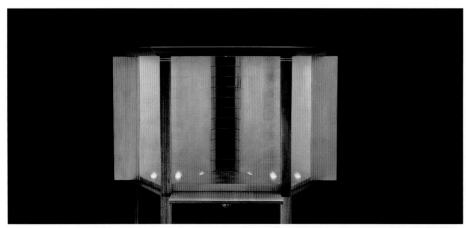

John Kennedy

Heartwood Craftsmen
312 West Columbia Avenue
Philadelphia, PA 19122
(215) 236-3050

John's furniture blends function and aesthetics in a subtle, clean, elegant style that harmonizes with many contemporary environments. His designs are carefully executed in combinations of domestic and foreign woods. The pieces are finished in either Tung oil or lacquer depending on the woods used and the protection required.

John is co-founder and co-owner of Heartwood Craftsmen, formed in 1978. His original designs for corporate and residential furniture are available through Heartwood. Commission work is also accepted. Delivery is usually within 12 weeks.

(top left) Coffee table, "A Striping Table," 52"L, 28"W, 17"H, curly maple with padauk striping.

(top right) End detail of dining extension table, "Dots and Stripes Forever.Qq2, 111" Open, 87" Closed, 43"W, 29"H Bird's-eye Maple with Padauk Striping.

(bottom) Four variations of the coffee table, "A Striping Table." Clockwise: Curly Cherry with Rosewood, Curly Maple with Padauk, Alligator Oak with English Brown Oak, Bubinga with Satinwood.

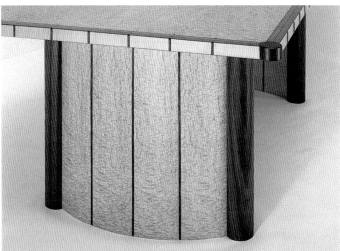

Stephen R. LaDrew

Custom Furniture and Interiors
Old Reliance School
Rt. 1 Box 1920
Reliance, VA 22649
(703) 869-6710

Stephen La Drew produces fine contemporary furniture for commercial and residential interiors. His background in architecture enables him to design durable and functional artistic solutions to meet client needs. In both one-of-a-kind and production designs, execution in rare and unusual hardwoods is a specialty.

The chair and executive desk shown here are built using traditional methods of construction including mortise and tenon joinery and bent lamination. Made of muiracatiara, a Brazilian hardwood, these are two in a series of works designed in 1986 for office or home environment. Information about these and other pieces is available on request.

(top) Tripod chair prototype; several variations available.
(bottom) Executive three drawer desk; 78"L × 32"W × 31"H.

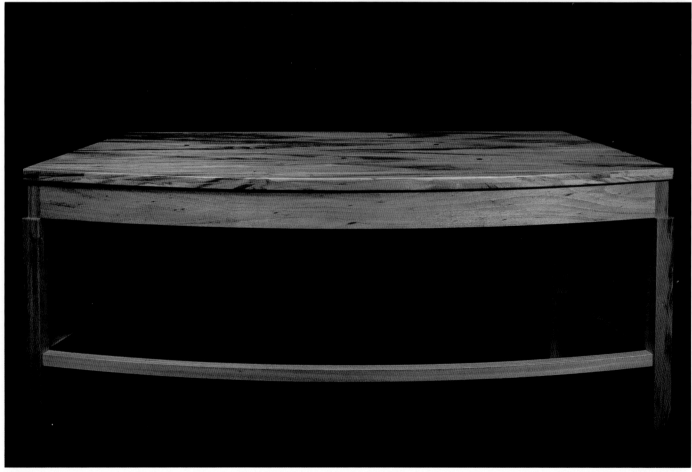

Mark S. Levin

Levin Inc.
1611 Simpson Street
Evanston, IL 60201
(312) 328-6541

Mark S. Levin's work is collected by corporations, museums, and private collectors. Approximately forty to fifty works are commissioned per year with a lead time of six to twelve months.

His work exudes beauty, sensuality and power.

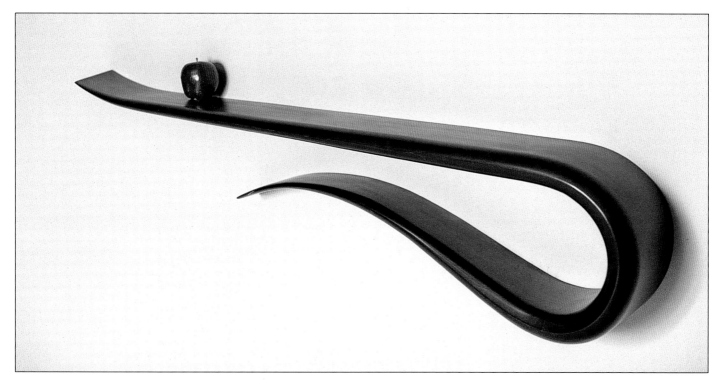

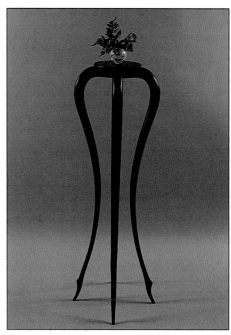

Monte Lindsley

Ptarmigan Willow
P.O. Box 551
Fall City, WA 98024
(206) 392-5767

Monte Lindsley has been designing contemporary willow furniture since 1978. His work has been shown nationally and featured in noted magazines and newspapers. His kinship with nature and movement is the backbone of his work.

All works constructed in limited individual editions. Using native materials of the Northwest (Willow, Maple, Aspen etc.), all materials are gathered by hand. Each piece is individually constructed and sealed with a protective finish and seasoned in the sun. All his works are created with function in mind.

One of his goals is to create a more eloquent contemporary look to a traditional craft form. This is achieved through his flowing loop designs. His work consists of bark, peeled and dyed pieces. Dyed colors include purples, blues, greens, whites, etc.

Brochure available—colorchart.

John McAlevey

100 Memorial Street
Franklin, NH 03235
(603) 934-3241

I have been designing and building furniture since 1964. My furniture is made from domestic and imported hardwoods and I use an oil finish unless otherwise specified.

Drawing upon my knowledge of traditional joinery and an ever present interest in fine art, I attempt to convey a strength of line and an attention to detail in my work.

Depending upon the size of a commission, the time from initial contact to delivery can be from three to six months.

I accept residential and corporate commissions.

(top) Library ladder Cherry
48"H × 18"W × 20"
(bottom) Credenza Mahogany
42"L × 20"W × 29"H

Jeffrey T. McCaffrey

McCaffrey Designs
1404 S.E. 26th Avenue
Portland, OR 97214
(503) 239-5367

Jeffrey T. McCaffrey designs and produces custom and limited edition furniture for private and commercial clients. Since completing his Master of Fine Arts Degree at the University of Wisconsin in 1982, McCaffrey has headed the Wood Department at the Oregon School of Arts and Crafts, and his studio has produced work for homes and offices across the country. Taking on an endless variety of shapes and forms, furniture by McCaffrey is unusual yet useful. Carefully defined line and simple, but powerful, forms are the essence of his art. McCaffrey is a recognized authority on bentwood, and brings this experience to much of his work. Pieces are usually commissioned from an existing portfolio with alterations incorporated to suit a particular environment.

(top) Writing Desk, 56" × 32" × 30"
White Oak
(bottom) Dining Set with two of six chairs shown, 60" diameter walnut. Similar design available in an oval with matching armchairs.

Bronwyn Rex Moore

607 Corona
Denver, CO 80218
(303) 744-0746

Artist and designer Bronwyn Rex Moore produces folding screens that are each unique works of art—paintings freed from walls. Vivid rhythmic patterns are enhanced with glittering metallics and hot flashes of color.

Each panel is entirely wood covered with gesso and painted in acrylic latex. All surfaces are finished with polyurethane for durability. Standard panel sizes are 12", 18", or 24" wide; 80" tall; and 1.5" thick. Three, four, or six panels are hinged together.

Screens are shipped assembled and crated by air freight. Delivery time one week on completed pieces.

Also shown are Sculpture Boxes assembled from found wood and painted in similar colors and designs, animal and fruit themes dominate.

Slides of currently available pieces provided on request. Custom projects welcome.

Thomas Moser

Thos. Moser Cabinetmakers, Inc.
415 Cumberland Avenue
Portland, Maine 04101
(207) 774-3791

Thos. Moser Cabinetmakers builds chairs, cases and tables suited for both the residential and contract markets. Known for their integrity in construction, commitment to utility and reverence for wood, their designs are gracefully proportioned interpretations of classic American furniture. They work predominantly in solid cherry, hand selected for it's distinctive color and clarity of grain.

A list of contract representatives for the architect and design community is available upon request.

(top) Thos. Moser Continuous Arm Chair. An American Classic. 41"H × 23"W × 17"D.

(bottom) Eastward Arm Chair. All the cherry components are faceted, giving the Eastward a highly-crafted feeling.
41"H × 19"W × 19"D.

Richard Scott Newman

66 Frost Avenue
Rochester, NY 14608
(716) 328-1577

Exquisite handmade furniture for the most discriminating clientele, corporate or residential. Providing a fresh approach to neoclassicism, Richard Newman's original designs offer fine materials, painstaking attention to details, and the best of modern and traditional technology. Recent commissions: Boston Museum of Fine Arts, Coca Cola Corp., Gannett Corp.

(top left) Umbrella stand, 33" × 14", Swiss pearwood, ebony, bronze
(top center) Demilune table, 40" × 17" × 29", figured maple, ebony
(top right) Fluted chair, 35" × 19" × 19", cherry, gold ormolu, silk
(bottom) Dining table, 70" × 46" × 30", opening to 118", Swiss pearwood, ebony, curly maple, gold-plated silver castings

Craig Nutt

Craig Nutt Fine Wood Works
2014 Fifth Street
Northport, Al 35476
(205) 752-6535

A fine example of Art Dino, "Deinonychus Desk" is based on a bipedal dinosaur whose name means 'terrible claw.' The 84" × 35" × 30" curved-top desk is carved from mahogany and sports ebony claws. A shallow drawer is concealed in the molded edge.

A Governor's Arts Award recipient, Craig Nutt has established a reputation for successful execution of residential and corporate commissions.

His furniture and sculpture has been featured in significant exhibitions in such museums and galleries as Southeastern Center for Contemporary Art, Birmingham Museum of Art and Zimmerman-Saturn Gallery; in publications including Horizon and Fine Woodoworking ; and in the American Craft Council Crafffairs in Baltimore and West Springfield.

Edward C. Overbay

2095 S. E. Airport Rd.
Warrenton, OR 97146
(503) 861-1379

Designer craftsman Edward Overbay and crew produce a wide range of finely crafted works including entry doors, bars, mantle pieces, cabinetry, room divider and shoji screens, contract furnishings, limited edition and one of a kind furniture. Current limited edition information available upon request.

(left) China cabinet: Teak, ebony. 84"H

(right) Chest of drawers: Cherry, rosewood, bubinga, aromatic cedar. 54"H

Norman Ridenour

Furniture Designer & Sculptor
1060 17th Street
San Diego, CA 92101
(619) 239-0588

Norman Ridenour has been a professional artisan since 1974. He has completed over a hundred commissions for private and corporate clients. He designs and creates limited edition pieces that can be ordered in various sizes and woods. He has the capability and experience to design custom pieces or whole environments.

(top) Coffee table. Ed of 20. Available in numerous woods. Several other similar designs have been developed.
(right) Bentwood chair.
(left) "Z" rocker, available in three sizes and as a dining or desk chair with or without arms.
(bottom) Desk. In walnut, top size 84 × 34. Available in cherry, walnut, oak, bubinga. Companion credenza available.

Daniel Mack Rustic Furnishings

225 West 106th Street
New York, NY 10025
(212) 866-5746

My custom rustic furniture combines the romantic and the improbable—grace with humor.

The Forest-style works with the natural shapes and strength of hardwood saplings. The Log-style emphasizes large-scale mass and straight lines.

If it's furniture, it can be made from trees: indoor-outdoor, chairs, tables, couches, beds, ladders, railings... fences, gazebos, bridges and other outdoor structures.

Retail furniture prices range from $650 for chairs to $3,000 for elaborate beds. Delivery time averages 3 months.

"Mack's twig furniture is virtually ideogrammatic, skating the line between sculpture and furniture. The backs and legs have the suggestive, weightless feel of Chinese calligraphy." House and Garden

"It's imaginative, it's calculated and it costs. Whimsey comes high." The New Yorker

Current Catalog: $3.00

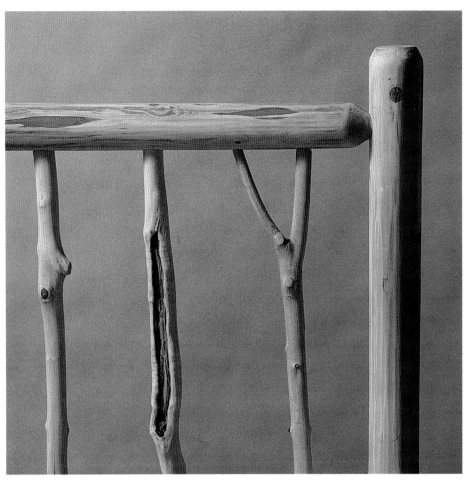

125

William (George) Rosenberger

13611 Beskeen Road
Herald, CA 95638
(209) 748-2679

George Rosenberger's sculptural furniture adapts well to both corporate and private decor. It is nothing short of excellent!

(top left) Tech One from the Contemporary Design Collection. This limited edition, the result of ageless tools, methods, modern equipment and techniques is fabricated of high quality 16 gauge stainless steel. Marble, ceramic, or glass surfaces available (34″ × 55″ × 12″)

(top right) Oriental Oak captures a decomposed granite garden in a collar of fine handcrafted oak, hovering above a natural river stone bed, all supported by a recessed stainless steel pedestal. (54″ × 54″ × 10½″)

(bottom) Any Which Way from the Abstract Collection. A six sided form which can present itself as a vertical freestanding sculpture, or expose a stainless steel or rusted black iron surfaced table. (24″ × 34″ × 16″)

Fred L. Saunders

Crechairs
6245 36th Avenue N.E.
Seattle, WA 98115
(206) 523-4604

Saunders has been painting and drawing since he could hold a crayon. More recently, his doodles have evolved into Crechairs; tables and chairs utilizing the shapes of wildlife. His creations vary from armadillos to wolverines, rocking chairs to work desks. Each piece is signed, dated and copyrighted.

The chairs and painted table parts are constructed of Medite©, individually painted by hand and air-brush, then four-coated with polyurethane. The table tops are lucite or glass.

Crechairs are unique, aesthetically and conceptually, collected for conversation, function and beauty. They complement any interior, providing a whimsical mood to their environment.

Call or write for a representative portfolio and price list.

Joel Shepard

Joel Shepard Furniture
12419 NE 124th
Kirkland, WA 98034
(206) 823-4545

Joel Shepard specializes in a degree of artistry and craftsmanship seldom found in the marketplace. Handcrafting one-of-a-kind or small number multiples of commercial and residential furniture from premium quality veneers and hardwoods has built Shepard's reputation as one of the finest craftsmen in America. Each project has its own set of challenges. Translating those challenges into the most appropriate solutions for the client has become the benchmark for Shepard's product. Nearly 20 years of experience in design and fabrication of custom pieces from strongly traditional motifs to slick contemporary designs have given Shepard the facility to be comfortable working in a remarkably wide variety of styles, materials and finishes. When you can choose nothing but the best for you or your clients, contact Joel Shepard.

Joel Shepard

Joel Shepard Furniture
12419 NE 124th
Kirkland, WA 98034
(206) 823-4545

(Facing page)Dining table. Wenge, brushed brass, glass. 40" × 72" × 30" extending to 108" with two wenge leaves.
Side chairs. Elm, fabric.

(top) Desk. African mahogany crotch veneer, wenge, Honduras mahogany.
36" × 60" × 30"

(bottom) Game table. Walnut, walnut burl, exotic burled chess board with backgammon on reverse. 36" × 36" × 30".
Chairs. Walnut, walnut burl, fabric.

Portfolio of representative work available upon request.

Peter Superti

Trans Hudson Design, Inc.
49 Harrison Street
Hoboken, New Jersey
(201) 798-3018

My work encompasses a variety of materials and techniques, used in a way that interprets an idea, attitude or style. I've never felt hell-bent on any one particular approach. I see my work as a series of phases affected primarily by my own stimulation. I've had extensive training in traditional furniture construction and apply these standards to ensure the integrity of my work.

(top) "Day at the Beach" Black slate/Yellow Pine 15"h x 30"d x 48" w
(bottom) Blake Table Birds Eye Maple/Cocobola 60" diam x 28" h

Thomas Swift

Pin Oak Design
Route 1 Box 122B
Paw Paw, WV 25434
(304) 947-7109

Fine modern furniture for both residential and commercial interiors. A catalog of limited edition pieces is available. Commissions are also accepted.

(top) Hall Table, detail, ebonized walnut, 32"H × 67½"L × 17"D
(bottom) Table for Three, padauk and maple, 29½"H × 46" on a side. Part of a commission for the restaurant New Heights in Washington DC.

Joseph Tracy

Joseph Tracy Woodworks
Rt. 102
Mt. Desert Island, ME 04660
(207) 244-7360

A small company specializing in the design and construction of commissioned and limited-production furniture of simple line, using domestic and imported hardwoods. Tracy studied woodworking and furniture design for six years at the School for American Craftsman, Rochester, N.Y., and an additional year studying furniture design in Scandinavia.

An unbound collection of photographs is available which includes other tea cart designs in wood and stainless steel, tables, lamps and a descriptive price list. The cost of the photo collection is $10, which is refundable.

(below) Tea cart, maple, plate glass, plexiglass wheels, rubber tires, 36"L × 24"W × 32"H

Trans-Time Design, Inc.

Fine Furniture & Cabinetry
1915 7th Avenue
Ybor City, FL 33605
(813) 247-3015

For the past eight years Trans-Time Design, Inc. has been specializing in custom furniture for the architectural and design community.

Although Florida is our primary market, we have completed projects throughout North America, including Montreal, Minneapolis and Honolulu.

Our style is contemporary with expertise in laminates, lacquer, faux finishes and Avonite.

Past and present clients include:

General Telephone of Florida
Lincoln Properties Corp.
North Carolina National Banks
First Florida Banks
Shearson/Lehman American Express

(top) Wall unit, private residence
Constructed of Plastic Laminate
Designer: Thom Thibodeau
(bottom) Reception Desk, Lincoln Properties
Corp., Tampa, Florida
Constructed of Plastic Laminate
Designer: Thom Thibodeau

A Partnership

When you commission a piece of furniture, you are entering into a partnership with the artist. You are the catalyst that initiates a chain of events resulting in the creation of a unique work.

You present the furniture maker with a problem to solve, or a set of parameters to work within. Typical considerations include function, size, type of wood, color, or a mood or tone that you want to create. The finished piece can reflect something of your own personality as well as the creative vision of the artist.

In order to successfully integrate your needs with the furniture maker's artistic goals, it is important to search for common ground. If you have seen some of the artist's work that you like, the chances are good that you share some common interests or sensibilities.

What is it about the work that appeals to you? What are some of your likes and dislikes? What other things are you comfortable with, or excited by?

While your input into the process is vital, the artist needs to have as much latitude as possible in the creation of the work.

As you discuss the potential piece, it is possible that your interests may not be compatible. If this turns out to be the case, do not be discouraged. There are other artists who may be perfect for the job. However, it is probable that you will find that common ground and can proceed with designing the piece.

Each artist works a little differently. The presentation I make is usually in the form of a scale drawing or drawings, but sometimes it will be a model or photograph of a model. For this work, I charge a design fee. This fee, which varies according to the complexity and size of the job, pays for a portion of the time I spend on the design. To me, it represents a certain amount of commitment to the project.

Once I have completed the design, I am able to provide a realistic estimate of the cost of the piece, and project a delivery date.

If the customer is pleased with the design and satisfied with the price, we proceed to the best part: the realization of a unique and personal piece of furniture. It is even possible that along the way the customer will become hooked on the notion of commissioning art. I have seen it happen.

Craig Nutt

Craig Nutt
Furniture Maker and Sculptor
Northport, Alabama

Stephen Turino

Designer/Craftsman
P. O. Box 343
Fort Ninigret Road
Charlestown, RI 02813
(401) 364-3511

Turino designs and executes one-of-a-kind pieces of furniture for the residential or commercial setting. Fine cabinetry and special architectural details can also be accommodated. The techniques employed vary to meet the individual design requirements of each piece. Attention to detail, construction and finish are upheld as in the finest furniture tradition. Being a small versatile shop makes it possible to meet the needs of a wide variety of commissions.

Education includes: Peters Valley Craftsmen, Layton, NJ, and Boston University Program in Artisanry: BAA in Woodworking and Furniture Design.

(top left) Mirror/Lamp, Purpleheart, Ebony, Curly Maple, sandblasted glass and mirror. 74" × 17" × 7"
(top right) End Table, Rosewood, Curly and Birdseye Maple. 26" × 24" × 15"
(bottom) Bed (Queen Size), Ebonized Mahogany. 86" × 65" × 56"

Preston Wakeland

Rt. 4 Box 40
Lockport, IL 60441
(815) 838-1285

Almost all of my work is commissioned by my clients. As such, I must adapt my taste and training to their needs so that I can produce a piece that pleases them as much as it does me. As a result, I find all periods of furniture design artistically challenging. The fact that wood is moisture sensitive dictated many early designs such as the wide use of frame and panel construction. The modern woodworker has the advantage of more stable materials like plywood. Such products permit the construction of large flat panels so prevalent in contemporary designs. Some of my traditional designs speculate on what seventeenth century furniture might have looked like if the cabinetmakers of the day had had these modern materials to work with.

(top) Credenza (speculative piece). Solid Ash with Walnut and natural cane accents. 60" Wide × 30" High × 22" Deep.
(bottom) China cabinet for private residence. Solid Walnut with Carpathian Elm burl accents on doors and drawer fronts. Marble top and mirrored back. 10' Wide × 8' High × 2' Deep.

Leslie Wicker

Artist/Designer
P. O. Box 5077
Asheville, NC 28813
(704) 687-0583

Original decorative folding screens crafted of finest quality hardwoods and opalescent stained glass are available in limited editions and one-of-a-kind designs. An expressive decorative element as well as an aesthetic solution for dividing space, these screens furnish privacy or background settings, and with the addition of back lighting, a dramatic light source. Smaller screens, (top) can create a colorful focal point in front of a fireplace not in use. All screens feature double folding hinges which allow many possible variations in standing form.

Inquiries will receive photos and pertinent information on screens currently available.

(top) "Irises" Oak, 36 ½" H x 52 ¼" W

(bottom) "Magnolia" handcarved Mahogany, 78" H x 68 ¼" W

Rick Wrigley Furniture

80 Race Street
Holyoke, MA 01040
(413) 536-2034

Corporate Fluency: In the realm of executive suites, each piece of furniture must communicate eloquently.

Articulate image-making demands a sensitivity to design, absent in standard mill work.

Rick Wrigley Furniture has taken its place in the executive suites of HBO, Bell of Pennsylvania, and Pandick Inc., as well as in the Legislative Office Building in Hartford, Connecticut.

Interior Design Magazine called the HBO headquarters, which showcases the Wrigley/KPFC table shown on this page, "One of the best installations of 1985." In mahogany and wenge with inlays of sterling silver, mother-of-pearl, and marble, this table is fourteen feet long and five feet wide.

Whether you envision furnishings of your own design, a Wrigley design, or a collaborative venture, Rick Wrigley Furniture will speak well for you.

TEXTILES AND FABRICS

Patsy Allen

Designer/Quilt Artist
P.O. Box 5699
Greensboro, NC 27403
(919) 272-0912

Patsy Allen designs and makes one-of-a-kind quilts for private, corporate and architectural settings. She specializes in large scale and multi-panel works. The quilts are made of prewashed, 100% cotton fabrics with poly batting and are machine pieced and quilted.

Patsy Allen's quilts are exhibited nationally and internationally. Her bold geometric designs and sophisticated colors have garnered numerous awards. Ms. Allen's works are in many corporate collections including IBM, Steelcase, NCNB and Farm Credit System Building. Publications include Fiberarts, Metropolis, Threads and The Quiltmaker's Art.

Commission information: $200. per square foot, retail; $250. design proposal fee; Average delivery time—6 to 8 weeks.

(top) ©1986 DECO PINWHEEL III: CARNIVAL; 51″ × 15′; Commissioned by IBM, Boca Raton, Florida.
(bottom) ©1986 DECO TEPEE I: ARROWHEAD; 43″ × 92½″

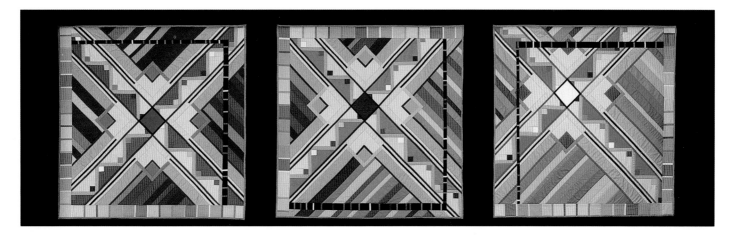

Tafi Brown

Artist/Designer
The American Wing
HC 63 Box 48
East Alstead, NH 03602
(603) 835-6952

Tafi Brown's consistently award-winning wall quilts have been acquired and commissioned by private collectors as well as banks and corporations. They have appeared in both international and national juried shows since 1976.

Tafi builds fiber art from cyanotype photographs, using the original archival method of blueprinting developed by Sir John Herschel in 1840. The interaction of the subject, the photography, and design result in a truly unique fiber art form that employs the essence of the separate disciplines and ends as more than the sum of its parts.

(top) "Hammerbeam Variations", machine pieced cyanotype prints on cotton, hand-quilted 46" × 46"
(bottom) "Compound Joinery", machine pieced and quilted cyanotype prints on cotton. 60" × 37"

Catherine Creamer

Creamer Textile Design
41 Union Square West
New York, NY 10003
(212) 255-6210

State of the art computer equipment is used to design fabric for corporate and residential interiors. As a prototype center for many major mills throughout the U.S., the studio provides technical expertise and design consulting to develop and execute woven concepts. Applications vary from upholstery cloth to free hanging textiles, including screens and draped or framed wall treatments. Prices range from $30.00 to $150.00 per square foot.

Catherine Creamer, designer and owner, is coordinator of the Textile Program at Parsons School of Design as well as a member of the faculty at both Parsons and The New School in NYC. Her work is represented throughout the country in collections and galleries. Creamer received her training in Norway and at the School for American Craftsmen in Rochester, NY, and currently lectures on computer aided textile design.

Ann S. Epstein

Fiber Artist
2316 Walter Drive
Ann Arbor, MI 48103
(313) 996-9019

Ann Epstein's painterly ikat-woven hangings integrate color and texture to express the interior landscape and universal emotional themes of our everyday lives. Her work has been shown around the country at juried exhibitions, invitational shows, and galleries, and has been featured in Fiberarts magazine. The one-of-a-kind multi-panel weavings are of fine, hand-dyed, cotton yarns in complex twill patterns. Individual panels can be any length and up to approximately three feet in width, combining to produce pieces whose total dimensions can meet any space requirement. The color range is unlimited, and weavings are backed with velcro for easy installations. The artist accepts both residential and corporate commissions.

(top left) Separations, 44″ × 79″; (top right) Inner Outerspace 45″ × 55″; (bottom) Home Fires 44″ × 69″

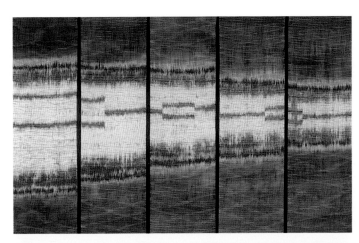

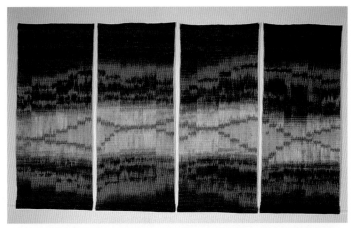

Pamela Hill

Imperial Hotel Building
P.O. Box 221
Amador City, CA 95642
(209) 267-0670

Although frequently used as wall pieces, the quilts are designed and constructed to be durable for everyday use as bed covers. All are filled with PolarGuard and are machine-washable. Commissions are accepted.

"Occasionally one finds a genuine 'power object': Something with the presence, the intensity, that one associates with a genuine artistic statement; most notably Pamela Hill's vivid, geometrically patterned quilts."
Thomas Albright
San Francisco Chronicle

(top) Detail "Praiser"
(bottom) "Praiser," 108" × 120", machine-pieced and quilted of pima cotton, satin and metallic fabrics.

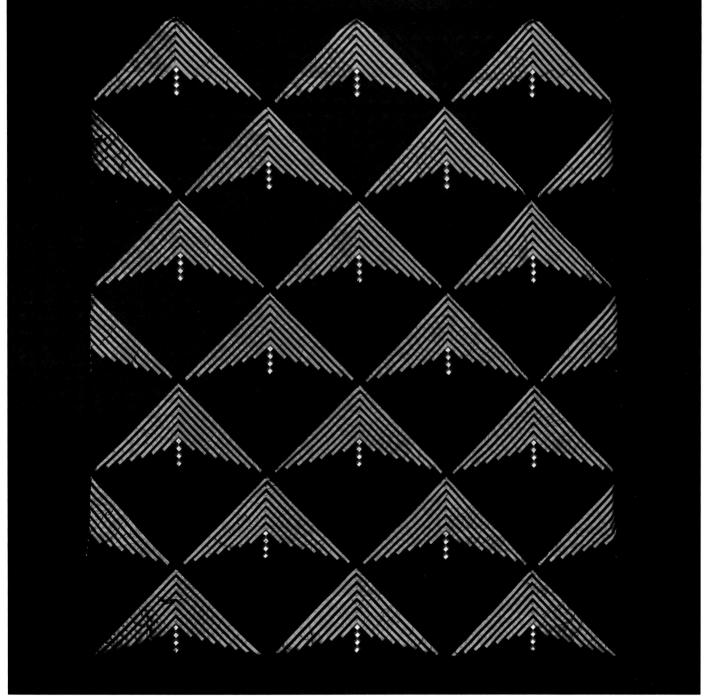

Judith Larzelere

254-C Westfield Street
Dedham, MA 02026
(617) 329-4936

Judith's colorfully evocative, intricate quilts have been selected for Quilt National '81, '83, '85 (individual choice '87) and other national and international shows. Corporate commissions include Biogen, Inc., Weston Hotels, General Electric Company, DEC. Many private collectors enjoy her work.

Commission information: $85 per square foot - retail price; $2,000 minimum retail prices; $250 rendering fee.

Available quilts - slides upon request; retail price $1,200 and up.

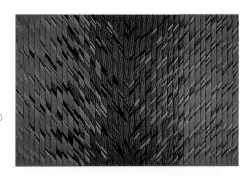

(top) MARRIAGE OF BLUE AND ORANGE, 78" × 110", machine quilted 100% cotton, collection of Kathe Gregory, New York, NY, © 1980.

(bottom) DAYGLOW, 78" × 72", machine quilted 100% cotton, © 1986.

Nancy Lubin

Western Maine Weavers
13 Pearl Street
Camden, ME 04843
(207) 236-4069

Handwoven throws in luxury fibers for all seasons.

For ten years Nancy Lubin has been working with interior designers across the country to provide a resource for custom- designed throws. In addition, her company has an excellent inventory for immediate choice. Her throws appear frequently in major home design magazines. Nancy exhibits regularly at prestigious national craft fairs as well as national trade shows.

All: 48" × 72" plus fringe, mohair and brushed wool throws

(top) Turquoise/rose plaid
(bottom left) Pastel plaid
(bottom right) Celadon/moss plaid

Solid colors available.

Maeve Matthews

M. Matthews Handwoven Fabrics
21 Hillcrest Drive
Rochester, NH 03867
(603) 332-6779

Custom Weaving of Yardage and Home Accessories

Our fabrics are carefully woven by hand of natural fibers in original designs to complement contemporary and traditional decors. These handwovens may be used for window treatments and tabletop. We also create custom designs and fabrics for other unusual settings and uses.

Shown are fabrics of silk, cotton, and rayon blends in a variety of weaves and textures with special fringes for tabletop pieces and window treatments.

Suzanne Punch

560 West End Avenue, 1-W
New York, NY 10024
(212) 595-8531

The ancient art of painting on silk is revived here in luminous color. Framed and under plexiglass, a series of orchids grace a Tokyo restaurant. As free-hanging banners, a large abstract painting completes the atrium of Oyster Point Hotel in Redbank, New Jersey. Now working in association with Basia Poindexter, these paintings can be seen in galleries across the country:

S.A. Stockton - Los Angeles
Incorporated Gallery - NY, NY
Shirley Scott - Southampton, NY
Sylvia Ullman - Shaker Heights, OH
Roche Bobois - Philadelphia, PA

Steve Stratakos

100 North Stone
LaGrange, IL 60525
(312) 354-6218

Chicago artist Steve Stratakos creates textile collages—detailed quilts that combine appliqué techniques and unique fabrics. The images—ranging from historic and current events to legend and myth—reflect the artist as a quiltmaker who defines fabric as a medium of unlimited expression.

The artist will produce "fabric paintings" in any size quilt or banner for public or private space in homes, offices, and other institutions including libraries and museums.

Stratakos will present preliminary sketches with photographs of more than 40 major works and will meet with clients as needed to create a unique product with which to decorate or commemorate.

(top) Little Big Horn
 quilt 61" × 71" (155cm × 180cm)
(bottom) Hors d'oeuvres
 quilt 80" × 42" (203cm × 107cm)

Jill Wilcox

36 West 20th Street, 4th Floor
New York, NY 10011
(718) 858-0868

Ms. Wilcox makes hand-painted textiles in one-of-a-kind and limited editions, suitable for banners, wall hangings and bed coverings. Designs range from realistic forms found in nature to abstract patterns drawn from her work as a painter.

She draws also upon her extensive experience as an artist and designer in the New York textile industry for her meticulous attention to color relationships and design detail.

(right) Shell hanging 59" × 28".
(left) Child's butterfly quilt 41" × 36".

FLOOR COVERINGS

Patricia Ancona

19 Lovell - Studio B
San Rafael, CA 94901
(415) 258-9790

Patricia Ancona is a designer-sculptor. She is a recipient of a National Endowment for the Arts Fellowship and lived in Italy where she created designs for the ceramic tile industry and worked in collaboration with Architect Ebe Montanari on interiors. In addition to the rugs shown here, she is presently creating ceramic wall pieces and is an artist for Kohler Company Artist Editions, Kohler, Wisconsin.

The rugs can be placed on the floor or walls and are 60 line hand-knotted wool. Designs are original and are available by either commission or non-commission in limited editions of 5. Portfolio of designs is available. Colors range from rich to subtle. Color and rug samples available. Many sizes. Each rug individually produced upon order. Delivery approximately 3 months or less.

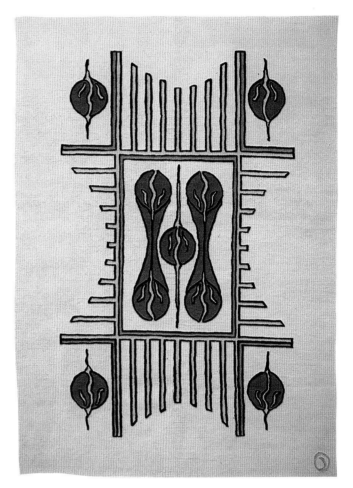

Carolyn and Vincent Carleton

Carleton Designs
1015A Greenwood Road
Elk, California 95432
(707) 877-3540

Carleton Designs is a weaving studio dedicated to the art of fine rug-making. Working in a traditional American summer-winter weave, Carolyn and Vincent Carleton create rugs that are reversible, with one side the inverse image of the other.

Each design is limited to an edition of ten, all signed and dated. Yarns of the finest worsted spun Argentine wool are hand-dyed, using Swiss dyes for optimum wash and light-fastness. The rugs, handwoven on a warp of Belgian linen, are offered in standard as well as custom sizes, ranging from area rugs and runners to large room-size carpets. Custom dye-matching is also available.

Major shows include "For The Floor," American Craft Museum, New York, and first place award at Convergence, Dallas, by Handweavers Guild of America.

Top: "Diamondback", 20' × 22'

Bottom: inverse of "Diamondback"

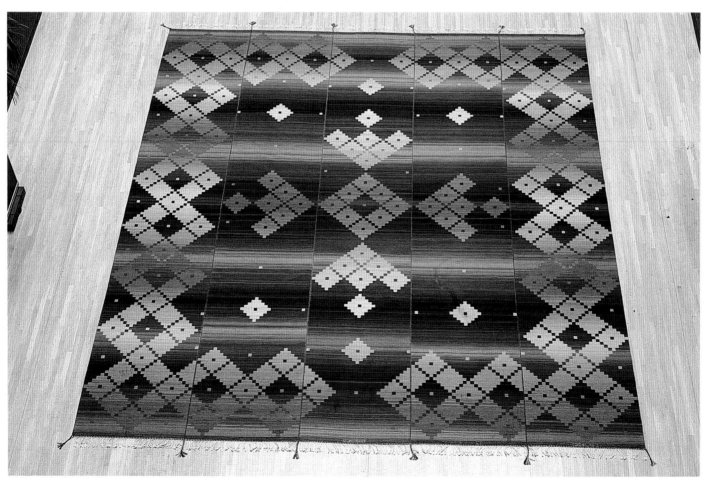

Kathy Cooper

Orchard House Floorcloths
Rt. 5 Box 214
King, NC 27021
(919) 994-2612

Cooper specializes in whimsical designs, using animal, vegetable and abstract imagery. Custom work is available. Made of heavy canvas, each floorcloth is hand-painted, then receives several coats of varnish for a durable yet flexible surface. The colors will not fade. Floor canvases are intended for practical use on hard floor surfaces, or may be hung on the wall. The floorcloth is cleaned with mild soap and a damp sponge. Periodic waxing recommended to protect the varnish.

Cooper's canvases have been featured in New York magazine, House Beautiful, Metropolitan Home, Better Homes and Gardens Decorating and Country Homes.

(top)"Hawaiian Flowers and Stripes" © 1986 2½' × 3'

(bottom) "Abstract Floral with Checks" © 1986 3' × 12' (interior: Dean Farris)

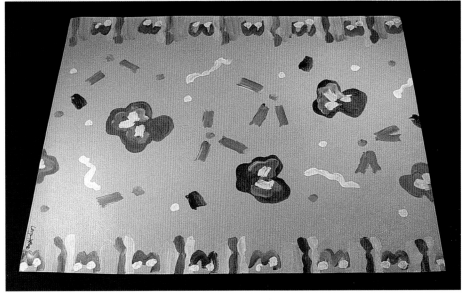

Gwen-lin Goo

596 Broadway
Suite 902
New York, NY 10012
(212) 925-5523

Vision, finesse, and technical expertise are combined uniquely in the works of Gwen-lin Goo.

Unexpected layers of color and pattern are spirited and enduring in her one of a kind silk screened heavy canvas floor and wall coverings.

Duality and illusion, repetition and subtle changes are shimmering elements in her imagery of fishes, flowers, and geometric patterns. Multiple layers of shellac enhance the richness of colors, durability and ease of maintenance.

The artist works on special commissions from her Soho loft. She has exhibited nationally from the showroom of Jack Lenor Larsen to the permanent collection at the Renwick. In addition to special commissions she has reproduced Wiener Werkstätte printed textiles for the Metropolitan Museum of Art.

(right) Humuhumu, Phase I 25" × 70"
(below) detail-Humuhumu, Phase II
26" × 54"

Sara Hotchkiss

Sara Hotchkiss, Handweaver
P.O. Box 4213
Portland, ME 04101
(207) 871-1426

Custom designed tapestry rugs for wall or floor, handwoven of cotton warp and fabric in soft shaded color variations. Design motifs of borders, squares, diamonds, stripes or visual images are constructed in a traditional tapestry technique. Quality materials and a dense weave structure make for rugs that will withstand years of use. Larger sizes available. Produced by commission, as one-of-a-kind pieces, or in limited edition.

(top left) "Bermuda Checkerboard" 3' × 5', limited edition, rug or wall hanging.
(top right) "Reflecting Triangles" 3' × 5', limited edition, rug or wall hanging.
(bottom) "Madd Apple Mandela", 36" × 38", commission, wall hanging.

Ayalah Jonas

1525 West End Drive
Philadelphia, PA 19151
(215) 473-3664

Represented by:
J.M. Sorkin
616 West Lancaster Avenue
Wayne, PA 19087
(215) 964-0333

Contemporary art pieces for the residential or corporate floor. Hand-tufted in limited editions of 100% wool. Actual production time 10-12 weeks. Delivery, F.O.B. Philadelphia. Color renderings will be submitted within four weeks of receiving specifications and a design fee. Strike-off follows placement of order.

Ayalah Jonas, a teacher at the Parsons School of Design, New York, graduated with an MFA from the School for American Craftsmen. Jonas' fabrics could be found in her line of scarves commissioned by Henri Bendel's and in a signature collection of winter coats.

(top) 6'6" × 9'9" © 1985
(bottom) 6'6" × 9'9" © 1986

Interiors by Leslie John Koeser,
Roche-Bobois/Philadelphia.

Connie Kindahl

364 Daniel Shays Highway
Pelham, MA 01002
(413) 253-5572

Connie Kindahl has been designing and weaving flat woven rugs since receiving a Master Weavers Certificate in 1981. She has also studied in Norway. Her work has been shown nationally and is in a number of private and corporate collections.

The rugs are woven on a Swedish countermarch loom with Irish linen warp and high quality wool rug yarns, washed, moth-proofed and with a high resistance to fading.

The weaving technique is done with superior craftsmanship to give a firm rug which will lie flat on the floor or hang flat against the wall. They are reversible and are woven to be functional and durable. They are easily maintained.

Designs are one of a kind with emphasis placed on colors and their constantly occurring changes and relationships to each other.

Beth Minear

1115 East Capitol Street, SE
Washington, DC 20003
(202) 544-1714

Beth Minear's rugs are noted for their original designs, distinctive use of colors, and tight construction. They are individually woven using techniques with historical origins in colonial America and Scandinavia.

Usable as floor coverings or wall hangings, they add a dimension to both living and office space. High quality wool weft on Irish linen warp assures durability whatever the setting. Rugs for wall mounting available with Velcro or plexiglass rods. An assortment of sizes is available, including floor runners. Commissions are welcome.

Minear's work has been shown in recent years at exhibitions and galleries in Maryland (at the American Crafts Council shows), the District of Columbia, New Jersey, Pennsylvania and Virginia. Her rugs hang in the corporate offices of Citicorp in Washington and Sulzer Ruti in Switzerland.

(top) "Strange Imaginings", 46" × 75"
(bottom) "Aegean Aurora", 42" × 75"

Lyn Sterling Montagne

476 Bryan Street
Atlanta, GA 30312
(404) 577-6007

Lyn Sterling Montagne operates a weaving studio specializing in custom and limited edition handwoven rugs. A variety of materials and styles are available. Prices range from $15 to $80 per square foot. No size limitation. Ten week delivery on most orders.

Represented in private and corporate collections. Rugs have been shown in museums across the country. Design Award, American Craft Museum, 1985.

(top) 5 × 6 ikat painted pattern, linen and rayon
(bottom) 3½ × 5 painted pattern, linen and rayon

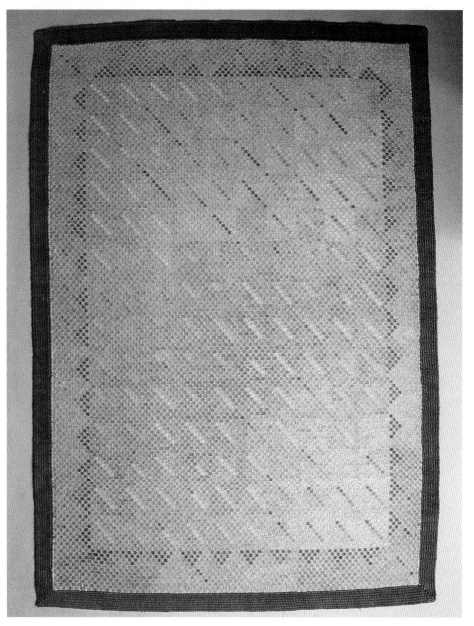

Dianne Carol Roach

Handweaver & Fiber Artist
1314 Rhode Island Avenue, N.W.
Washington, DC 20005
(202) 234-4941 and 232-5325

Specializes in one-of-a-kind and commissioned rugs and wall pieces in linen warps with wool surfaces, often with reversible designs. Suitable for interior installations for corporate, commercial and residential locations.

B.F.A. Textile Design, Moore College of Art, 1970, Philadelphia, Penna.

(See also Floor Coverings)

(below) Private residence, Washington, D.C., McCartney-Lewis, Architects, Washington, D.C.
Wall piece, 24″ × 60″, floor piece, 42″ × 72″

Kate Rohrer

Designer/Weaver
Plainweave Studio
Winter: P.O. Box 64
Middleton, WI 53562
(608) 831-0424
Summer: 6345 Hwy. 57
Rt. 3
Sturgeon Bay, WI 54235
(414) 823-2129

I weave contemporary wool or rag rugs for floors and walls. The rugs are tightly woven with high quality materials, resulting in a sturdy but thin, flexible product. Designs range from bold to subtle, colorful to neutral; input from the client is welcome. Plainweave rugs are currently in private and corporate collections. Wool rugs are $30-$75 sq/ft, based on the complexity of design and whether hand dying is required. Rag rugs cost $8-$20 sq/ft. Design fee is $50-$100, waived upon signing of contract. Size limitation: 5' width, 20' length.

(left) "Baffled", 3' × 5'. Wool, tapestry weave.
(right) Rag rug, 3' × 5'. Cotton strips, log cabin weave.

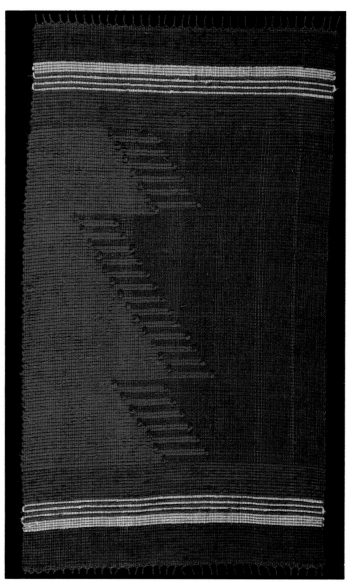

Sally Vowell-Gurley

Rug Designer/Weaver
609 Valle Street
Ft. Worth, TX 76108
(817) 448-9525

Each rug is custom designed to fit the needs and personality of the client and the space it will occupy. Using 100% wool weft, durable Irish linen warp, and all natural custom dyeing she designs and weaves rugs for the floor. They are flat weave rugs and reversible. Size is unlimited. The maximum unseamed width is ten feet.

Her rugs are found in corporate and private collections throughout the United States. There is a design fee that includes consultation with the client, a colored rendering drawn to scale, and a "mock-up" of the design with the actual yarns. The price is $50 per square foot plus a minimal dyeing charge, with 50% due when contract signed, 50% due on completion.

Brochure available on request.

(top) "Interaction" 9'4" × 14'4"
(bottom) "Calculated Risk" 6' × 9'

TAPESTRIES

Annie Curtis Chittenden

190 Neck Road
Madison, CT 06443
(203) 245-4925

I design and weave framed architectural wall pieces and free-hanging tapestries for public, corporate and residential spaces. On site-specific commissions, I work closely with clients, considering the interior and exterior dynamics of the location for inspiration.

My representational landscapes often act as windows, bringing the outdoors inside to provide the illusion of greater space. My more abstract designs also contain three-dimensional illusion to create a sense of expanding and receding space.

Installations are durable and virtually maintenance free. Choice blends of silk, wool, cotton and linen yarns soften and add warmth to contemporary interiors. Brochure and General Terms available on request.

Collections/Commissions:
Connecticut Commission on the Arts: Attorney General's Offices (Hartford, CT)
Scovill Corporation: World Headquarters (Waterbury, CT)
Automatic Data Processing (N.Y.C.)
County Federal Savings (Stratford, CT)

Larry Edman

739 Jenifer Street
Madison, Wisconsin 53703
(608) 255-0648

Edman designs and weaves for you—
tapestries, hangings, rugs and other textiles
for both corporate and residential interiors.

Tapestry designs which unite and complement your interiors while providing an
impressive focal point are a specialty. They
are woven in traditional flat and pile weaves
from a color palette of over 100 colors of
wool on a linen warp foundation.
Unseamed widths of up to seven feet and
lengths up to thirty feet are possible. Design
images range from abstract geometric
compositions to representational realism.

Corporate commissions include banks, hospitals, churches; insurance, publishing,
video production and telephone companies; government, law and medical offices
in Wisconsin, Illinois, Iowa, Minnesota, Kansas
Oklahoma and Florida.

(top) Oscar Mayer Inc., Madison, WI. Geometric Tapestry, 98" × 62"
(bottom) American Family Ins., Madison, WI.,
Landscape Tapestry, 26' × 4'

170

Louise Weaver Greene

Louise Weaver Greene Tapestries
2304 Ashboro Drive
Chevy Chase, MD 20815
(301) 585-1011

Original-design flatwoven weft-faced tapestries handwoven of Norwegian wool weft and Irish linen warp. Available as one-of-a-kind production pieces or woven by commission.

Represented in private and corporate collections throughout the United States and in Canada.

Prices and further information available upon request.

Exhibitions:
American Craft Museum, New York, NY
Smithsonian Institution, Washington, DC
University of Toronto, Canada
Delaware Art Museum, Wilmington, DE
Meredith Gallery, Baltimore, MD
Detroit Gallery of Contemporary Crafts, MI

(Above) "Color Field", 50" × 72".
Corporate collection, Gannett Co., Inc.
Washington, DC. Commissioned, 1986.
(Below) "Winter Gothic", 50" × 36".
Corporate collection, Dominion Federal Savings and Loan, Tysons Corner, VA. 1986

Silvia Heyden

2729 Montgomery Street
Durham, NC 27705
(919) 489-0582

Heyden tapestries originate as a spontaneous dialogue between the vision of the weaver and the possibilities of the loom. Tapestry is a progression in space and time, more akin to music than to that of painted design.

MAJOR SOLO EXHIBITIONS: Duke University Museum of Art, Durham, NC; Bank of America, San Francisco, CA; BM Centrum, Mannheim, Hamburg and Dusseldorf, Germany; Landis and Gyr Foundation, Zug, Switzerland; and Stadtmuseum, Graz, Austria.

LARGE COMMISSIONS: Bank and Trust Company, New York, NY; Nordfinanzbank, Zurich, Switzerland, Judea Reformed Congregation, Durham, NC; Royal Davis Library, UNC, Chapel Hill, NC; Warner Lambert Pharmaceutical, Morris Plains, NJ; Round Hill Community Church, Greenwich, CT; Choate Rosemary Hall, Wallingford, CT; Hilton Gateway, Newark, NJ and New York Hilton Hotel, New York, NY.

(top) "Sierra", 5' × 5½', CCB, Winston-Salem, NC

(bottom) "Ready to Fly", 6' × 5' Private Collection

Pamela Hird Klein

6805-4 Panamint Row
San Diego, CA 92139
(619) 267-2997

Each tapestry is individually designed and handwoven by the artist, Pamela Hird Klein. Her pieces are of an abstract nature, varying from a leaf motif or landscape, to geometric expressions of color. Pieces have been woven in rectangular, square, and circular shapes depending on the size and shape needed. A scale drawing of the piece and dyed yarn samples can be provided for prospective commissions. Finished pieces are usually available for inspection. Prices are determined by square footage.

Major commissions and collectors: Sutton Construction, Cole-Wheatman, Flak Corporation, and Scripps Memorial Hospital.

Pamela received her B.F.A. from Pratt Institute, with prior weaving and tapestry training in Sweden.

(top) "Windows", 52″ × 55″.
(bottom) "Rolling Along", 42″ × 70″

Michelle Lester

15 West 17th Street - 9th Floor
New York, NY 10011
(212) 989-1411

Michelle Lester earned a BFA from the Cleveland Institute of Art and an MFA in Design from Syracuse University. Her original designs often suggest stylized landscapes, yet her Studio has also produced works of photographic realism. It is equipped to execute any size and number of wool tapestries. Although most corporate clients require large scale work, Michelle has developed miniature tapestries in silk and wool for smaller spaces.

Major Commissions and Collections:3M Company; Manufacturer's Hanover Trust; Women's Hospital; R.J. Reynolds Industries; Art Museum University of Kentucky; IBM; Federal Home Loan Mortgage Corporation; Toyota; Texaco; Carter, Hawley & Hale; Southwest Bell; Prudential Insurance Company; Herman Goldman Foundation; Neiman Marcus; New York Power Authority; General Electric.

(right) "Spring," 30' × 10' tapestry
One of four "Seasons" for a corporate client,
© 1986 Michelle Lester

(bottom) "Betatakin," 8' × 6', © 1985
Michelle Lester.

Nancy Lyon

35 North Mast Road
Goffstown, NH 03045
(603) 497-2084

In my work I create impressionistic land-scapes in fiber. I use weaving techniques and structures to describe the many ways color, form, and atmosphere interlace.

My wall hangings come in different hand-woven fabrics—brushed mohair with sur-face decoration, lustrous cotton in a matted, ready-to-frame format, and shining, reflec-tive, rayon and metallic yarns with surface decoration. They are available in limited editions and by commission. Commissioned work ranges from $50-$90 per square foot.

Recent commissions include work for: IBM, Honeywell, New England Telephone, John-son and Johnson Medical Services, Sanders Corp., Indian Head Bank (partial listing)

Slides and price information on request.

(top right) "Red Sky at Night" 48" × 46"
(bottom right) "Evening Landscape: Sky View" 24" × 30"
(bottom left) "Sand, Sea, and Clouds" 50" × 60"

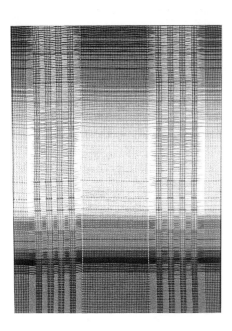

Ilona Mack

205 Seventh Avenue #1
New York, NY 10011
(212) 645-1157

Ilona Mack was trained at the Viennese Academy of Applied Art as a painter and tapestry weaver. She finished her MFA in Linz/Austria at the School for Artistic and Industrial Design.

Her work has been exhibited in the USA, Canada, and Europe. Her tapestries are in several private and public collections and she has executed numerous commissions such as those for the UNO in Vienna, The Austrian National Bank, etc.

Her abstract tapestries are woven with 100% custom dyed wool on cotton warp in the gobelin technique. They are durable, easy to install and suitable for corporate and public as well as private spaces. A selection of work for sale may be seen by appointment.

(top) Tapestry by Ilona Mack 1986
Title: Reminiscence
Size: 5' × 6½'
Material: Wool weft and cotton warp
Technique: Gobelin
(bottom) Tapestry by Ilona Mach 1984
Title: Wedding
Size: 3' × 8'
Material: Wool weft and cotton warp
Technique: Gobelin

Sharon Marcus

Tapestry
4145 S.W. Corbett
Portland, OR 97201
(503) 222-2454

Utilizing classical techniques learned directly from French master craftspeople, Sharon Marcus designs and executes one-of-a-kind handwoven tapestries for residential and corporate interiors.

Premium quality natural fibers (cotton, wool and linen) are used to create woven images in a wide range of colors and textures which are convenient to install and maintain. A variety of installation options are available.

Sharon Marcus welcomes the opportunity to work directly with clients or their chosen representatives in the creation of tapestries suitable for specific sites. Every effort is made to meet the budgetary, conceptual and aesthetic demands of the project. Please allow a minimum of three months from final approval of design to delivery.

Biographical and pricing information available upon request.

(top) detail from "Refuge"
(bottom) "Refuge", cotton and wool tapestry 34"H × 30"W

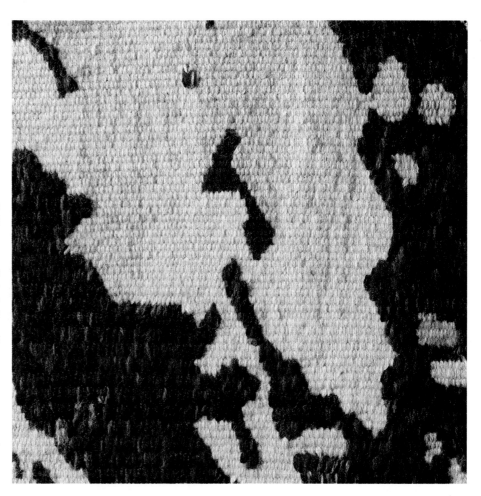

Mary Jane Miller
Valentin Gomez

700 TAPESTRIES
Rt. 3 Box 299
Abingdon, VA 24210
(703) 628-9258

One-of-a-kind custom woven tapestries.

All tapestries are suitable for wall hangings or floor coverings, and designed to accent any decor—professional or residential. We use only selected high quality industrial rug yarns, commercially spun and dyed, for our weaving.

Design and colors to meet your specifications. Size 4' × selected length; panel designs and triptychs also available. Hanging apparatus can be ordered with tapestries.

We have a new commercial collection marketed through Alpujarra Textiles in Mexico. This collection features larger rugs 6' × 9' and 9' × 12'. Detailed information and designs are available.

Resumé, slides, and yarn samples gladly sent upon request.

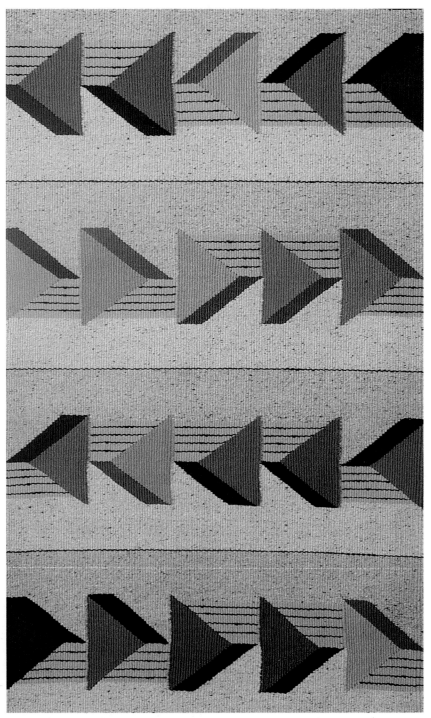

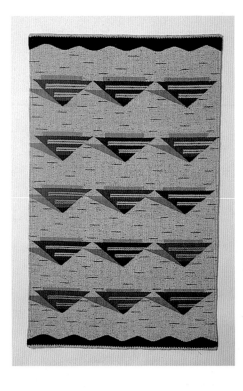

Cynthia Neely

282 Durham Road
Madison, CT 06443
(203) 245-4917

Cynthia Neely's hangings and rugs display an artistry and elegance of design that transcends function. Weaving since 1973, Neely has developed a style and an original technique to accommodate it.

Each wall piece is handwoven with a handsome blend of select yarns—silk, wool, rayon and linen—"mixed" to achieve a texture and color rich with light and depth. Rugs are designed with equal style and technique in subtle shades of 100% carpet wool. All work is painstakingly hand-finished with a sturdy linen warp, assuring that both hangings and rugs are attractive and durable.

Neely custom designs by commission, working with the client to incorporate a color scheme or to complement an architectural style.

Her work is in numerous private collections, has been exhibited widely and published in several international magazines and books.

(right) "Rain Dance" 4' by 5' wool
(bottom) "Aerial Boundaries" 4' by 5' silk, wool, linen, rayon.

Inge Nørgaard

Norgaards Studio
1740 Franklin Street
Port Townsend, WA 98368
(206) 385-0637

Inge Norgaard was educated in Denmark. She has been designing and weaving free style goblin tapestries since 1975.

Her work has been shown internationally for the last ten years. The tapestries are woven with handspun and vegetable dyed wools on a linen warp.

The durability of this method is proven in the old Goblins which are still hanging in European castles and museums hundreds of years later.

Her major work is a series of seven tapestries depicting Skandinavian Mythology, with life-size figures.

Designs are originals, one-of-a-kind.

Average price $175. per square foot.
She accepts commissions for special colors and sizes

(top) Detail of Gefion and her four bull oxen. 4' × 10'. Norse Mythology
(bottom) The Tree of Life, the ash Ygdrasill 5' × 12'. Norse Mythology.

Moshe Novak

Art-Nova.k
P. O. Box 4508
Annapolis, MD 21403
(301) 268-9520

Moshe Novak designs and creates hand tufted tapestries of colorful abstract images using a technique he calls 'Painting with fiber'. Each piece is individually hand tufted with 80% - 100% wool yarn and available in varying heights and widths, custom designed with an unlimited range of hues. The densely tufted tapestries are moth-proofed, colorfast and extremely durable. They are hung by loops attached to the canvas backing. All are suitable for large homes, galleries, public spaces and corporate offices.

Novak has exhibited internationally in galleries and museums and has also been commissioned by corporations and individuals.

Prices are determined by square footage and the amount of detail in a particular piece.

A representative portfolio is available upon request.

(top) Chariot of Fire, 8' × 8'

(bottom) Red Sea Fish, 7' × 7'

Myra Reichel

6437 Park Avenue
Philadelphia, PA 19126
(215) 224-9986

Bold color splashes and strong geometric lines tamed to textural softness for your commercial or residential areas.

Myra Reichel tapestries enliven interiors while softening harsh, angular spaces. Sound is absorbed. Attention focuses on the pliant, giving textural variations, creating fascination with the endless color and light enhancing the architecture and the decor.

Myriad shapes and myriad sizes. Whether 2 or 2,000 square feet, each panel is customized to your specifications and approval.

Myra Reichel invites you to contact her personally to view for selection her nationally exhibited award winning work.

(top) Night Tales 96″ × 90″ × ½″ Traditional tapestry technique. Three rearrangeable panels each 30″ × 96″ × ½″ ©1986.

(bottom) Miroian Dream 33″ × 78″ × ¼″ Unstretched inlaid tapestry. Private commission New York, NY ©1985.

Neil Rhoads

Box 84
Monte Rio, CA 95462
(707) 865-1464

Museum quality, one-of-a-kind fiber works, hand-woven in wool and hand-dyed in vibrant colors; exhibited nationally and included in numerous collections.

Neil Rhoads' rhythmic, geometric designs express simultaneously a strong personal statement and universal vision. His juxtapositions of line and color impart a richness of movement unusual in the static arts. The works contribute the warmth of texture and an invigorating artistic presence to offices and private residences and, on a large scale, to corporate and public interiors. Mr. Rhoads also creates dramatic contemporary floorcoverings.

The weavings are constructed with the highest integrity and are light-stable. Commissions are accepted and a limited number of works are available from the artist's collection. Price and dimension information on request.

(top) "The Healing Touch" 14' × 4'
(bottom) "Day of Fire", detail

Scheuer Tapestry Studio

167 Spring Street
New York, NY 10012
(212) 431-7500

The Scheuer Tapestry Studio is unique for its contemporary approach to the classical French tapestry technique. Trained at the Manufactures Nationales des Gobelins in Paris, founder Ruth Scheuer works with studio weavers and apprentices to create original works of art in tapestry. Tapestries from the studio have been exhibited in museums and galleries throughout the U.S. and Canada, and are included in many major collections.

The fine tapestries offered by the Scheuer Tapestry Studio are especially durable and easily maintained. Made with any of five available textures, work is produced in a variety of sizes suitable for corporate, residential and public spaces. Commissioned tapestries are designed in close consultation with the client. A selection of finished works for sale may be seen by appointment at the studio.

(below) Taxi #1 - The Urban Chase 4' × 4' ©1986. Designed and woven by Ruth Scheuer
(opposite) Taxi #2 - The Urban Chase 4' × 4' ©1986. Designed and woven by Beverly Godfrey.

**Scheuer Tapestry
Studio**
167 Spring Street
New York, NY 10012
(212) 431-7500

Stephen Thurston

Stephen Thurston Tapestries
660 West Grand Avenue
Chicago, IL 60610
(312) 829-1183

Thurston produces finely handwoven tapestries and handcrafted fiber constructions primarily for corporate interiors. A master craftsman with over twenty years of professional experience, he works in both the classical flat tapestry style and hand-tufting processes. He is noted for the range of his comprehensive design versatility. Each of his pieces is custom-designed and site-specific. Professional renderings, a fiber color and texture palette, and technical samples are submitted for a basic design fee. Fees are applied to the total commission cost. Pieces range from $150 to $500 per square foot. Commissions range from private collectors to Fortune 500 corporations. (Largest commissioned tapestry to date - 12' × 95'.)

Photos:
(top) Commission, Private Collection, 1986, 3' × 4'6"
(bottom) Detail.

Restoration

Ersi Valavanis

105 McDougal Street #29
New York, NY 10012
(212) 460-5504

Ersi Valavanis
Specialist in conservation—restoration and mounting of archeological and antique textiles.

Mrs. Valavanis has ten years of experience in this field. She has worked on textiles that where purchased by museums, institutions and private collectors in the United States and abroad.

Category: Restoration Work

(top) Nazca Poncho 6th - 8th century AD. (wool 44½ × 25¼).
(bottom) Khosu Chinese 17th century. (silk 19½ × 13½)

FIBER INSTALLATIONS

B.J. Adams

Art In Fiber
2821 Arizona Terrace, N.W.
Washington, D.C. 20016
(202) 364-8404, (202) 686-1042

B. J. Adams creates paintings with **flexible** materials... fabric and thread. Flat fabrics in juxtaposition with manipulated ones are combined with rows of stitching to add **brush-stroke** interest. The textural, colorful, yet dramatic wall hangings are designed to effect a synergism with contemporary and traditional interior design. These one-of-a-kind framed works can be designed in any range of colors and size adding dimension to commercial as well as residential surroundings.

Commissioned works are in the collections of: TRW, Inc., Rosslyn, VA.; Kaiser Permanente, Washington, D.C.; two banks of Naperville, Illinois; Alabama Power Company, Birmingham; The Methodist Hospital, Indianapolis; Terre Haute Heart Center, Indiana; and numerous private residences.

Commission information and resumé provided on request.

(top) "UTSUROI" 5 panels total size 47" × 90"

(bottom) "FREE SPIRITED GEOMETRY" 30" × 24"

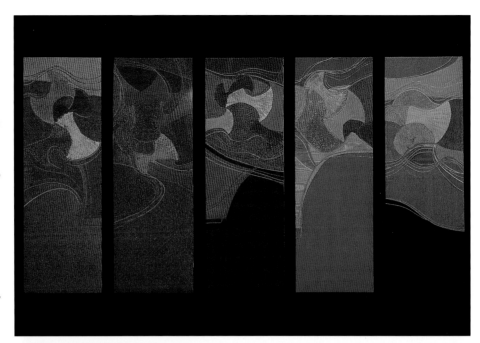

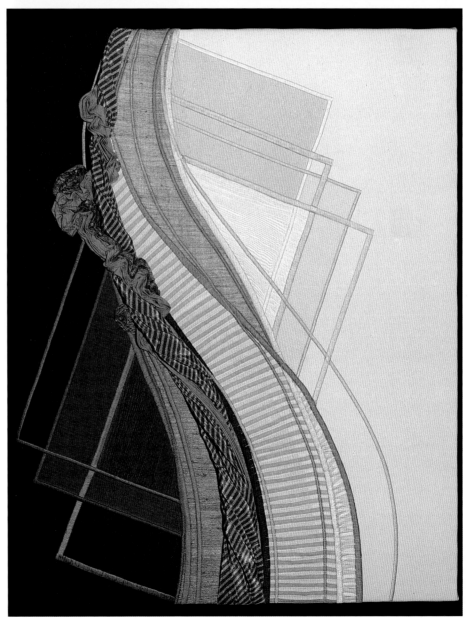

Carol Adams

2355 Main Street
Peninsula, OH 44264
(216) 657-2681

My work is created with fiber of various types, hand-made felt, enamel fired on copper, carved wood and sometimes other metals such as brass and steel.

The edges of large pieces are frequently wrapped copper tubing which allows them to be bent to undulate on the wall and provides structure and strength. They are executed in the format of Shell II: Conch and have great flexibility as far as overlap and wall arrangement. I specialize in odd shaped walls.

The pieces pictured here can be plexiglass boxed and done in series for an extended composition.

The concepts involved are based mostly on the land and my travels. I create the feel and mood of an experience rather than a photographic image.

For the client who wants to enhance the interior of a building, office, or home, I can offer a unique composition in fiber and/or enamel that relates to the furniture, the color, and the decor found within a space to bring the entire room together.

(top right)"Outerspace II: Satellite I" 1985 enamel on copper/handmade felt/stitchery 15" × 12" × 1"
(bottom right) "Sunset I: San Blas" 1984 enamel on copper/handmade felt 22" × 21" × 3"
(bottom left) "Shell II: Conch" 1984 tapestry/enamel on copper 28" × 19" × 3"

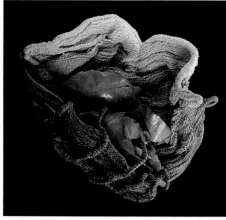

Donna Braverman

Donna Braverman, Ltd.
7920 E. Camelback Rd.
Suite 511
Scottsdale, AZ 85251
(602) 946-2633

Braverman creates modular fiber sculptures ideally suited for interior artspace in a corporate environment. Natural fibers of linen and silk introduce textural elements of warmth and color into contemporary architectural settings. Procion yarn dying techniques lend sun and fade resistance to finished art. Completed sculpture dimensions satisfy individual client needs. Modules are easy to handle and install. Artist can provide detailed scale models and dyed yarn samples for pre-project analysis and has extensive experience in meeting specialized architectural crafts requirements. Braverman has exhibited widely, e.g. "Paper/Fiber VIII;" Tucson Museum of Art "Primavera" Arizona Women Artist Invitational; "The Wichita National '86;" and has won numerous awards. Her work is featured in several publications, including Fiber Arts Design Book II and Architectural Crafts: A Handbook and Catalogue. Major commissions: Sohio Petroleum, Phillips Petroleum, Reichold Chemical, Rolm Telecommunications.

(top) Arizona Biltmore Estates, Phoenix, AZ
5' × 12' × 20" ©1986
(bottom) Desert Highlands Development, Scottsdale, AZ   Sculpture over fireplace.
4' × 4' × 9" ©1986.

Lois Bryant

722 Broadway #2
New York, NY 10003
(212) 777-5932

Unique woven hangings of luminous colors in cotton, linen, and silk. Sizes range from 1 foot to 120 feet. Price per square foot is $100 for most prices, less for large installations. Delivery time 2-6 months.

Clients include:
United Airlines, New York Times, Greater Detroit Chamber of Commerce, residences.

Publications include:
Interior Design , June 1986, p. 152
Fiberarts, May/June 1986, p. 54
 Jan/Feb 1985, p. 34
American Craft, April/May 1985, inside back cover.

Exhibitions include:
Cooper-Hewitt Museum, Smithsonian Institutions, NYC: 1984 and 1983.
Fiberworks Center for the Textile Arts, Berkeley, CA: 1986
Three Rivers Arts Festival, Pittsburgh, PA: 1986
"Textiles for the Eighties," Rhode Island and traveling, 1985-87
Conduit Gallery, Dallas, TX, 1985 and 1987
John Cusano Gallery, South Norwalk, CT, 1986

(right;) "Passages Series: #8" cotton, linen, silk, metallics; 29" × 21"
(top left) Untitled 1985 (detail) cotton
(bottom left) "Floats" linen; 60' × 30' × 10', co-designed with Cameron Taylor-Brown

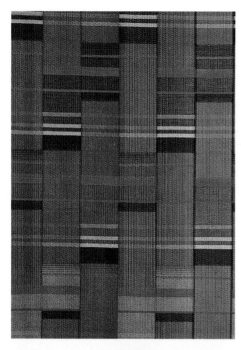

Joyce Marquess Carey

Pliable Planes
913 Harrison Street
Madison, WI 53711
(608) 256-1537

Richly textured wall pieces for residential or corporate settings are constructed of commercially dyed fabrics in a broad range of colors. Each one-of-a-kind piece is precision sewn by Carey on an industrial machine for strength, with extensive hand sewing to assure a well-tailored finish. Work is Scotchguarded™, easily maintained with light vacuuming and is dry-cleanable. Available work ranging in size from 30″ × 60″ to 60″ × 90″ may be selected from slides. Custom designed work is unlimited in scale and color selection.

Carey's work is shown in several publications, in juried, invitational and one-person shows. Commissions include the State of Wisconsin Percent for Art Program, the Ralston Purina Corporation, and many private and corporate sites.

(top): "Lumiere" 54″ × 81″
(bottom): "Wild Goose Chase", 43″ × 66″

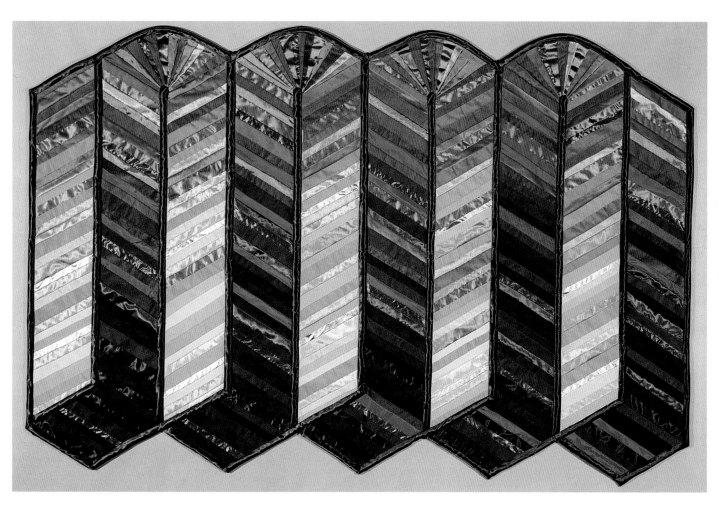

Martha Chatelain

Artfocus Ltd.
P.O. Box 127238
San Diego, CA 92112-7238
(619) 234-0749

Martha Chatelain specializes in custom designed, handmade paper wall sculptures. Created from 100% cotton fiber, her works are richly textured and enhanced with fiber reactive dyes, acrylic paints, and iridescent mica powders.

Call Chatelain to discuss design specifications and client environment, corporate or residential. Chatelain can work to drawings, interior photographs, fabric swatches and color samples. Allow 6-8 weeks from design approval and price contract. Prices, from $500-$4000, depend on size and complexity of work. Works shipped FOB San Diego unframed or in plexiglass frames built to order.

(top) "Waves Upon The Shore,"
48" × 70" × 5"
(bottom left) Detail, "La Cumbre"
(bottom right) "La Cumbre," 40" × 34" × 4"

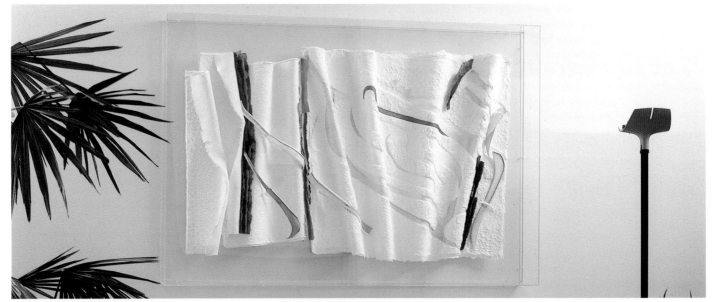

Martha Chatelain

Artfocus Ltd.
P.O. Box 127238
San Diego, CA 92112-7238
(619) 234-0749

In her San Diego studio, Martha makes 100% cotton, museum-quality paper, combining classic European and Japanese paper-making methods with the latest vacuum-casting techniques. Chatelain's artwork enhances the architectural and design features of the interior space for which it is created. Pictured below, "Odyssey", 24" × 79" × 3", has embossed surfaces with acrylic paints and iridescent mica powders.

Prices, from $500 to $4,000, depend on size and complexity of work. Allow six to eight weeks from design approval and price contract. Works shipped FOB San Diego unframed or in plexiglass frames build to order.

Major commissions: Sheraton Hotels, IBM, Potlatch Corporation, Nordstrom

Susanne Clawson/Fibercations

5093 Velda Dairy Road
Tallahassee, FL 32308
(904) 893-5656

Susanne Clawson designs and produces original wall sculptures in two media: handmade paper and fiber.

The handmade paper works are of 100% cotton and abaca fibers, ensuring a long life expectancy. The paper fibers are dyed by hand, with careful attention to color. These fibers are often mixed with an array of silk threads, iridescent chips, and pearlescent pigment, which become embedded in the paper to produce unique and striking effects.

The fiber pieces are created from wool, silk, rayon, and other materials. They are constructed with on- and off-loom techniques to yield rich texture and sculptural relief.

Commissions are custom-designed and site-specific, based on close consultation with corporate and residential clients and can be requested in a wide range of colors and sizes.

(bottom) "Satay", wrapping/wool, rayon, cotton, bamboo, 14" × 22" × 2"
(top) "Stegosaurus", handmade paper/100% cotton, abaca, silk threads, iridescent chips, pearlescent pigment, 48" × 84" × 4".

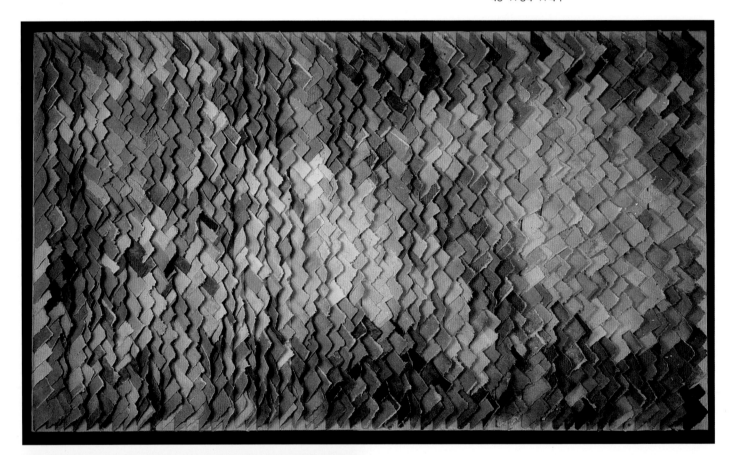

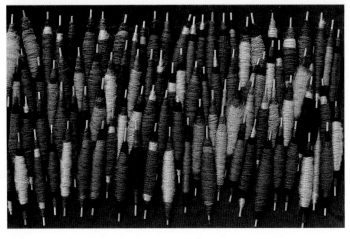

Beth Cunningham

33 Lower South Street, Suite 220
Danbury, CT 06810
(203) 798-6245

Beth Cunningham designs and executes commissioned wall pieces for commercial, corporate and residential interiors. The canvas surface is built up with acrylic paint, cotton strips or squares, and silk tissue paper, and is sealed with an acrylic polymer. The washable surface resists dirt and pollution, and is sun/fade resistant.

Multiple panel series are designed for larger public spaces in banks, hotels and reception areas while smaller single panels are suitable for private offices and home interiors.

(top) "Iced Desert", 1985, 44" × 36", private collection.
(bottom) "Cutty's Corporate Haze", 1985, 36" × 48", private collection.

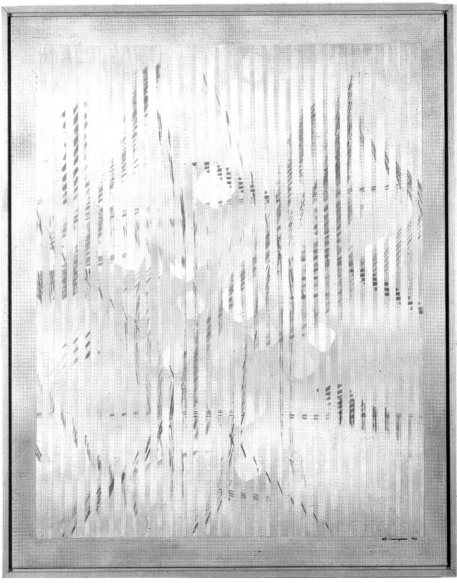

Ann Dunn Designs

Designer/Handmade Paper
30100 Town Center Drive
Suite #0-286
Laguna Niguel, CA 92677
(714) 499-1729

Ann Dunn, well-known southern California handmade paper artist, has created her own unique style of paper wall installations. She is currently working on the layered series of handcast paper and the knot series of hand pulled papers using abaca and natural fibers on a woven bamboo structure. These works offer a variety of sizes, textures and colors. Ms. Dunn's handmade paper artworks are in corporate and private collections around the country and have been shown nationally and internationally.

(top) "CHOICES", 30" × 40" handmade abaca paper and bamboo. (bottom) "Canyon Suite", 44" × 27" handcast cotton and abaca paper.

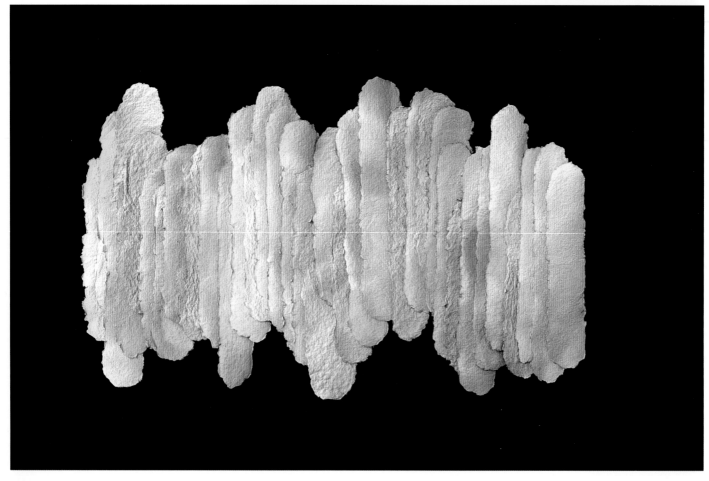

Margaret Getty

Box 1733
Media, PA 19063
(215) 565-1564

"Serenity … beauty, flawless execution … " Juried show April, 1986.

Using hand dyed, woven linen and wool units she calls "Kwers", Margaret Getty creates warmly textured fiber compositions inspired by a landscape, poetic phrase or musical passage. The individual Kwers are arranged as brush strokes in a painting. Pieces may be detailed with flax, rayon, paper, and collagen, until the essence of her inspiration has been achieved.

"Among the standouts are two works by Margaret Getty … who garnered first place in … fiberarts with 'Origins and Endings', an abstract of linen, paper, rayon, and shells … (and) in wall hangings (with) 'Aurora 2', a vibrantly colored creation … " Philadelphia Inquirer, May 29, 1986.

Margaret Getty is a well-known Pennsylvania artist who is represented in galleries across the country and has executed commissions in the East, Mid-west and Far-west.

On display at The National Craft Showroom in New York City

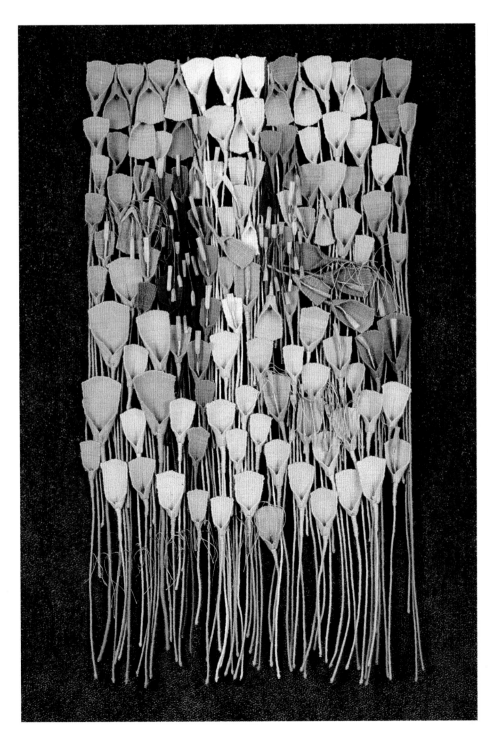

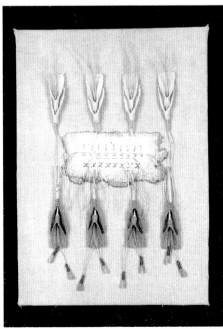

James R. Gilbert

James R. Gilbert Woven Structures
P.O. Box 474
Bloomfield Hills, MI 48303-0474
(313) 545-8229

In working with architects and designers, the space is examined for concepts and ideas. Proposals, color cards and drawings are rendered, from which a final decision is made. Color development is a special consideration.

The curved form and translucent structures have been a trademark of this well-known artist's style for more than fourteen years.

(top) PAS de DEUX AT DUSK
Living room wall installation
14' wide × 1' deep × 5½' high
dyed rayon, lurex
(bottom) AN ILLUSION
Seven story sculpture
Amway Grand Plaza Hotel; Grand Rapids, Michigan
44' wide × 17' deep × 76' high
dyed rayon, lurex

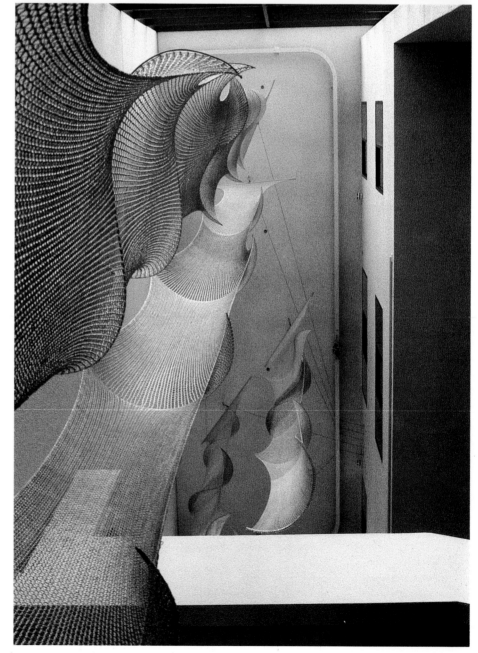

Barbara Grenell

1132 Hall's Chapel Road
Burnsville, NC 28714
(704) 675-4073

Tapestries in two and three dimensions, free-standing screens and columns.

Collections and commissions include: Bankers Trust of New York, I.B.M., R.J. Reynolds-Nabisco, Art In Architecture Program—The Tennessee Valley Authority. Awards include: The National Endowment for the Arts—Crafts Fellowship.

Specializing in site specific commissions. Completed tapestries also available. Additional information on request.

(top) TIDAL FLATS. 52" × 36" × 7" 1986
(bottom) QUINTET. 52" × 30" × 7" 1986

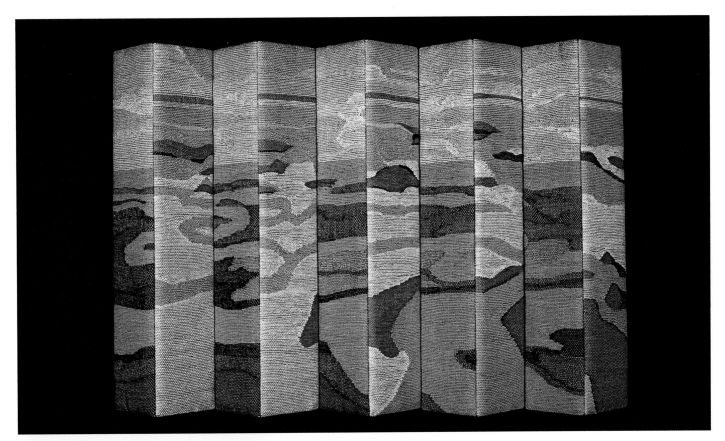

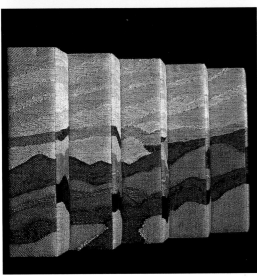

Hollie Heller

2080 Arrowwood Drive
Scotch Plains, NJ 07076
(201) 232-7852

Textural constructions might be the most descriptive title for her work. Hollie Heller uses hand-made felt as her canvas that is made from fleece that has been dyed in rich hue gradations. The felt is embellished with a variety of material such as nails, wire, plastic tubing and different types of natural fibers to subtle color gradations that change as the viewer walks around the piece. Custom work in any size, shape or coloration is available. Samples are available upon request.

Hollie Heller has been working in fiber for the past eight years and has received her Masters of Fine Arts degree from Rochester Institute of Technology. She is presently on the faculty of Stratford College of Fine Art in Hilton Head, South Carolina.

Detail "Snowfields", 2'8" × 2'8" (1986) Materials are felt, masonry nails, paint, wire, banana fiber and plastic tubing.

"Masai Dancers", 2'8" × 2'8" (1986) Materials are felt, masonry nails, paint, and pine needles.

James Kirkell

19 Vestry Street #5
New York, NY 10013
(212) 966-7002

Visit companies like IBM, TRW and Metropolitan Life... they all feature the distinctive works of artist James Kirkell.

Kirkell's medium is painting on silk... the unique product of a contemporary talent adapting traditional methods to modern taste... an outgrowth of his study under an Indonesian batik master in Java.

Kirkell's banners bring dramatic interest to atriums, offices and open areas, as seen in 3 piece commission for Sibson Co., Princeton, NJ and geometric work hanging in Tower Suite, Chrysler Building, NYC.

Commissions are priced on a square foot basis and include scale drawings and color swatches in accordance with client's specifications. Completion, 4-6 weeks after approval of drawings. Smaller framed pieces, from artist's floral series are also available.

(bottom left) 4' × 14' installation
(bottom right) 4' × 12'

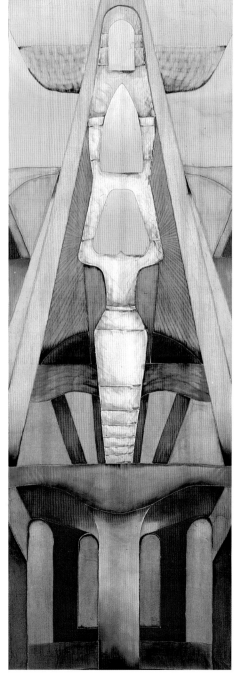

Ellen Kochansky

Route 2 Box 630
Pickens, SC 29671
(803) 868-9749

Ellen Kochansky's collage works depart from the traditions of quilting to humanize and soften corporate and residential settings. Original techniques involve laminating, overdyeing, transparent fabric, airbrushed fabric dye and pigments. Eight years commission experience. IBM, Florida National Bank, and other collections. Proposal (10% fee) consists of actual color fabric swatches, scale color rendering, and contract confirming date of delivery, price, terms, installation arrangements and care procedure. Easily installed mounting system provides formality and security. Plexi framed format available.

(top) "Redbud" commissioned by John Portman & Assoc. for ballroom of R. Howard Dobbs University Center, Emory University

(bottom) "Redbud" quilted triptych, each panel 5' square.

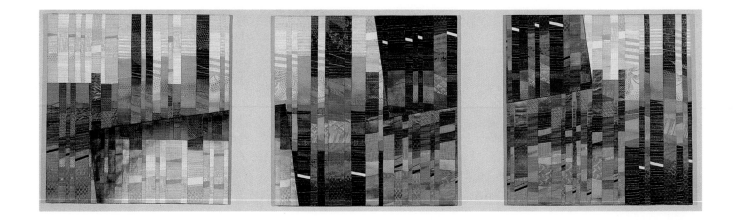

Susan Kristoferson

2040 Abbott Road
Brookville, IN 47012
(812) 775-9066
(513) 529-6032

Kristoferson creates dynamic fabric sculptures and two-dimensional work for architectural spaces. She is experienced in developing and adapting concepts independently or in concert with the client. She is adept at solving problems unique to a client's intended aesthetic and functional requirements.

Kristoferson is knowledgeable in a variety of color processes ranging from silkscreening, airbrushing, and fabric painting to all dye methods. Processes and fabrics are chosen in order to optimize lightfast and washfast qualities. Prices range from $300-$3,000 for two-dimensional and from $2,000-$20,000 for sculptural works.

Her works have been in many national and international exhibitions, published by Kodansha Press in Shibori: The Inventive Art of Japanese Shaped Resist Dyeing; purchased by AT&T, Cincinnati; Hyatt Regency, Austin; and Bank One, Dayton, and commissioned by the Mariotte Mariner Hotel, Huntsville Texas, and Paragon Group, Inc. Louisville.

(left) "Skylight Suite" Paragon Place, Louisville, KY
(right) "Shibori Cascade" Middletown City Building, Middletown, OH

Gail Larned

Larned-Marlow Studios
144 S. Monroe Avenue
Columbus, OH 43205
(614) 258-7239

In twelve years as a professional fiber artist Ms. Larned has produced a broad range of work for both residential and corporate settings.

The work is created by wrapping sisal or cotton around a jute core-producing coils which are dyed to specs. and then assembled. Her sculptural pieces like the "Great Goddess" have immense presence and power, while the vibrant colors of her many wall designs are the cohesive element of any interior.

Larned's work is represented in over 40 corporate collections nationwide including Bordon, Dow Chemical Co., Chi Chi's Restaurant, as well as banks, hospitals, health care centers and numerous residences.

The wall pieces are mounted on cast acrylic rods and include installation instructions.

Prices range from $30.00 - $75.00/sq. ft. Brochure or video tape available.

(top)"The Great Goddess", Private Collection - 3' × 10' × 12' Chester and Betty Osborn

(bottom)"Elements of Chance", Huntington Trust Building, Columbus, Ohio - Commission - 5' × 7'

Cal Ling Paperworks

441 Cherry Street
Chico, CA 95928
(916) 893-0882

Gardens, architecture, wall papers, fabric, patterns and de-patterning... The paper art works of Cal Ling vary from impressionistic 'paper paintings' to very graphic assemblage 'tile' pieces, both whimsical and architectonic. The work is produced with 100% rag pulp, exclusively the finest quality cottons, silks, rayons, and other anthropomorphic sources. Size ranges from an intimate 11" × 16½" to larger 3' × 6', 6' × 6', as well as room size 'wallpapers'. Diptychs and triptychs are also available. Larger pieces are reinforced for durability and longevity. All work is color/fade fast. Commissions are accepted.

Cal Ling Paperworks is marketed nationally through major shows, galleries, and representatives.

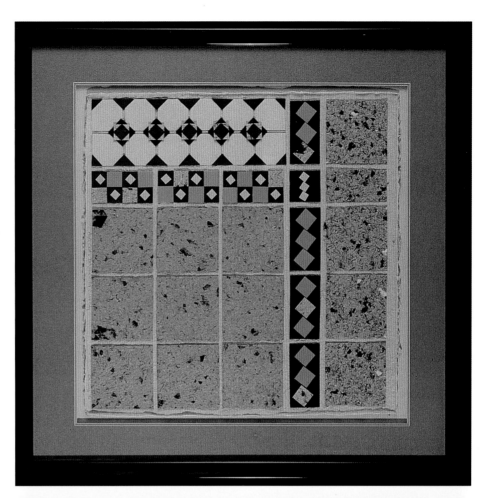

Professional Collaborations

There are those who believe that to bypass a high-level corporate job in order to pursue a dream is about as risky a venture as one can undertake. But many do. In fact, open *The Guild* to any page and you'll encounter someone who believes that he or she has the talent and skill to be a craft artist running a successful enterprise.

There is no doubt that crafts are on the rise and that the independent craft artist has an important role to play. Combined with a talent in one or more of the craft media, the artist has learned to direct all business aspects of the studio, and has the ability to plan, to manage and to make money.

Craft artists know they need an effective plan to put that dream in motion. They need a background that includes both formal course work and apprenticeships in the studios of established colleagues. They need to overcome the image of an artisan selling mugs and macrame hangings at local street fairs.

For an initial presentation, the craft artist has to be prepared to show examples of recent work by offering a combination of slides, drawings, videotapes and maquettes. The artist will also include original designs for unique pieces or limited edition series, all geared to providing the client with the best work at the most competitive price.

Despite the informality of their surroundings and often their non-traditional business attire, crafts people operate first-rate businesses. They take pride in their workmanship and respect the contractual agreement to deliver on time.

As anyone who's witnessed the splendor of the San Francisco Airport, Hyatt Hotels or specialized corporate collections such as *U.S. News & World Report* and International Paper, you know what fine crafts can tell you; the word "splendid" doesn't even come close to describing their impact on the space and its ambience. Craft artists are creating new expressions for residential and public places that can exceed great expectations.

On the practical side, the craft artist will present you with a complete array of facts and figures: price range, availability of work, deposit and return policies, cancellation and warranty terms. In addition, both parties must know who is responsible for shipping and installation, maintenance and repair.

Not every job is suitable for the craft artist, but when a job is, the architect or designer can find the collaboration is a dream come true. Furthermore, today's craft artist is a professional in every sense of the word.

Rosanne Raab

Rosanne Raab
Director, Rosanne Raab Associates
New York, New York

Mary Ann Lomonaco

50 Webster Avenue
New Rochelle, NY 10801
(914) 633-8824

Unique assemblies of pattern, texture, color and movement.

Three dimensional handmade paper wall-pieces. Specially dyed colors in sophisticated pallettes. Made from cotton, hemp, manila, linen and sisal fibers. Framed in lucite for protection

Constructed to any specific dimensions. Designed as individual modules or in a series. Can be installed as multiples to form larger scale pieces. Extensive color variations. Can be coated for protection to hang unframed

Touche Ross. World Bank Library. American Ultramar. United Federal Bank. Neutrogena Corporation

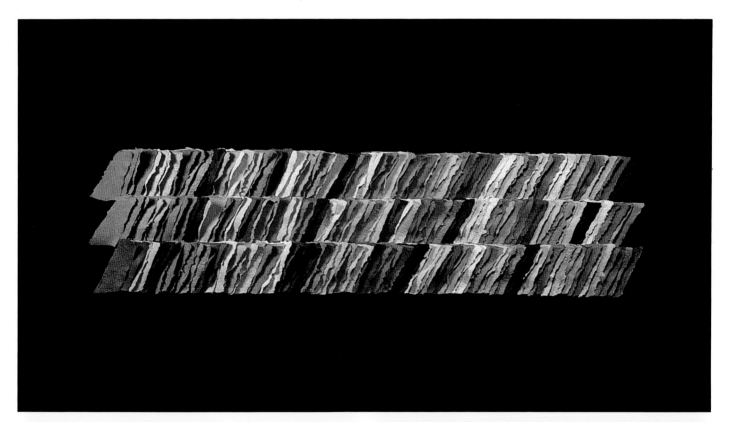

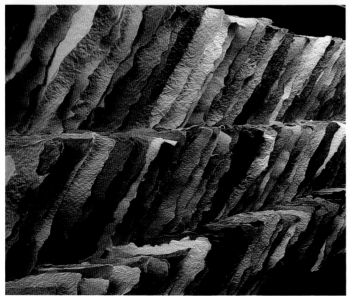

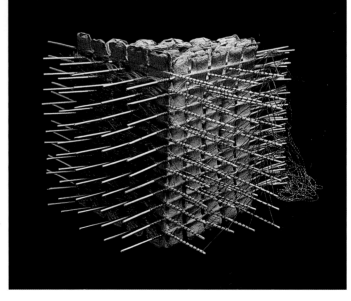

Joyce P. Lopez

Joyce Lopez Studio
927 Noyes Street
Evanston, IL 60201
(312) 491-0545

Joyce Lopez is one of the most versatile and innovative artists working in the U.S. today.

Successfully working in the areas of sculpture and weaving as well as painting and drawing, she has over 15 years of experience doing commission work to her credit in both the private and corporate sectors.

Her experience is appreciated by architects and designers with her designs reflecting her sensitivity to sites as well as to the clients' special needs.

This award winning artist is included in the newly published book AMERICAN ARTISTS by Krantz Publishers.

Write for further information.

(top left) detail, "Musikantow Corp.", chrome, wrapped French thread, 17' × 7'
(top right) "Bank of America-Sears Tower", chrome, French thread 14' × 4'
(bottom left) "Fort Lee Executive Park, New Jersey", chrome, French thread, 5' × 4'
(bottom right) "Illinois Institute for Legal Education", wool weaving, 17' × 7'

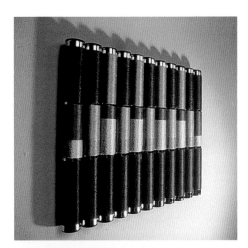

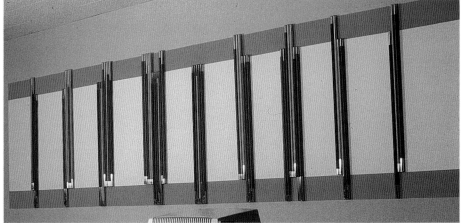

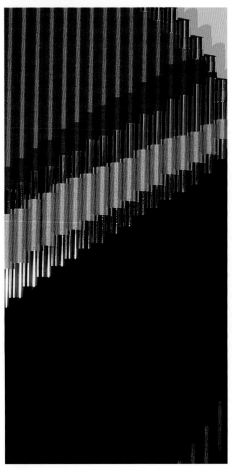

Patricia MacGillis

2201 San Dieguito Road
Del Mar, CA 92014
(619) 259-0589

Patricia MacGillis uses her handpainted torn canvas with weaving techniques to create unique, contemporary, one of a kind, textured wall pieces and installations. They are well crafted, durable, and fade resistant. Painted canvas, functional basket forms are also created in various shapes and sizes. Custom design and color is available.

For the last ten years the artist has been exhibiting nationally and has been doing commissions for hospitals, hotels, and corporations, as well as for private homes.

Further information is available on request.

Irene K. Pittman

Weaver's Studio
115 S. Lincoln
Tampa, FL 33609
(813) 870-0527

Irene Pittman has been a fiber artist for 15
years, creating hand-painted silks, as shown,
hanging mobiles for atrium spaces in silk
and aluminum, and wall tapestries in both
two and three dimensional configurations.
Each work of art created by the artist is one-
of-a-kind and is designed specifically for a
particular project and space.

The silks are economically priced from $300
to $1500 and can be made in any design,
realistic or abstract.

The artist also paints on cotton, does mar-
bling, and works in all resist techniques.

Prices vary according to size and design for
tapestries, wall sculptures and mobiles.

Clients include development companies
for lobbies and atriums, hospitals and hotels
(Holiday Inn, Hyatt, Marriott, Ramada Inn).

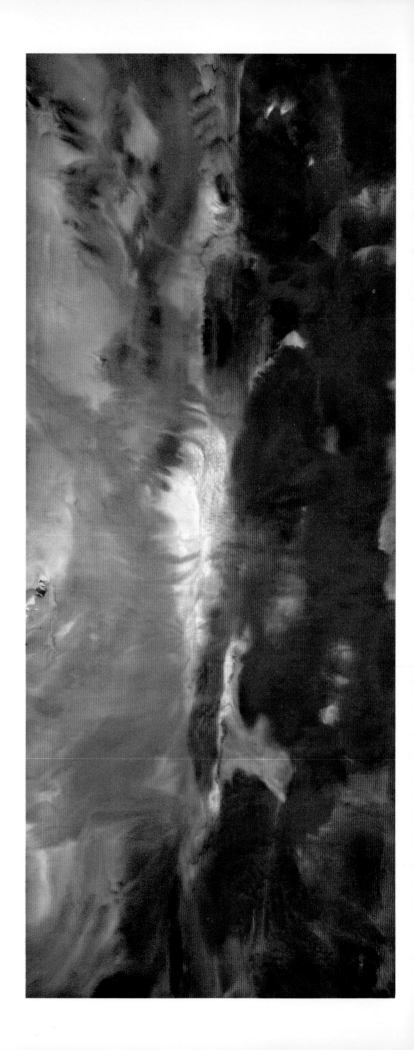

Dee Ford Potter

Artist-Weaver Studio
45 N. W. Greeley Ave.
Bend, OR 97701
(503) 382-4797

Dee Ford Potter designs and creates weavings for special spaces. Her richly textured wall sculptures are in homes, galleries, and corporate collections in the United States and in Paris.

Dee trained in architecture and interior design, has experience in specialized installation requirements, works to drawings, photographs, fabric and color swatches, and makes models for design approval.

The highest quality fibers are used to introduce textural warmth and embracing color ideally suited for her sculptures which bring presence and artistic inspiration to the interior artspace.

Reduced scale woven sculptures in plexiglass frames and monotypes of weavings are available to coordinate the extended interior artspace.

Maintenance: routine vacuuming.
Prices: weavings $1,000 to $10,000; monotypes $200.

ONE WON 1
7' × 17', 1986
Commissioned for The First Street Office Building
Ketchum/Sun Valley, Idaho.

Karen Rhiner

Fiber Wall Sculpture
2649 Elyssee Street
San Diego, CA 92123
(619) 278-7306

Karen Rhiner's one-of-a-kind fiber wall sculptures consist of flexible cylinders called wrappings and stress motion, color and design.

In the past six years she has completed almost fifty commissions for commercial and residential sites from La Jolla to Mexico City to Manhattan, has had two one-person shows and has participated in numerous group, invitational and juried shows.

She believes that meeting client's needs from design to installation is a top priority. Slides of other styles in which she works are available.

(top) "Lickety Split" 30" × 90" × 8"
(bottom) "Cause" 56" × 26" × 8"

Bernie Rowell

Bernie Rowell Studio
1525 Branson Avenue
Knoxville, TN 37917
(615) 523-5244

Bernie Rowell has been professionally producing fiber art for residential and commercial interiors for 7 years.

Her canvas collage works combine a stitchers' skill with rich painted surfaces. Canvases are cut, woven, torn, pleated and layered to achieve three-dimensional textures. Geometric shapes interact with smoothly modulated color. Iridescent and metallic paints in combination with sewn line drawings add detail interest to these one-of-a-kind works.

Glazed, padded and stretched for a durable "soft-surface" presentation. Completely wrapped edges require no additional framings.

Commissions/custom colors/$35 per sq. ft.

(top) Ross/Fowler Architects, Knoxville, TN, Commission Padded/Stretched, 84" × 48" × 4"
(bottom left) "Saw-Toothed Moon" padded/stretched, 36" × 48" × 3"
(bottom right) "Eclipse" 30" × 40"

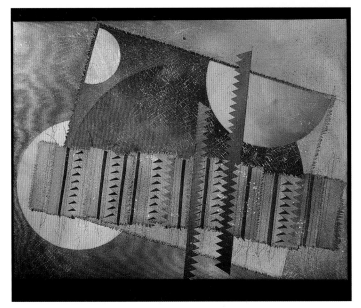

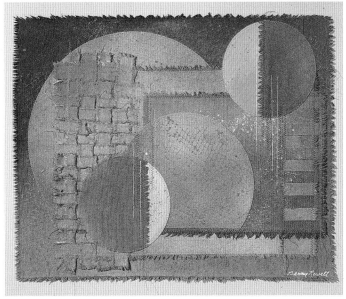

Alice C. Sanders

Textile Designer
1500 Cunliff Lane
Sarasota, FL 33579
(813) 366-4121

Represented at: Manifesto, Chicago, IL

Site-specific art textiles for commercial and residential interiors.

The challenge to design every textile within a given setting — floor, wall and fabric—is avidly sought.

"Such resolute intentions, a natural out-growth of this artist's manifest vision, are well buttressed by her recognized style." Al Alschuler, Design South Magazine.

Commission information, references, etc. available on request.

(top left) Detail, pattern runner, 2½' × 7', wool with linen warp
(top right) Detail, knotted rug, 4' × 6', wool with linen warp
(bottom) Construction for the wall, 5' × 7', raffia and linen

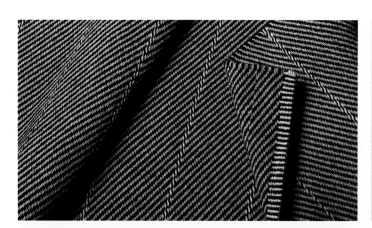

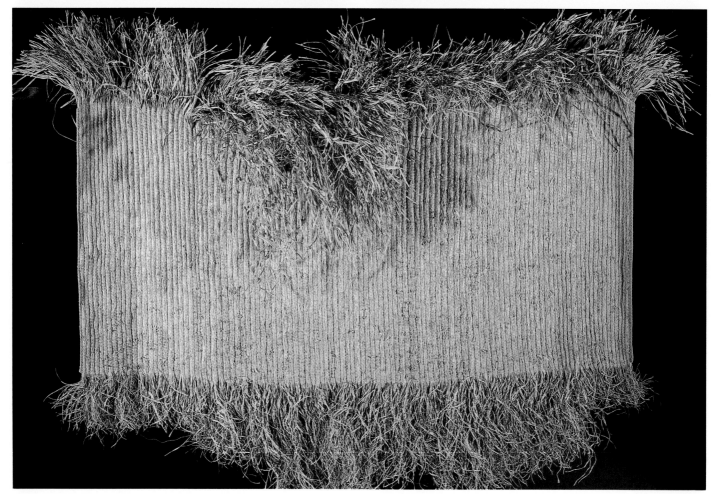

Beverly Semmens

2359 Flora Street
Cincinnati, OH 45219
(513) 421-1894

Beverly Semmens specializes in one-of-a-kind and commissioned fiber works, handwoven of hard surface yarns, such as linen, and non-tarnishing metals. The pieces are shaped when off the loom, creating a dramatic play of light, shadow and color. The works range in size from the intimate to the architectural.

Easily installed and maintained, these fiber pieces enhance both commercial and residential spaces. Corporate collections include: IBM, Chi Chi's Restaurants, Linclay Corporation and Mead Data Central.

Color renderings and sample yarns are available for a basic design fee, deductible from final commission payment. Allow 8 to 12 weeks average delivery time after design approval and price contract.

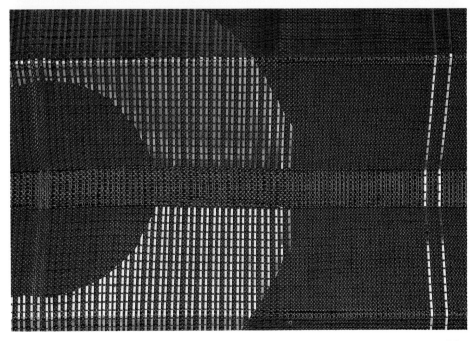

Bob Simpson

8751 Mariposa Street
La Mesa, CA 92041
(619) 464-7188

Bob Simpson creates a variety of expressions in hand-made paper. Using pure cotton fibers, he vacuum-casts and hand forms his unique shapes. He specializes in abstractions of forms found in nature, and in the explorations of visual language systems and symbols that are personal yet universal. They are painted, stained, and sealed with permanent acrylic pigments, and are fade-resistant; they do not require framing under plexi-glass. Prices average from $500 to $3000 depending upon size and complexity. Residential and corporate commissions are welcomed.

One's Personal Rosetta 45″ × 30″
Luminous 7′ × 6′

Mary Jo Sinclair

10 Milton Street
St. Augustine, FL 32084
(904) 824-1441

Sinclair creates sculptural statements from the intimate in size to large scale environmental works—wall, suspended and free-standing—capturing the essence of images drawn from the desert and the sea. She seeks visual symbols for weathered rock formations, shifting sands, changing skies, the sense of limitless lands, oceans, and ancient cultures.

The mixed-media sculptures are a merging of paper and metal. Woven copper and brass wires and sheet metals formed with layers of translucent conservation papers. Color applied with permanent acrylic pigments. Small to medium-sized works are enclosed in plex boxes. Free-standing and large scale wall pieces protectively sealed. Commissions drawn from the artist's present series—"Desert Song"adaptable to client's environmental situation.Slides of available works upon request.

(top) "White Feathered Soul"
5"L × 5"H × ½"W
(bottom) "Running Ridge" Four sections
total 16'L × 7'H × 11"W.

Barbara Lee Smith

Smithworks Inc.
205 North Euclid Avenue
Oak Park, IL 60302
(312) 383-0577

A strong sense of space and transparency is often the first impression when viewing Barbara Lee Smith's modular wall pieces. Closer study reveals a richness of detail, intricate color relationships and strong contrasts of form. Thus, the work can be appreciated in large, public spaces as well as intimate ones. Smith first creates a painting on a sturdy cotton/silk base, then adds more color and texture with machine embroidery creating a second design upon the initial painting. Each piece is stretched and hung by a hidden frame. Her work has been purchased or commissioned for numerous private, corporate and university collections in North America and Europe. Some of the corporate collectors are: American Express, Sohio Petroleum, Marshall Field and Co., and Baker, Knapp and Tubbs.

(top) Capturing the Sun, 34"h × 81½"w
(bottom right) The Ways of Light, 30"h × 32"w
(bottom left) The Ways of Light, detail

Raymond D. Tomasso

Inter-Ocean Curiosity Studio
2998 South Bannock
Englewood, CO 80110
(303) 789-0282

I have worked in three-dimensional cast handmade rag paper since 1974. Each work is made of laminated hand formed sheets of 100% cotton rag paper, ensuring a life expectancy of 100 + years. The color is a combination of pure pigment, colored pencil, and latex paint, which has a surface coat of clear flat lacquer. Display may be with or without a plexiglas box depending on the security of the piece and its environment. I welcome both corporate and residential commissions. The work can be designed to fit architectural specifications. Selected collections include: AT&T, American Bell, Coca Cola Co., Emory University, Hyatt Regency, IBM, Mountain Bell, Prudential-Bache Securities, Sheraton Hotel, University of Arizona.

(top) "The Boarder Line Between Reality & Illusion" 22" × 27"
(bottom) "A Lattice of Coincidence in the Evaporating Mist of a Memory" 26" × 36"

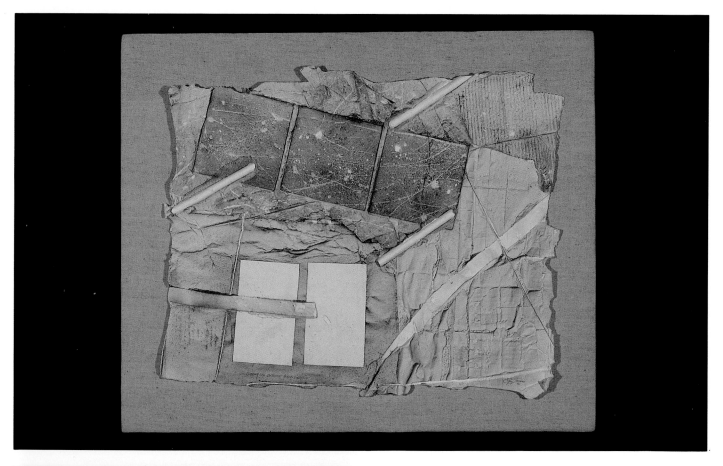

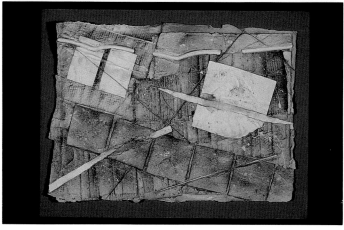

P.C. Turczyn

438 Broome Street
New York, NY 10013
(212) 925-6717

P.C. Turczyn works primarily in a mixed-media, bas-relief format. Large wall installations are executed and hung using a modular system. Favored materials are: wood, metal leaf, vinyl, mylar, fabric, paper, polyester resin, beads, paint and bamboo.

Her background in textile design is reflected in both her patterned imagery and in her ability to work with architects and designers in creating color moods for interiors.

In addition to the wall pieces, P.C. Turczyn has developed a line of handsome resin coated mulberry paper and gunmetal torchere lamps.

She has taught and exhibited nationally, and in Canada, and been featured in several publications including, The Fiberarts Design Book II and Textiles: A Handbook

(top) "Autumn Leaves",
24"H × 57"W × 3½"D
wood, copper, aluminum leaf, paper, mylar, vinyl, paint
(bottom) "Summer", 27"H × 57"W × 3" D
wood, gold leaf, graphite, mylar, vinyl, oil paint.

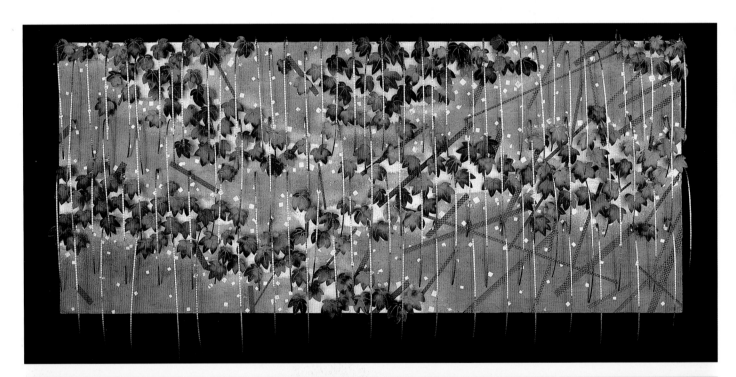

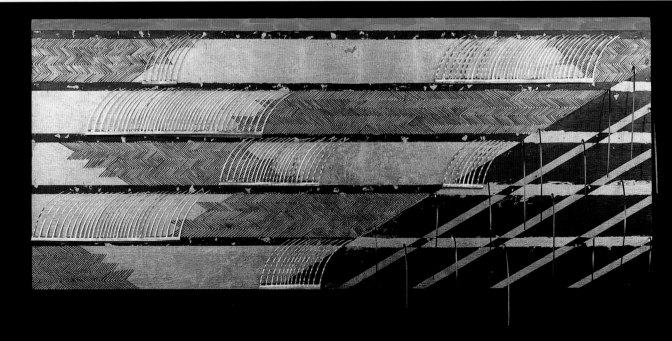

Pamela Twycross-Reed

117 Lamarck Drive
Snyder, NY 14226
(716) 839-2691

Woven abstract landscapes using subtle changes in color and texture to create the design. Custom designed or limited edition tapestries are available. The weavings are durable, cleanable, easy to install and suitable for home, commercial and corporate use.

Work is in numerous private collections and corporations throughout the USA, Canada and Europe.

(top) "Dreams Of The West". Set of 3 panels each 30" W. × 40" H
(bottom) "Shoreline" 54" W × 35" H oval

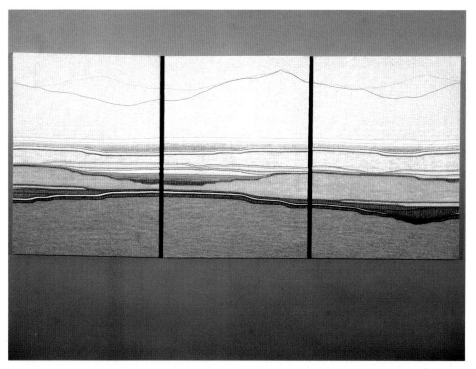

Alice Wand and Dennis Kalma

R.D. 1, Trudeau Rd., Box 347A
Saranac Lake, NY 12983
(518) 891-5506

These artists produce decorative hand-made paper objects, lamps and shades. They use abaca pulp for both production and one-of-a-kind pieces.

Alice Wand designs wall saucers as well as fans, bowls, boxes and framed paper collages. She has worked with pulp for 12 years and has exhibited across the US in galleries and at major craft shows.

Fascination with light and shadow led Dennis Kalma to papermaking. Several styles of hanging and table lamps use textures and/or laminations to modulate the warmth of light. Papers are off-white or colored as are the bases and trims.

(top): wood framed lantern, inspired by Japanese woodcut 9" × 9" × 22"; hanging lamp, inspired by seed pods 10" × 10" × 16" (bottom): saucer set, large diameter 21", medium 18", small 16".

Illustrated brochures available. Photos also available, $5. refundable deposit.

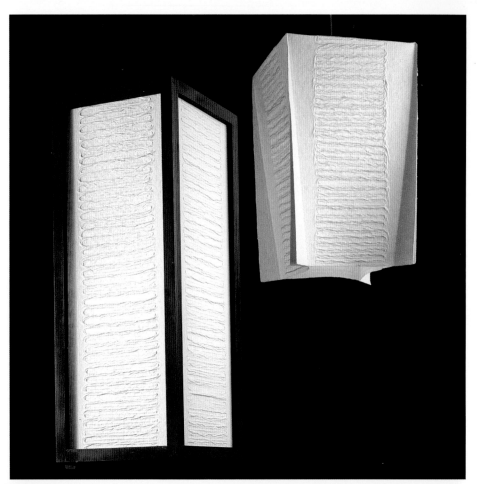

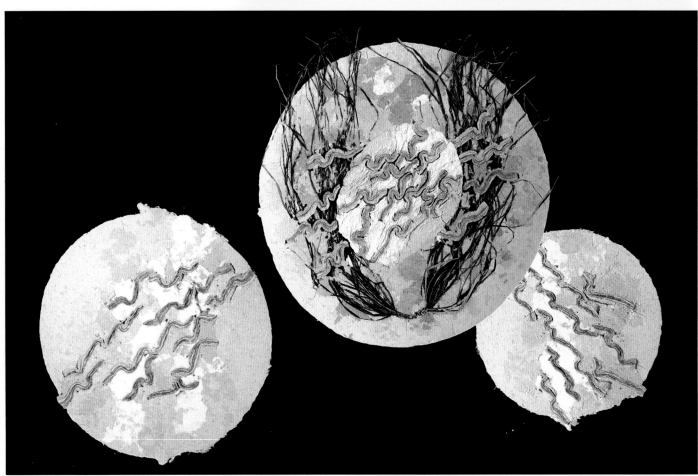

Leanne Weissler

50 Webster Avenue
New Rochelle, NY 10801
(914) 235-7632

Represented by: Roseanne Raab Associates
167 East 61 Street
New York, NY 10021
(212) 466-1399

Leanne Weissler specializes in elegant and durable handmade paper reliefs, of linen and gampi fibers, using transparent overlays with embedded handpainted fabric and drawn additions. They are easily framed and installed, and suitable for indoors (homes, lobbies, hotels, hospitals). These images can be used singly, in multiples, as free-standing sculptures or paneled screens, framed or unframed, and are available in a choice of colors. Each design is one-of-a-kind; signed, dated and copyrighted. Most images are involved with tactile and translucent surfaces.

Commissions for IBM, Coffee and Sugar Exchange, Westchester Medical Center, Mercy College, Mayor Edward Koch, Joy Licht Interiors, Trig Graphics, and installations for restaurants, law, public relations, advertising and typography firms. Commissions accepted for special colors and sizes, and a representative portfolio is available upon request.

(top) "Environmental 1 Teepee", handmade gampi paper 20" × 19" × 15" unframed
(bottom) "Damask Fan", handmade linen and gampi paper, 29" × 38" framed.

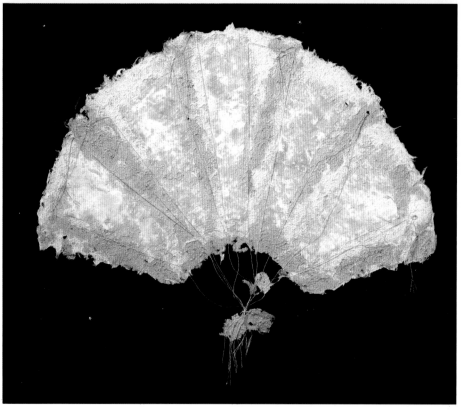

Joen Wolfrom

104 Bon Bluff
Fox Island, WA 98333
(206) 549-2395

Joen Wolfrom specializes in creating two-dimensional commissioned site-specific textile art for residential and contractual interiors. Her versatility enables her to translate her conceptual imagery into simplistic or complex abstract and scenic designs, ranging in mood from calm subtleness to dramatic boldness. Wolfrom's color use, design style, and construction techniques are recognized in the field as being uniquely her own. Her work reflects her desire to create beauty while maintaining excellence in workmanship and quality.

Commission work can be created to fit any color treatment, space, or design theme. It is suitable for placement within private living spaces, lobbies, conference rooms, executive offices and other similar environments.

The artist's work has been exhibited internationally, and is included in public, private and corporate collections in North America and Europe.

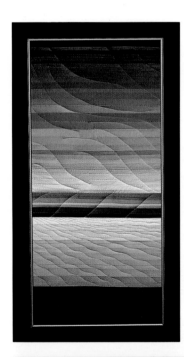

WALL INSTALLATIONS

Therese Albert

13910 S.W. Walker Rd.
Beaverton, OR 97005
(503) 644-1314

Therese Albert's tile murals may be commissioned for any wall space and customized to one's personal fantasy.

Hand painted directly with glazes and fired at a low temperature, the tiles acquire an infinite variety of jewel-like depth of color which extends through the embossed surface. The colors blend in muted shades or stand out in sharp-edged detail. One's hand is drawn to touch the surface.

Therese Albert received her degree, Diploma National Superieur des Beaux Arts, in Paris. She has shown and sold her work nationally and in Europe since 1960.

(bottom) 5' × 10' mural using 200 six inch square tiles. Eight inch square tiles are also available.

(top) 19" dia. plate showing detail work.

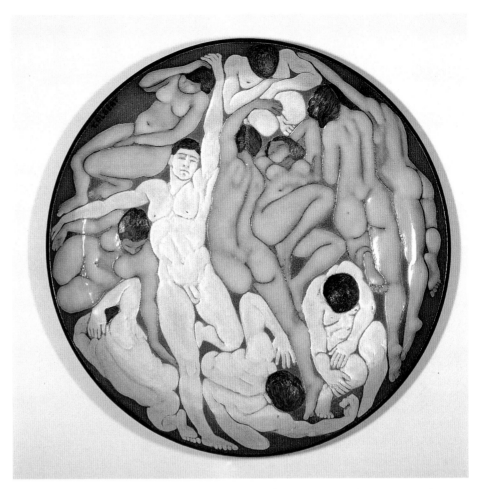

Melinda Ashley-Masi

16 Savin Ave
Norwood, MA 02062
(617) 769-6321

3 Rue Du Professeur Leroux
Chatenay-Malabry 92290
France
(14) 350-67-77

Melinda Ashley-Masi maintains residencies
in the United States and in France. Her studio
is in Norwood, Massachusetts.

She works in high fire porcelain, utilizing celadon and chun glazes, with brushed-on
oxides. Her work ranges from decorative vessels and platters to large-format tile wall
murals. The drawings on her pieces are primarily nudes and floral forms.

The tile murals are one-of-a-kind, and are
appropriate for interior and exterior installations. The artist will accept commissions.

Ashley-Masi is represented in craft galleries
throughout the U.S., and in many private collections in Europe and in Japan.

(Right) "Sauna" high-fire porcelain tiles
3' × 4½'

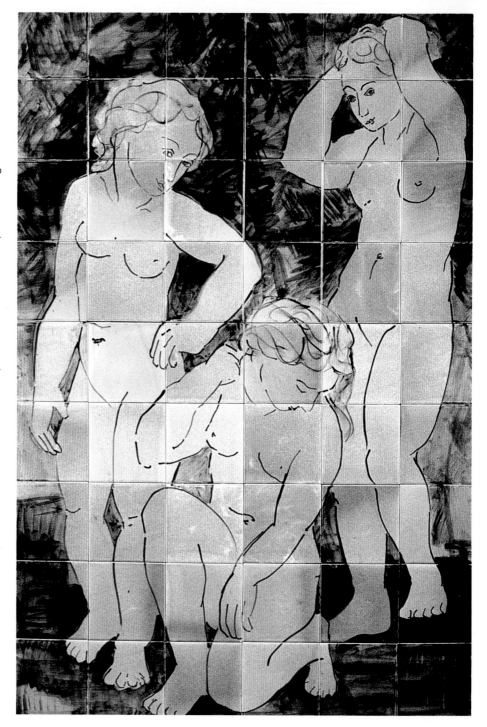

Jamie Davis

Rt. 2 Box 63
Pickens, SC 29671
(803) 868-9749

These extruded red earthenware wall reliefs are durable and maintenance-free. Hung by a single screw each, these modules exhibit great versatility in configuration and spacing. Color, which can be coordinated with any site, shifts as the viewer moves past the piece. Metal, fired into the piece, is painted with bright enamels. The form and length of each module can be varied, and a large group can be formally or informally arranged.

Artist will submit a sketch of the proposed piece after visiting the site or viewing photographs and sample materials. Delivery is 4-6 weeks.

(top) "Party Favors II" 1986 overall 3' × 2' × 3"
(bottom) "Shimmy" 1986 overall 4' × 5' × 3"

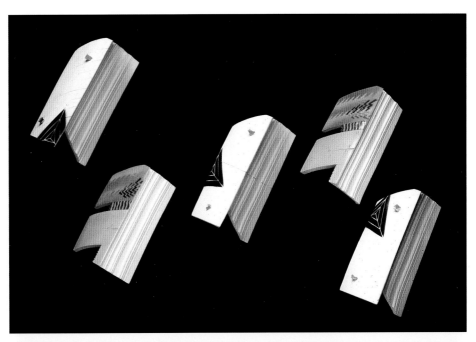

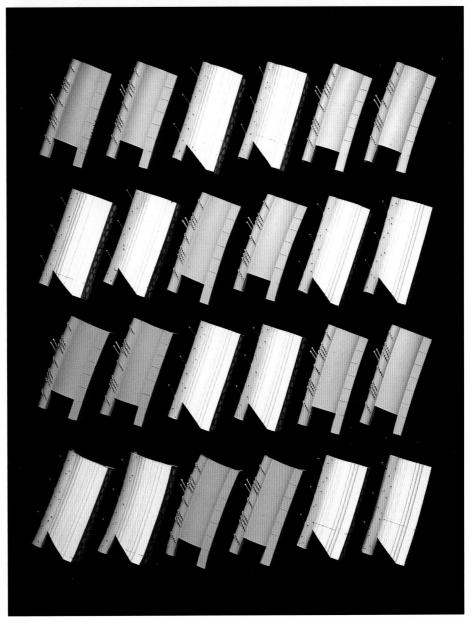

Ruth Duckworth

3845 North Ravenswood
Chicago, IL 60613
(312) 935-0088

Collections: (selected)
Stuttgart Museum, Germany
Windsor Castle, England
National Museum of Modern Art, Japan
Stedelijk Museum, The Netherlands
Smithsonian Institutions, Washington, D.C.
Museum of Contemporary Art, Chicago
Museum fur Modern Keramik, Germany
Philadelphia Museum of Art, Philadelphia
City Museum. Bassano Del Grappa, Italy
Boston Museum of Fine Arts, Boston

Rodger Dunham

6566 Lincoln Street
Bloomfield, CA 94952
(707) 795-8827

Design approach follows two categories of orientation:
1) Architectural—commissioned designs which harmonize with formal and functional elements of a given site and which reflect the esthetic preferences of its occupants, and

2) Autonomous—self-motivated pieces independent of prescribed requirements.

Custom projects (kitchens, bathrooms, etc.) are executed according to a scaled rendering of the specific site as supplied by client. Lead-time of eight weeks is encouraged.

An updated portfolio is available for serious inquiries. The latest schedule for gallery exhibits and shows is available upon request.

Shown below: single and multi-course tile murals, sponged-on underglazes and glazes.

(top right) "VIVA CISNEROS", 30" × 45" × 5", Northwind Gallery, Mill Valley, California.
(top left) "SILICON CARNE", 7' × 4½' × 6", divided diagonally with seven separate attached units, Uniquity Ltd., Highland Park, Illinois.
(bottom) "A RUNNING FENCE", mural for hearth, facade, and soffit, private residence, Sebastopol, California.

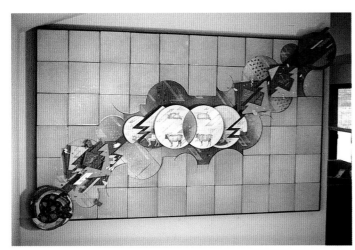

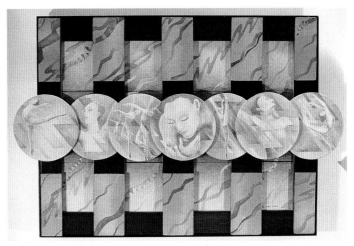

235

Kerry Feldman

Fineline Studios
4228¾ Glencoe Avenue
Venice, CA 90292
(213) 827-8692

Drawing from a fascination with the desert
and the southwest, Feldman creates luminous, abstract and literal landscapes with
fabricated and fused glass panels. Pieces
are designed to hang freely on the wall or
can be architecturally incorporated into
interior spaces. Commissions for specific
sizes and spaces are welcome.

(top) Diptych, "Blue Plane", 12"h × 24"w
(left) "Violet Room", 24"h × 24"w
(right) White Room, 16"h × 10"h

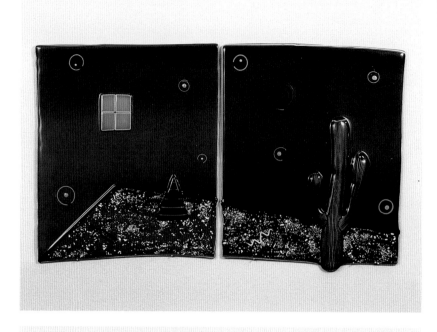

Penelope Fleming

7740 Washington Lane
Elkins Park, PA 19117
(215) 576-6830

Penelope Fleming's inspiration for her wall pieces is derived from rock and earth studies. She is a colorist whose forms intersect space and invite the viewer to discover their many different angles. Much attention is given to surface and form details. Each of the many individual forms acts as a thread to carry various modulated colors to the total piece. The primary materials are clay and/or anodized aluminum which together create both intense, as well as more subtle, color vibrances. There is no limit to the color palette in both materials.

These site specific wall pieces have established a following by many architects, designers, galleries and private collectors. A current portfolio and/or video cassette documents all phases of these wall pieces as well as other smaller pedestal pieces and can be sent upon request.

(top) "Dawn's Mist", 24" × 24" × 3"
private collection, Morristown, NJ
(bottom) "River Styx" 60" × 60" × 6"
lobby entrance of Great Valley Board of Education, Penn via grant from the Pennsylvania Council of Arts.

Scott Goewey

Architectural Ceramics
139 Benham Street
Penn Yan, NY 14527
(315) 536-9614

Since 1978 Scott Goewey has specialized in stoneware wall reliefs for boardrooms, offices and private homes.

Working primarily in earth tones, his custom-designed wall pieces feature a high degree of sculptural relief and are shaped from a combination of slab and coil building techniques, then refined by extensive carving of the leather-hard clay.

These reliefs can be installed permanently or mounted in such a way that they can be moved from one location to another. There are no mortar joints to detract from the movement and integrity of the work which is suitable for interior or exterior locations, such as entry ways, lobbies, homes and offices.

Scott Goewey has exhibited nationally and internationally. His work is in numerous public and private collections.

A minimum of three months is required for completion.

Michelle Griffoul

P.O. Box 588
Los Olivos, CA 93441
(805) 688-9631

The ceramic wall relief is a medium born of the combination of texture and color in clay. The viewer is invited to explore the work as both a tactile and visual experience. A graduate of the International School of Ceramics in Florence, Italy, Michelle Griffoul has been designing and executing thrown and slab works of clay since 1968. Her ceramic reliefs have been commissioned for major banks, hotels, schools, corporate offices and private residences. She accepts both site-specific and non-site-specific commissions and has wide experience in the development of proposals through the public competition process.

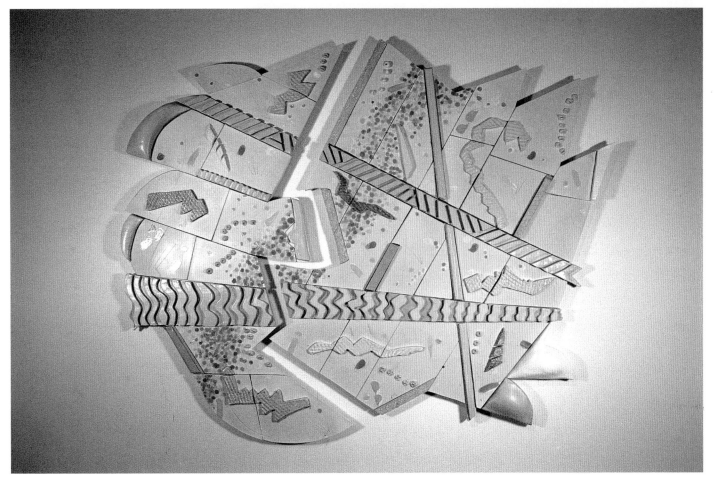

Margie Hughto

Ceramics/Handmade Paper/Screens
Margie Hughto Studio
509 W. Fayette Street
Syracuse, NY 13204
(315) 475-9906

This clay painting entitled, "Seasons," was commissioned by the Niagara Frontier Transit Authority in Buffalo, New York for the Utica Street Station. The artwork, installed in 1985, covers a wall area of about 1,000 square feet and consists of 7,000 lbs. of clay, and took eight months to complete.

The (top) photo shows "Seasons" in the afternoon light in almost its entirety along the stairway and escalator. The artwork begins at the main level and top of the stairs and is 12½' high and descends to the lower level, 32' high, for a total length of 30'. (bottom left) Additional artwork 9' high and 18½' long is at the lower level. (bottom right) the ceramic painting "Seasons" as seen from the bottom of the stairway.

Margie Hughto

Ceramics/Handmade Paper/Screens
Margie Hughto Studio
509 W. Fayette Street
Syracuse, NY 13204
(315) 475-9906

Margie Hughto is nationally recognized for her one-of-a-kind ceramic wall pieces. The ceramic paintings and collages made of colored stoneware clays, slips and glazes are known for their magnificient colors and lush, seductive surfaces. The pieces vary in size and are suitable for public, corporate and residential environments. The artist accepts commissions. Prices vary depending on size and complexity of the project.

Works are included in collections of:
Museum of Fine Arts, Boston, Massachusetts
I.B.M., Atlanta, Georgia
I.B.M., Charlottesville, South Carolina
U.S. News & World Report, Washington, DC
Everson Museum of Art, Syracuse, New York
Lincoln Center, Dallas, Texas
NYNEX, New York, New York
and many other museum, corporate and private collections.

(top) "Ancient Myth," 1986, 22" × 45"
(bottom) "Ancient Island," 1986, 42" × 38"

Martha Jackson-Jarvis

1215 Lawrence Street NE
Washington, DC 20017
Studio: (202) 667-0919
Home: (202) 529-1793

Jackson-Jarvis constructs site specific Architectural Ceramics Wall Installations for interior and exterior spaces. Wall sculptures are constructed of earthenware clay using sensual color applications of permanent glazes and stains.

Studio space includes 2,500 square feet of work space plus spacious kiln site to accommodate construction of large scaled wall environments. Jackson Jarvis is a recipient of the National Endowment for the Arts Sculpture Grant and the D.C. Commission on the Arts Fellowship Awards in both ceramics and sculpture.

Recent Exhibitions: Everson Museum, Syracuse, New York; 1986. Chicago Museum of Science and Technology, 1986

Commissions include: Lenkin Corporation, Washington, DC 10½' × 30'
Installations included in numerous private collections

Publications: The International Ceramic Text: Glen C. Nelson, Ceramics: A Potters Handbook (Fifth Edition)

Consultant
Red Stone Development Corporation
Florence Architectural Corporation
Senterra Limited
JBG Associates
Washington Post Company

Pamela Joseph

Metal Paintings
RR3, Box 140
Pound Ridge, NY 10576
(914) 764-8208 or 764-5732

Diamond K, installed in the Fall of 1986, was commissioned by Diane and David Kirtland for their Pennsylvania home. The work consists of curved aluminum panels that wrap around an exterior tower like diamond banquettes with a fourth flat panel acting as a vertical counterpoint. The formation is airbrushed in kinetically dynamic lacquers, pearl powders, prismatic metalflake and urethane. Specifically designed to interact with the focus at the front entrance.

(top left) Diamond K, detail
(center) Diamond K, detail
(top right) Embedded Blue Diamond, painting, 4'H × 3'W
(bottom) Diamond K, flat panel 80"H × 42"W, Three Curved Panels; 30" × 202"W

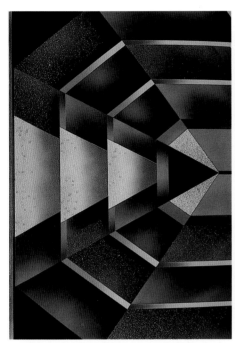

Architectural Ceramics

El Terry Leonard
P.O. Box 49645
Sarasota, FL 33578
(813) 923-6713 and (813) 951-0947

El Terry Leonard of Architectural Ceramics specializes in large scale, site-specific commissions in clay for residential and corporate clients. She produces handbuilt, originally designed ceramics for architectural application. Specialties include: relief wall murals, fountains, and custom surface treatment for walls, fireplaces and floors. Suitable for both interior and exterior installation, work is durable, maintenance-free and guaranteed for the life of the surface. Complete studio services range from concept to installation and shipping anywhere in the world. Major commissions include: Arvida Corporation, Longboat Key, Florida; Barnett Bank, Sarasota, Florida; Chamber of Commerce, Sarasota, Florida; Trotter's Restaurant, Springfield, Missouri

(top) detail
(bottom) "Ginger and Ibis". 5' × 7' relief wall mural, office entry, St. Petersburg, Florida.

Susan Livingston

241 23rd Avenue N
St. Petersburg, FL 33704
(813) 898-2746

Susan Livingston has been working with coil/handbuilt clay for twelve years. She has an M.F.A. in painting and is self taught in clay. Her work exhibits strong classical form and contemporary imagery. The technique of using different kinds of stoneware clays together has been her signature. The introduction of colored clays and more recently, slips, are exhibit in these works.

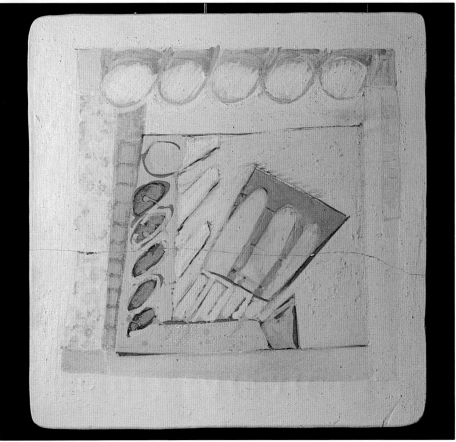

Elizabeth MacDonald

Box 205
Bridgewater, CT 06752
(203) 354-0594

"The misty, color-field wall pieces by Elizabeth MacDonald made of small, thin squares of rough-textured clay are fired with glaze powders and then mounted on a wooden backing. Each square - and there might be dozens or hundreds in a piece - turns out to be a variety of tones that blend with the adjacent squares." Liza Hammel, NY Times

"Nuances of sparkling colors evoke a penetrating mood of German romanticism as well as the utter joy of French Impressionism." Rozanne Kaplan, Art New England

Recent commissions include works for IBM in Boca Raton and the lobby of 155 Federal Street in Boston.

(top) Entrance lobby, Arrow International, Reading, PA. 3'6" × 11'. Tiles are 4", with each panel weighing 25 lbs.
(bottom left) 29" star
(bottom right) surface detail of 3" tiles

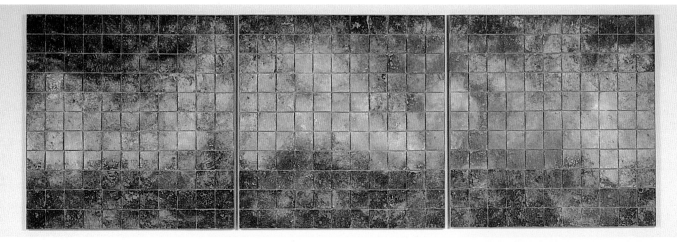

Thom Maltbie

P.O. Box 21
Dillsboro, IN 47018
(812) 432-3126

Thom Maltbie's wall-hanging plates are made from white fireclay, smoked and/or stained with underglaze colors and embellished with bamboo, wood, silk, and handmade paper in layered grid constructions.

The same motifs and materials have also been translated into large-scale tile wall installations.

Commissions include Saks Fifth Avenue at various locations, the Hyatt Regency in Cincinnati, and the Gannett Company, Inc., Arlington, Virginia.

(top) 18" plate, detail
(bottom left) 18" plate
(bottom right) 14" plate, detail

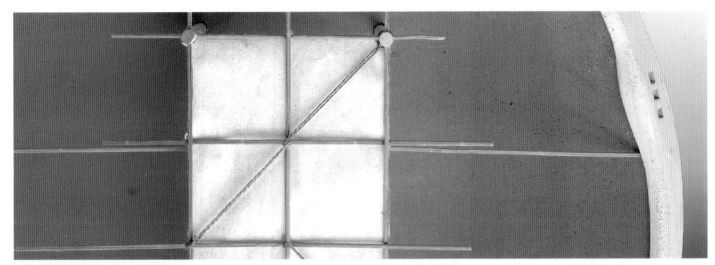

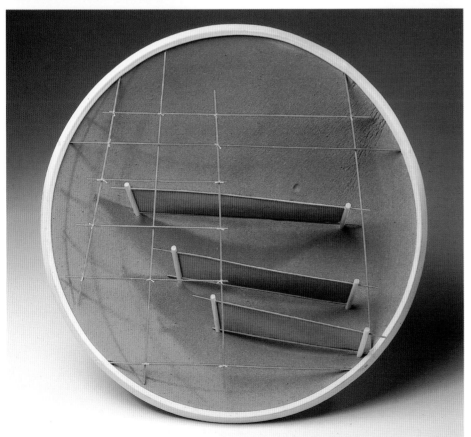

Lois S. Sattler

3620 Pacific Avenue
Venice, CA 90291
(213) 821-7055

Lois Sattler has been working in porcelain for many years. Her unusual handbuilding technique is inspired by her love of natural forms. After the clay piece is made and almost dry, underglaze paints are applied with an airbrush. The piece is then fired to cone one. Each piece can be made to any size and color. She also has a complete line of plates, vases, and bowls which are handbuilt and sculptural in form. Her work can be seen in galleries and showrooms throughout the United States.

On display at The National Craft Showroom in New York City

John Shedd

John Shedd Porcelain
200 Washington Street
P.O. Box 276
Rocky Hill, NJ 08553
(609) 924-6394

All pieces are executed in high temperature stoneware and porcelain glazes. Primary emphasis in all work is the coloration and texture of durable finishes that impart a permanence to interior and exterior surfaces. Surface material is color permanent and wear resistant. Colors and shapes can be adjusted to blend or contrast with any environment. Work requires 4-6 weeks for completion. Inquiries are invited, price quotes and brochures are available upon request.

John Shedd has designed and worked in ceramics on a professional basis for the past nine years. His work is shown throughout the United States. Wall tiles were developed in part through a grant from the New Jersey State Council on the Arts. Both residential and commercial commissions are sought.

(top) Triptych, 12"H × 36"W
(bottom right) Set of 9 Tiles, 36"H × 36"W
(bottom left) Altered Vase, 18"H

Susan Singleton

1101 East Pike Street
Seattle, WA 98122
(206) 322-9200

Susan Singleton Studio, established in 1973, specializes in site-specific artwork for both commercial and residential spaces.

Working in a variety of media, Susan's work includes sculptural pieces, large canvases and limited edition prints. With the assistance of her staff, whose areas of expertise include graphics, printmaking, photography, textiles, video and sculpture, Susan is able to create a variety of work for a diverse clientele.

The Singleton Studio will respond promptly to inquiries for commissioned artwork by providing a resumé, fabric samples and initial suggestions for the projected artwork.

(top) "Fields 1 & 2"
6' × 6' × 4'6" × 6'
Goldleaf Partners and Amberdon Corporate Pointe Ltd.
Culver City, California
Dyed canvas, hand colored and stitched.
(bottom) "Walk it Down"
135' × 45' × 3'
Embassy Suites Hotel
Boston, Massachusetts
Varnished Okawara paper, bamboo, leather lashings, and colored cotton cording

Drew Smith

7793 Bremen Road
Logan, OH 43138
(614) 385-2972

Drew Smith is a glass artist who makes architectural scaled sculpture of handblown and cast glass. His work is in major collections throughout the world. Select commissions: Anchor Hocking, Hooker Chemical, Indianapolis Museum of Art and the Ohio State Supreme Court.

Smith's sculpture is contemporary. It makes use of light and makes environmental glow. Neon is sometimes used.

Walls of any size or shape can be commissioned as well as unique sculptures for clients. Sculptured glass vessels on glass stills from 12" to 36" tall are also available.

(top left) "Sea Frame", 40" × 18"
(top right) "Orb Continuum", 30" × 17" dia.
(bottom) Large Spectrum Generators, 70" to 40" long × 5" dia. tubes.

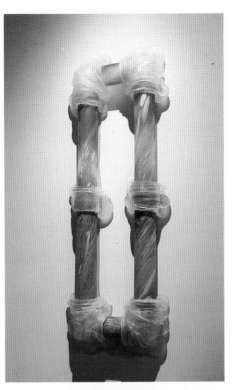

Darius Strickler

15 Castle Hill Avenue
Great Barrington, MA 01230
(413) 528-1866

Venturing beyond the tradition of paper-making, these works blend richly luminous tones, embossing, inlays, illustrations and electronics in both two and three dimensional forms.

Architectural-scale paintings, sculptural masks and limited edition plates are rendered in a style which translates as "humanistic encouragement" - utilizing classical references with touches of political, social and artistic satire. The tense but balanced compositional design evokes association to ages past and reinforces fresh contemporaneity.

Created as one-of-a-kind and limited editions, these pieces are appropriately mounted in custom-made plexiglass boxes or frames. Commissions are accepted for both individual and corporate clients. An expanded and descriptive brochure featuring additional sculptural works is available on request.

Plates: 16" diameter
Large Mask: 17 × 11 × 4
Small Mask: 11 × 6 × 3

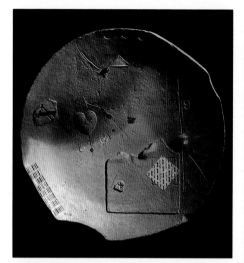
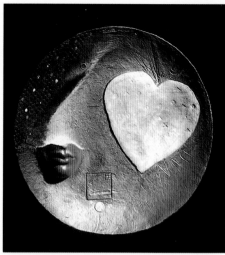

Neil Tetkowski

1530 Whitehaven Road
Grand Island, NY 14072
(716) 884-8463 and (716) 773-3266

Tetkowski makes large ceramic disks which hang as dynamic wall sculptures. Measuring from 2' to 4' in diameter these energetic, colorful reliefs have been installed in private and corporate spaces, including: the Dallas Ft. Worth Airport, Hallmark Cards of Kansas City, and the Museum of Modern Art in Tokyo.

Tetkowski's wall sculptures are strong and durable. They are easily and safely installed by means of a steel cable that wraps around the back of the piece. Tetkowski has recently made some of his works available in bronze.

(top) Kinetic Form #10, 1985, Diameter 36"
(bottom) Hyatt Regency Hotel, Buffalo, New York

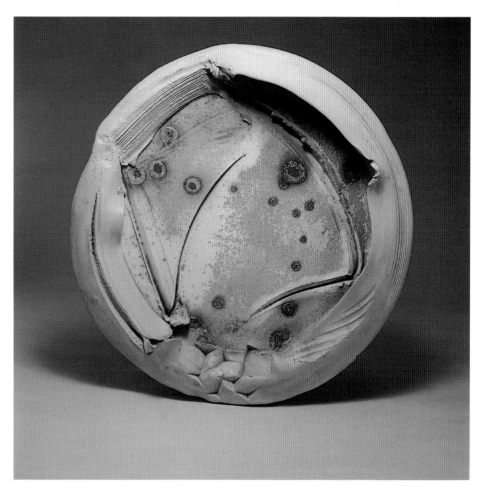

K. N. Whitcomb

Steel and Copper Enamellist
Whitcomb Architectural Enamelles
1631 Mimulus Way
La Jolla, CA 92037
(619) 454-0595

Enamelling, the art of fusing vitreous components (glass-like pastes or powders) to a metal surface, yields an art form which has the strength of the underlying metal and the weather resistant properties of the glass surface. Whitcomb is a master of many forms of enamelling including cloisonne and has achieved international recognition for architectural enamelles. Among the dozens of commissions are architectural enamelles in the Dubai UAE International Airport (running for 97 feet behind the entire ticketing area); State of Alaska School auditorium, Kodiak; University Hospital, San Diego; Town Hall, Gosselies, Belgium.

Whitcomb's artwork has been published in Craft Horizons, Better Homes and Garden (cover), Designers West, Ceramic Industry (cover), Applause, and Time-Life Books among others. Awards include International Biennale Prize: Limoges, France (1978), Tokyo, Japan (1981, 1985).

Whitcomb attended both the Rhode Island School of Design and the Cambridge School of Art on scholarships.

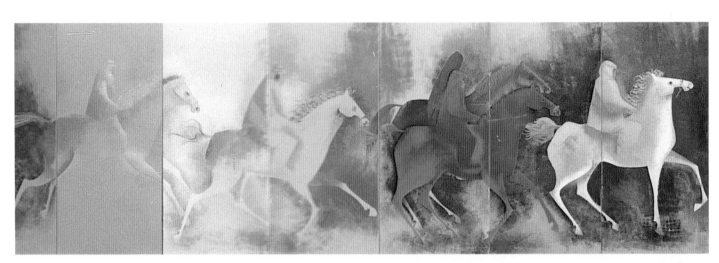

TILES AND MOSAICS

Priscilla Blake

Priscillas Ceramic Tiles
Erickson Street
Uxbridge, MA 01569
(617) 278-5490

Priscilla Blake fabricates custom ceramic tiles and murals for your personal specifications, all tiles are hand-executed, glazed and Kiln-fired for permanency.

Color samples, photographs, drawings, wallpaper and fabric samples, etc. provides better continuity of design. Combining the skills of consultant, designer, and artist produces the best ceramic tile setting. Artist provides a scaled drawing and fired tile samples for clients approval. Free from limitations, designs range from traditional to contemporary.

Phone or write to discuss your plans and objectives. Delivery on custom work varies by scope of project. All custom jobs are bid on an individual basis.

Ceramica Europa

Richard Sorrentino
P.O. Box 75211
Tampa, FL 33675
(813) 241-0055 ext. 498

Represented by:

Winston & Company
95 7th Avenue
Brooklyn, NY 11215
(718) 638-7942

Sunny McLean & Company
3800 N.E. 2nd Avenue
Miami, FL 33137
(305) 573-5943

Ceramica Europa, Inc. designs and produces hand made, hand-painted tile and ware. Our design services group, under the direction of Richard Sorrentino, works with architects and interior designers to create original tile environments.

Specialty: Large scale Venetian glass mosaics, hand-painted signature ceramic wall and floor tile installations.
Additional services: consultations; press molded, slip cast, hand-built slab construction, high and low fired clay bodies, custom color mixing; renovation and museum quality restoration.

Samples and brochures available on written request.

Major Commissions:
Mayfair in the Grove, Mayfair Hotel as seen in 1985 December "Ten Best" issue of Interiors Magazine; Treister and Cantillo Architects, Miami, Florida; The DeBartolo Corporation; Church Street Station; Paul Bocuse's "Morning Glory French Bakery", Orlando, Florida; Al Hirt, private residence.

Photo descriptions:
(top) The Columbia Restaurant, mural re-creation, America's oldest Spanish restaurant, Tampa, Florida
(bottom) The Tampa Theater Building, foyer flooring restoration, National Register of Historic Places, Tampa, Florida

Jamie Fine

4241 Crestline Drive
Ann Arbor, MI 48103
(313) 426-5298

Jamie Fine composes ceramic tiles into pictures whose colors and textures reflect the sky and landscape. Their subtlety belies the toughness and durability of the stoneware from which they are made. These ceramic "paintings" are suitable for indoor and outdoor spaces. They can be mounted directly to walls, hung as paintings, or attached to freestanding screens.

The tiles may be arranged in compositions of virtually any size and shape. This flexibility, combined with their wide range of color provides the designer with artworks which fit equally well into modern, post modern, and even classical decor. These pieces have been successfully used to enhance commercial and office spaces, homes, and public places.

Jamie Fine has been working with clay for twenty years, and her pieces are found in museums and corporate collections throughout the country.

Write for a selection of slides of current work, price list, and resumé.

(right) "Thinking of Halley's Comet" vertical triptych 18' × 3', I Financial Place, Chicago, Illinois, 1986.
(top) "Stellar Music" 9' × 2', SKR Records, Ann Arbor, Michigan, 1986.
(center) untitled screen, 6' × 6', private collection, Ft. Meyers, Florida, 1986.
(bottom) detail of 6" square tile, 1986.

Ronald L. Garfinkel

Monroe Salt Works
Stovepipe Alley
Monroe, ME 04951
(207) 525-4471

Salt-Glazed tiles are an excellent choice for floors, counters, and walls. They are rich in color and texture as well as extremely durable. They are unaffected by heavy usage, and can withstand high heat.

Garfinkel has been producing these unique tiles since 1969. His work appears in many prominent collections and has been featured in Ceramics Monthly, Studio Potter, and Salt-Glaze Ceramics. He has served as ceramic/design consultant in the United States and Latin America.

Geometric patterns also available.

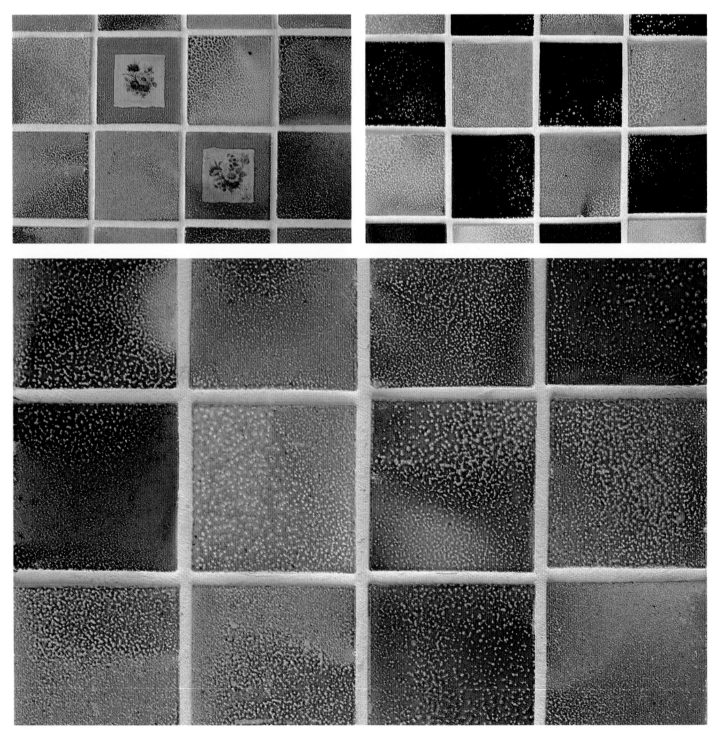

Jennifer Griffin

2401 South Ervay #305
Dallas, TX 75215
(214) 565-0323

Jennifer Griffin specializes in ceramic tile murals. Her designs are bold, graphic and colorful. Among her many influences are Navajo and primitive Indian art as seen in the furniture shown here. Having added the talents of a metalworker to her studio, Jennifer also designs the iron furniture that houses her tile work.

In addition to large murals, Jennifer can also be commissioned to produce single tiles used architecturally for embellishment. See below.

For three dollars, you will receive current information and photographs of installations and works in progress.

(top) One of four dining chairs. 1" hollow metal tubing and 6" bisque tile. Under and overglazes. (Tile also runs vertically up back of chair.) Plastic shoes inserted in legs to prevent scraping. Each chair produced in a different color. 20"L × 20"W × 38"H
(bottom) Coffee table, one of four commissioned by Norris Investments. ⟨3/4⟩" hollow metal tubing and 6" bisque tile. Under and over glazes. 38"L × 36"W × 19"H

C. Robert Markert

232 West Esplanade Avenue
Louisville, KY 40214
(502) 363-0952

Markert has 24 years experience, as a designer/artist in the area of glass and mosaics, including the painting and firing of glass, ceramic tiles, and terra cotta. A specialty is the covering of brick fireplace wall surfaces by the use of ceramic tile applications using hand made and painted clay pieces along with stock tiles available from tile manufacturers. The mosaic work uses hammer cut imported smalti, glass, and sliced stone. Design and material us is determinedly the specific needs of the project, especially in the area of texture, color, and budget.

Major commission: (top) Round mosaic at entry, 4 ft. in diam. (bottom) Ceramic wrapped free standing fireplace, 9ft. and three ft. deep; the Robert Prentice residence, Jeffersonville, Indiana.

Susan Parks

North Farms Pottery
32 North Farms Road
Haydenville, MA 01039
(413) 268-7429

Top quality ceramic tiles. Excellent selection of solid colors, images, patterns.

Custom colors and decoration. Images reproduced.

Complete design services include installation, layout and tile samples.

(top) 4" × 4" wall tiles
(bottom) 1' × 10' Three Cow Mural for Bart's of Amherst, MA ©1986

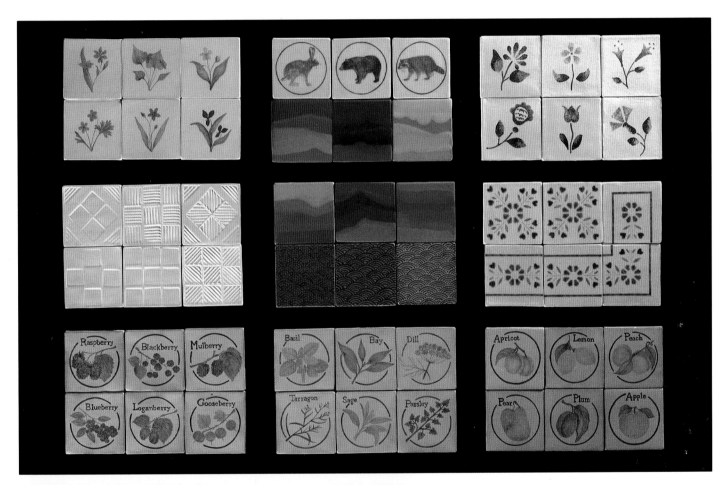

Judith Poe

P.O. Box 10156
Sarasota, FL 34278-0156
(813) 371-0234

Represented by:
NATIONAL CRAFT SHOWROOM, NYC

Each tile is hand cut from durable stoneware clay. After bisque firing, the tile is glazed by hand using a wax resist technique, colors are custom mixed from commercial glaze stains. The tiles are fired a second time to 2350°F, vitrifying them. They can be used for any usual tile application, e.g. splash boards and counters, roman tubs, shower enclosures, or as decorative borders for pools.

Prices vary according to complexity of design. Plain tile starts at ten dollars per square foot.

Custom colors and designs are available.

Write for price list.

Judith Poe has been a studio potter since 1976. She also produces porcelain tableware and decorative accessories which may be seen at National Craft Showroom, NYC.

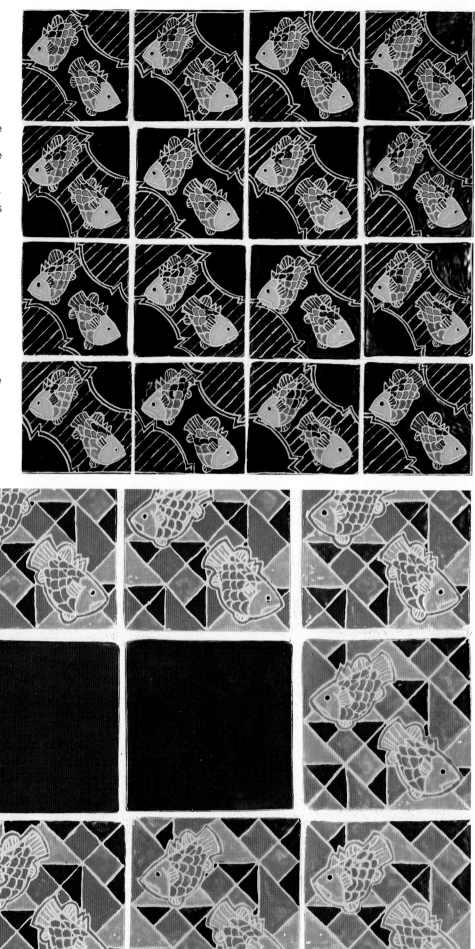

Will A. Richardson

1010 Garcia Road
Santa Barbara, CA 93103
(805) 965-5379

I began to study painting at the age of ten and have always enjoyed interiors and architecture. The tile mural is a fine way to unite these interests.

The tiles are commercially produced and are therefore of standard sizes. The painting, which can be a combination of hand execution, airbrushing and silkscreening, is low fired and suitable to both overhead and vertical surfaces. The designs are one-of-a-kind.

I have two degrees in painting and my varied crafts have been shown at the American Craft Museum in New York City, and in better crafts galleries throughout the United States.

(top) Benchback: 1' × 4'8"
(bottom) Ceiling: 13' × 14'

Joan Zerrien

Zerrien Ceramics
1624 West Washington Blvd.
Venice, CA 90291
(213) 392-4415

A ceramic artist for twelve years, Zerrien designs large scale tile paintings for interior or exterior installation. In addition to painting on commercial tiles, Zerrien has developed a variety of modular ceramic wall pieces that can be installed in an unlimited number of configurations. One series consists of raku-fired slabs, 10″ square, with a reduced copper glaze and eucalyptus leaf impression. Another option is a lightweight porcelain form, 10-12″ square, delicately textured and available in a wide range of colors. Slides available.

(top) Detail, tile wall painting.
(bottom) Tile wall painting, private residence, Los Angeles. Six-inch commercial tiles refired with low-fire pastel glazes to complement colors of house exterior and swimming pool. Dimensions 3 ½′ × 33 ½′

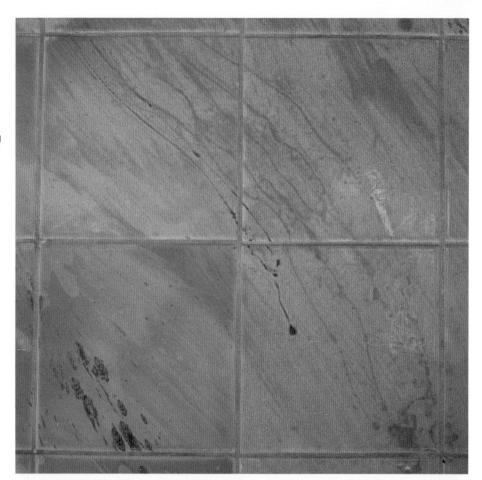

ARCHITECTURAL DETAIL AND PAINTED FINISHES

Timothy G. Biggs
Andrea M. Biggs

792 Eastern Parkway
Brooklyn, NY 11213
(718) 771-4221

Andrea and Timothy Biggs collaborate to produce:

Trompe l'oeil murals, specializing in architectural illusion;

Faux marbre and other faux finishes for ornamental pieces, walls, and ceilings;

Murals with large-scale floral, organic, or fantasy imagery;

Folding screens, each an original work of art painted on stretched canvas.

Andrea and Timothy work exclusively on a custom basis, producing original art works in our studio or on location, created for specific site installations. We welcome opportunities to work with designers and architects, integrating our work into the overall design program specific for each situation.

Andrea Biggs holds the MFA degree in painting from Bard College, and has exhibited her work in New York City and elsewhere. Timothy Biggs studied design and painting at Parsons School of Design. Their work appears on the walls and ceilings of both private homes and public and commercial spaces throughout the New York area.

Columbine

Bennett Bean
RD#3 Box 212
Blairstown, NJ 07825
(201) 852-8953

Developed for special site and need.

Columbine makes architectural terra cotta columns in a variety of matte glazes ranging from cool pastel colors to rich earth tones. Whether decorative or structural they are ideal for both interior and exterior applications from a single pedestal to a colonnade.

Available in modular sections of varying sizes and configurations the elements can be combined to produce endless variations. They may be purchased separately or assembled.

Don Drumm

Don Drumm Studios and Gallery
437 Crouse Street
Akron, OH 44311
(216) 253-6268

Drumm is both a Sculptor and
Designer/Craftsman. He maintains his own
aluminum foundry, where he produces an
emense variety of work. Here he creates his
"one of a kind" sculpture, a group of limited
edition sculptures, and an evergrowing
selection of functional craft objects.

Environmental art is his other love. His architectural sculpture and crafts are known and
owned world wide.

(right)
"Solar Totem"; Cement; 3 stories high;
Quaker Hilton Hotel, Akron, Ohio.

Brochures available on the Architectural
work, small sculpture, or the craft lines.
Please specify.

Scott Goewey

Architectural Ceramics
139 Benham Street
Penn Yan, NY 14527
(315) 536-8692

Since 1978 Scott Goewey has specialized in stoneware wall reliefs for boardrooms, offices and private homes.

Working primarily in earth tones, his custom-designed wall pieces feature a high degree of sculptural relief and are shaped from a combination of slab and coil building techniques, then refined by extensive carving of the leather-hard clay.

These reliefs can be installed permanently or mounted in such a way that they can be moved from one location to another. There are no mortar joints to detract from the movement and integrity of the work which is suitable for interior or exterior locations, such as entry ways, lobbies, homes and offices.

Scott Goewey has exhibited nationally and internationally. His work is in numerous public and private collections.

A minimum of three months is required for completion.

Conrad Malicoat

Brick Breakthroughs
Provincetown, MA 02657
(617) 487-0214

Conrad Malicoat has been using brick as a sculptural medium since 1974, designing and constructing one-of-a-kind nonlinear and rhythmic walls, fireplaces and free-standing sculpture. He is the recipient of a Massachusetts Artist Foundation grant and a National Endowment for the Arts grant for his work in brick. His particular use of brick lends itself to many applications, from creating sculptural walls and fireplaces in private homes and public places, to accenting and giving relief in conventional brick edifices. The basic unit of brick used in this manner creates general and implied forms, inviting and drawing in the observer to collaborate with the artist in supplying those forms with specific meaning. The themes in his work cover a wide range of both realistic and abstract content, depending on the site and client. Wherever brick is used, his treatment is a unique artistic achievement and enhancement.

Preservation by Design

The years bracketing 1850 saw publication of two books, each serving to define the development of two fields that even today remain distinguished—and heretofore distinct—in our contemporary culture: historic preservation and the arts and crafts movement.

Brandishing his pen before an increasingly industrialized society, John Ruskin published *The Seven Lamps of Architecture* in 1849. In his chapter "Lamp of Memory," Ruskin states, "There are two duties respecting national architecture whose importance it is impossible to overrate; the first to render the architecture of the day, historical; and the second to preserve, as the most precious of inheritances, that of past ages."

The Seven Lamps of Architecture continues to serve as a guiding light to preservationists engaged in the restoration of historic buildings. Practitioners in this field today include trades- and craftspeople providing services to conserve our artistic and cultural heritage.

The Stones of Venice, first published in 1851, laid the foundation for development of the arts and crafts movement by William Morris and others who were repulsed by products of the industrial age. Morris, in evolving his theory of design, wrote, "A designer... should always thoroughly understand the process of the special manufacture he is dealing with, or the result will be a mere *tour de force*. On the other hand, it is the pleasure of understanding the capabilities of the special material, and using them for suggesting (not imitating) natural beauty and incident, that gives the *raison d'etre* for decorative art."

The seedbed of preservation and crafts was cultivated by outcasts of the technocratic age—signaled by the brutal end of World War II. By the 1960's both fields were fast defining their respective ground. Nonetheless, today it is a rare instance when there is a common ground.

I suggest that such territory exists on each and every restoration job and new construction project—in the company of architect, designer, craftperson, artisan, artist and collector.

This can be achieved through 'preservation by design.' Not 'preservation vs. design,' which suggests a combative stance typifying the debate over the identity of art and craft. Not 'preservation or design,' which is optional or exclusive. Nor 'preservation and design,' this coupling appearing passive and without much objective. But 'preservation by design': a purposeful intent with a deliberate goal realized in a studious fashion.

The intent of 'preservation by design' is to address the two most important issues facing the field of architecture today: preservation of both our architectural heritage (past and future) and preservation of the artisan who created—and continues to create—this work.

First—the preservation of physical fabric, both old and new, can only be accomplished by integrating proper design into new construction, restoration, and even ongoing maintenance and repair of a building throughout its life. This entails designing for preservation from the onset and adhering to the very elementary principle of architecture: that a structure's primary function and design requirement is to protect itself and its occupants from . . . the elements. This task remains in the hands of architects and other design professionals.

Second—both the traditional trade techniques and contemporary craft skills can best be preserved through a common goal: an adherence to the finest principles of design—in the classroom, studio, workshop and field. With such a purpose, there is no distinction between an individual working on conservation of historic fabric and one engaged in construction of a new work.

Such principles appear separately in the fields of preservation and crafts. Let them combine to form a common ground over which a single banner flies reading *opus artificem probat*—the craftsman is known by the quality of his work.

Philip C. Marshall
Director, Architectural Artisanry
Swain School of Design
New Bedford, Massachusetts

Spring Street Studio

Richard Aerni/Michael Frasca/Allan Nairn
1311 Spring Street
Cincinnati, OH 45210
(513) 381-1463
Represented by Toni Birckhead
(513) 241-0212

Produce collaborative works in clay for architectural settings, including fountains, relief-carved murals, custom floor tile, modular wall systems and monumental thrown and slab-built vessels. Suitable for indoor or outdoor settings. The artists also produce a line of original decorative ceramics for designers and galleries. Brochures available upon request.

Commissions include: Omni-Netherland Plaza Hotel, Cincinnati; Atrium Two Wintergarden, Cincinnati; Wellington Corporation, Covington, KY; Bartlett and Company, Cincinnati; Central Trust Bank, Cincinnati; Rax Restaurants, USA; Zantigo Restaurants, Midwest Region; Saks Fifth Avenue, Cincinnati.

(top and bottom) Details of "Riverflight", hand-carved stoneware fountain executed for the lobby of Wellington Corporation, Covington, KY. Overall size is 8′ × 5′ × 10′.

Dennis Tillberg
J. Kenney Abrames

Renaissance Associates
Box 55, Annex Station
Providence, RI 02901
(401) 274-5354

Restoration Research
Original Design Consultation
Maquette Illustration

(top left) Detail. Environmental sculpture,
18' × 5' × 12', plaster structural steel,
mother-of-pearl overlay. Private residence.
(top center) Mural. Expanded detail derived from Fragonard's painting "The Swing."
Theater, Providence, R.I.

(top right) Detail. Gilding, stenciling, cornice, ceiling, walls, light cove. Theater, New
Bedford, Mass.
(bottom) Completed restoration of theater
in New Bedford, including ceiling mural
restoration

Dennis Tillberg
J. Kenney Abrames

Renaissance Associates
Box 55, Annex Station
Providence, RI 02901
(401) 274-5354

Decorative Artist in plaster and paint.

(top left) Detail. Plaster bench-drawn cornice, in progress. Chapel, Providence, R.I.
(top right) Reredos. Structural steel, plaster, scratch coat completed, for drawn-in-place, curved plaster cornice. Church, Providence, R.I.
(bottom) Chapel. Ornamental plaster, stained glass, stenciling, gilding, color composition

Mark Victor Venaglia

Designs for the New Age
132 West 24th Street, Box 7
New York, NY 10011
(212) 255-2772

Mark Victor Venaglia fools the eye with exquisite "trompe l'oeil" from the island of Manhattan. Fooling the eye is serious business to us. Take a closer look at the photos on the opposite page. Each design for the New Age is a work of fine art and an accolade to an ancient craft joyously revived. Whether wall or ceiling mural, floor treatment, "faux" finish, or flight of fantasy, each project is limited only by the client's imagination. Each work is created over a minimum of three months, and a limited number of commissions are accepted over any one period to insure close collaboration with the clients. All works are one-of-a-kind and are completed in the Designs for the New Age studios, where we encourage clients to visit. Created to be easily shipped and installed, murals are produced on canvas to provide maximum durability and are executed with paints that duplicate those used in Renaissance frescoes. No matter the size, they can move with the client. All works are covered with our exclusive protective patina that adds to the painted illusion. In each design for the New Age, we acknowledge the fine traditions that have preceded us and their application to contemporary design and lifestyle. Estimates upon request. Consultations encouraged.

ARCHITECTURAL GLASS

Frederick S. Abrams

3218 B. Highland Avenue
Santa Monica, CA 90405
213-392-1884

Abrams' unique use of glass, in terms of function, purpose and imagery, is distinguished by its relationship to environmental, architectural, cultural and anthropological influences, which become integrated design elements in his work. Varying shades, densities, opacities and textures of glass are composed to create multi-dimensional effects.

His works include mass transportation maps, economic charts and other diagrammed biological and industrial forms, which are interpreted as metaphorical icons. They have been exhibited in major university art galleries, a Bicentennial exhibition sponsored by the Xerox Corporation and received critical acclaim in publications ranging from art and scientific journals to TIME magazine.

Private and public commissions accepted. Portfolio available upon request.

(top) "Les routes de La Grande Odalisque (The Large Brain)" 1983, in 10' × 11" modular wooden frame w/glossy black lacquer finish.

(bottom) detail.

Mark Anderson

Anderson Art Glass
105 N. Union Street, Studio 316
Alexandria, VA 22314
(703) 683-7655

Color Light Line Form
Fine contemporary design in glass, capitalizing upon the greatest strengths of the medium.

Mr. Anderson's work plays with its setting, picking up architectural details, echoing forms as design motifs, then interrupting the patterns, teasing them with other patterns.

Whether the need is for rich explosions of color, the subtle grace of muted tone and texture, the interplay of light and shadow in 3-D wall pieces, plates and bowls, or the special effects of neon, you and your clients will find much pleasure in the work of this versatile and prolific artist.

Mark Anderson has executed scores of successful public and private commissions in thirteen years of working with glass. A master of traditional and contemporary techniques, his work has been exhibited in museums and galleries throughout the U.S.

Winner of the 1985 Schwarzschild Award for Glass.

Art Glass Studio

Kathleen Burns & Edward Grout
P.O. Box 295
Hollywood, MD 20636
(301) 373-3634

Specializing in Architectural Glass—
residential and commercial applications.
Emphasis on original design and versatility of
style. Dividing screens, etched mirrors,
autonomous panels and cabinet inserts are
available.

We maximize design potential by enhancing its elements with a variety of materials
and techniques which include hand-blown
imported and domestic glass, textured
optic glass, sand etching, and multi-layered
laminations. Construction is lead, zinc, and
copperfoil. Design alternatives are explored
with each client giving practical consideration to aesthetics, environment, structural
problems, light control, privacy, and thermal
properties.

(top right) Solomon's Pier Restaurant
Solomon's Island, Maryland
(bottom right) Entryway (70" × 75")
Private Residence
Potomac, Maryland
(top left) Dividing Screen (71" × 69") Exotic
hardwood frames available.
(bottom left) Detail of Private Residence
Potomac, Maryland

David Bellantone/ George Cirocco

Salamandra Glass
133 Market Street
Portsmouth, NH 03801
(603) 431-4511

Founded in 1975, Salamandra Glass is the registered name for the studio collaboration of David Bellantone & George Cirocco. Credits include extensive museum and private collections and international corporate clients.

Design and fabrication service offered include:

One-of-a-kind and limited edition art glass, handblown and cast multiples, lighting and custom bullseye windows.

Salamandra Art Glass Block & Tile: Hand-carved and cast modular glass block suitable for structural and decorative application. For use where light, color and privacy are key ingredients.

Top left and right: "Milky Way" transom construction—blown rondels embedded in cast glass tiles, 9" × 36" × 1½". Each tile 4½" × 4½" × 1½".
Bottom: walls lights—blown and decorated glass with brass hardware, 17" in diameter.

Sandra Christine Q. Bergér

Quintal Unlimited
100 El Camino Real, #202
Burlingame, CA 94010
(415) 348-0310

A sympathetic response to a client's environment, philosophy, and taste make Quintal Studio an innovator in custom designed glass (see also Sculptures).

Applying modern techniques and materials to an old world artform delivers an upbeat style of lasting quality.

Bergér evokes an oriental theme (below) by infusing a splendid mix of design, color, prisms, and architecture.

Sandra Christine Q. Bergér
Quintal Unlimited

Ed Carpenter

1812 N. W. 24th Avenue
Portland, OR 97210
(503) 224-6729

Ed Carpenter specializes in working with architects and interior designers to solve architectural problems through unusual uses of glass. Since 1972 he has designed windows, skylights, screens, lighting and a university clocktower for projects around the country, as well as undertaking a variety of consulting contracts. Some recent commissions have dealt with entire interior environments. His work has been published in Architecture, Architectural Record, Progressive Architecture, Neues Glas, American Craft, and many other journals. He has received grants and awards from the Graham Foundation for Advanced Studies in the Fine Arts, Western States Arts Foundation, and National Endowment for the Arts, among others.

Justice Center, Portland, Oregon 1983
Foyer window 30' × 24'
Fabricated by Tim O'Neill
(top) Interior view
(bottom left) Exterior view
(bottom right) Interior detail

Ed Carpenter

1812 N. W. 24th Avenue
Portland, OR 97210
(503) 224-6729

Kaiser Permanente Medical Center
Portland, Oregon 1985
24' × 14'
Broom, Oringdulph, O'Toole and Rudolph,
Architects
Fabricated by Tim O'Neill
(top right) Exterior
(bottom right) Exterior
(bottom left) Interior Detail

Josiah Dearborn

TransparentFabrications
36 West 20 Street 4th Floor
New York, NY 10011
(718) 858-0868

Decorative plexiglas construction and design, by commission. Mr. Dearborn has worked with acrylic plastics since 1975. Design experience includes as well, extensive work in silver, and interactive museum exhibits with Edwin Schlossberg Incorporate.

(left) Floor indicator for elevator lobby, with dyed and sandblasted pieces. (Sections light as each floor is reached; interface provided to existing control system.) 45" × 8" × 8".
(top)Transparent front for player piano. 60" × 36" × 6".
(bottom)3-dimensional logo in form of a griffin. 24" × 18" × 12".

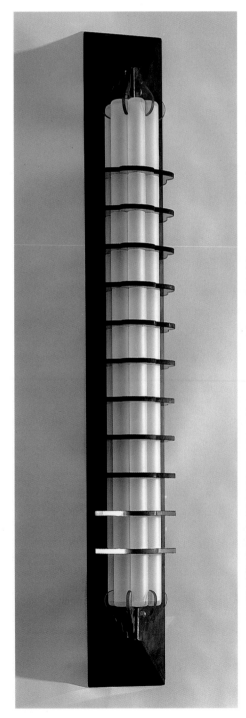

Fredrica H. Fields

Member of the Stained Glass Assoc.
of America
561 Lake Avenue
Greenwich, CT 06830
(203) 869-5508
By appointment only.

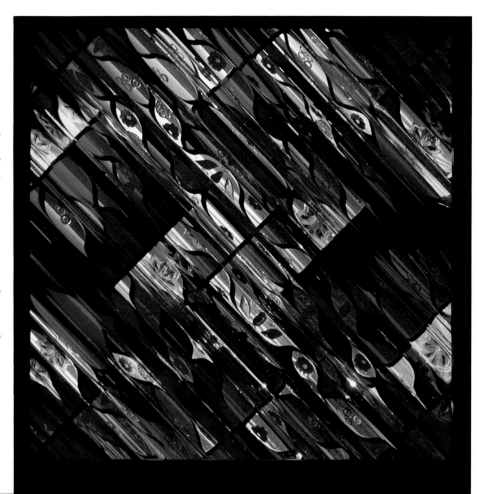

Specializing in a three-dimensional abstract
stained glass unique with us. Installed and
autonomous panels. Sizes from 6" by 6" by 3"
deep, to 48" by 24" by 5"- 6" deep, or equivalent space. Multiple individual panels can
be combined to make up a larger
installation.
Prices from $300 and up.

(bottom) "Mirage" 23"W by 17"H by 5½"
deep
Autonomous panel. $10,000
Second award in "Best Stained Glass of '86"
competition, sponsored by the Professional
Stained Glass Magazine.
(top) "Diagonal" 23"W by 23"h by 5½" deep
Autonomous panel. $8,000.
Public Installations:
Washington Cathedral, Washington, D.C.
Marie Cole Auditorium, Greenwich Library,
Greenwich, CT
Y.W.C.A., Greenwich, Conn.
The Association for Research and Enlighten-
ment, Virginia Beach, VA
The Connecticut Hospice, Branford, Conn.
Concordia College, Bronxville, N.Y.

Anita & Bob Flanigan

The Glass Works
300 Long Street
Nevada City, CA 95959
(916) 265-6700

Stained glass is a jewel. It tells a story. The story that it tells is of our heritage, our mood, our affluence or the life style in which we follow. Stained glass is very hard to describe. It is as life itself, ever changing. The Glass Works is a studio dedicated to the client. It is our responsibility to transform the soul of the client into the world of light and color. To do this, The Glass Works offers over twelve years of experience, and, internationally known designers who are available to our studio.

The Glass Works has been a studio member of the Stained Glass Association of America since 1978, and also specialize in repair, restoration and safety glazing.

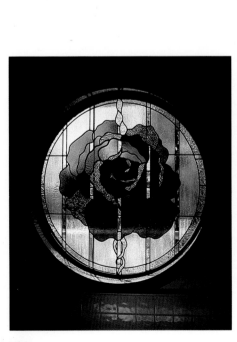

John David Forsgren

2856 N.E. Rodney
Portland, OR 97212
(503) 287-0020

Forsgren's training and experience in architecture is evident in his work as well as in his approach to his work. Context, client, and designer provide important direction for each project. In the ten years he has been designing and executing glass commissions, Forsgren has utilized traditional leaded glass techniques in an uncommon fashion. In addition to creating a surface which can be used in both window and wall installations, his approach to glass gives his work depth and subtlety. Slides are available upon request.

(top) Sandlbasted and grouted leaded glass wall panels with sandblasted aluminum frames. 5½'-11½' × 50'. United Virginia Bank headquarters, Richmond, Virginia.
(bottom) Heffer En Pointe,
autonomous panel   5' × 4'.
Sandblasted and grouted leaded glass window.

Saara Gallin

142 Sherman Avenue
White Plains, NY 10607
(914) 592-6930

Saara Gallin's work is almost always in relief. Often the relief is on both sides of the work. This is quite effective in a space where a room divider is desired. Only the finest hand-blown glass is used. Sculpting with light, working with transparency, texture and forms which have their shape radically changed by the heat of kiln, the use of wire and metal mesh, are among the distinguishing characteristics of her work.

Installations: Library of Sarah Lawrence College, Bronxville, N.Y.; Sommer Center, Concordia College, Bronxville, N.Y.; Appleby's Restaurant, Mt. Kisco, N.Y.; Temple Beth Abraham, Tarrytown, NY; Goldmuntz Academy, Netanya, Israel; Simpson Townhouse, N.Y. City

(top) Room Divider - Private Collection 6' x6' contains antique Lalique, Norman slabs, Tiffany and other turn of the century jewels.

(bottom) Detail of slumping from the screen "Profiles in Glass."

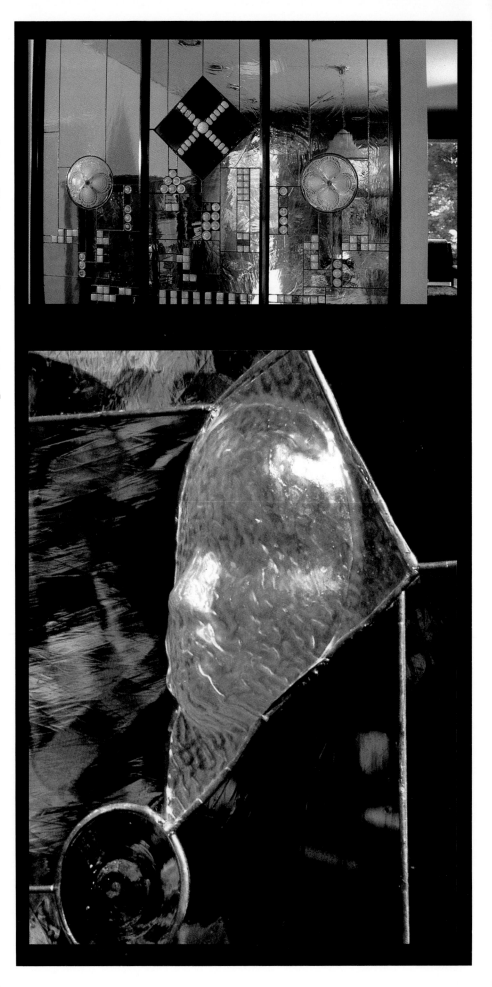

Jane Asta Godfrey and Sondra Radcliffe

Ambiente Stained Glass Studio and Gallery
2218 Lee Road
Cleveland Heights, OH 44118
(216) 321-6396

Ambiente has extensive experience in commercial and residential commission works. Their one-of-a-kind designs use the finest imported and domestic glass. These unusual creations, translate into free standing screens, installed or hanging panels, tables, cabinets, doors and wall pieces, easily complement the traditional or contemporary setting.

Designing exclusively for your client, collaborating on your design concepts or creating stained glass inserts for your pieces, Ambiente permits the architect, interior designer or builder to offer a visually exciting alternative in the field of handcrafted work. In addition to their current finished selection, Ambiente offers a wide choice of hardwood and color-enameled screens, tables and frames available for their customer designs. Please write or phone for further details.

Nancy Gong

Gong Glass Works
P.O. Box 10344
Rochester, NY 14610
(716) 586-1993

Brochure available upon request.

Decorative glass work.

(right) Front entry side lite
76"h × 18"w
Leaded glass, sandcarved
Private Residence
Copyright 1985 Nancy Gong

(lower left) Installation of front entry side lite.

Nancy Gong

Gong Glass Works
P.O. Box 10344
Rochester, NY 14610
(716) 586-1993

Brochure available upon request.

Fine Art Glass Work

(top right) "Strength of Spirit"
Interior French doors off main entry.
Leaded glass, sandetched
Each door 76"h × 24"w
Also "Floating Through the Mist"
Front entry side lite.
Leaded glass, sandcarved.
Private residence.
Copyright 1986 Nancy Gong.
(bottom right) "Vestige of the Past"
Art Glass wall piece.
30"h × 38"w × 6"d
Leaded glass, sandetched, sandcarved and painted.
Private Collection.
Copyright 1986 Nancy Gong.
(bottom left) Multiple-layered sandcarved fireplace screen. Standing 30"h × 48"w × 12"d.
For off season use or non-functional fireplace. Copyright 1985 Nancy Gong.

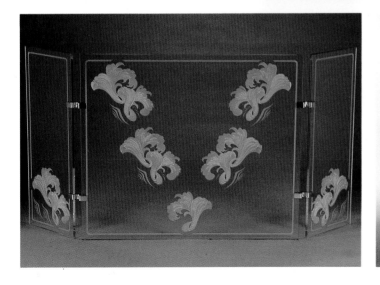

Joan Freeman Goodyear

George Clark Goodyear

Art Glass Studio
5077 Peachtree Road
Atlanta, GA 30341
(404) 455-4447

Joan and George Goodyear have been working together in flat glass since 1974.

Joan is a graduate of Virginia Commonwealth University with a BFA in Interior Design. "I like to work with designers and architects that are bent on a particular historical theme. My most satisfying recent commissions include carved grid system curtain walls for corporate headquarters and banks, hanging glass assemblages for homes and fancy traditional beveled glass doors."

George is a lifelong artist and native of Atlanta.
"In beveled glass, I value line quality and visual harmonic balance. I strive for precision and technical excellence in my work and my satisfaction comes only after satisfying the customer."

Prices begin at $20.00/square foot etched; $40.00/square foot stained; $50.00/square foot beveled.

Mark Eric Gulsrud

10213 Peacock Hill N.W.
Gig Harbor, WA 98335
(206) 858-3236

Gulsrud conceives architectural glass works as strong personal artistic expressions which simultaneously work with and enhance their environment. Design and fabrication are his own, resulting in high-quality and individual statements. Working in conjunction with Fremont Antique Glass Factory, in Seattle, Washington, he is able to formulate specific colors and textures in handmade glass. He is thus enabled to complement an existing palette in paints, fabrics and such, opening tremendous potential for the integration of artwork with an environment. Designs are executed in leaded glass, cast and slab glass, or cut crystal plate as determined by the specific project.

(top) Entry, private residence, Westwood, California, leaded antique glass, 8' × 22'. (bottom) 15th floor reception area, Tacoma Financial Center, created for Weyerhauser and Cornerstone Development Corporation, 17' × 38' leaded antique glass with cut and cast crystal accents.

Dale Gyongyos

Dale Gyongyos Art Glass & Design
2530 Superior Avenue
Cleveland, OH 44114
(216) 696-7930

Focusing on contemporary architectural glass installations, Dale Gyongyos provides successful solutions for architects, interior designers, and ecclesiastical building committees. Aesthetic and functional considerations guide Dale's creativity in producing distinctive glass panels for windows, entrance ways, skylights, partition screens and doors.

Large scale commissioned projects incorporate studio services including preliminary consultation, model concept proposal, fabrication, shipping and on-site installation. Fabrication skills include glass painting, sand abrasion, glass fusing. Also available, repair, restoration and protective glazing.

Education - The Pilchuck School, Stanwood, WA
w/Narcissus Quaqliata, Jochem Poensgen and Ed Carpenter

(top) Chapel screen, 34"w × 84"h, permanent collection—The Hallinan Center, Case Western Reserve University, Cleveland, Ohio
(bottom) Model proposal for 10" diameter rose window, 1st Evangelical Lutheran Church, Strongsville, Ohio

Gene Hester

Genesis Art Glass Studio
2704 Sackett
Houston, TX 77098
(713) 522-2950

From visual conception through fabrication and installation, Gene Hester emphasizes professional integrity in the quality of glass he produces. Working with a combination of clear texture glass, bevels and German antique glass, Hester's unique designs are both architecturally sound and aesthetically pleasing.

Hester has over 13 years experience of producing glass panels for use in commercial and residential projects. He has received state, national and international recognition, is represented in the permanent collection of the Downey Museum of Art in California, and has been published in Glass Studio, Glass Magazine, American Art Glass Quarterly, Texas Monthly, and The Houston Chronicle.

Pricing structure is based on square footage which varies with the type of glass and intricacy of design. Hester can and will work within your budget and time schedule.

Photos shown of a doctor's home in Austin, TX. Combination of clear texture, bevels and German antique glass.

Virginia Hoffman

Glasslite, Inc.
P.O. Box 2313
Sarasota, FL 33578
(813) 365-7450

Virginia Hoffman works closely with designers and architects to create Architectural Leaded Glass and Sand-carved Glass, utilizing her own individual style and approach. She uses the finest glass and glass elements in her work, and structures each window as an individual work of art intended for a particular architectural environment. Ms. Hoffman specializes in both architectural and ornamental glass work and problem solving in lighting and other design factors for a varied clientele, including banks, corporations, schools, home builders and owners, liturgical entities, hotels, restaurants and other commercial clients. She also creates autonomous panels. More of her work can be seen on pages 10 and 242 of the GUILD 1986

Shown here are two leaded glass front door panels, assembled from handblown reamy, crackle and antique glass, and custom beveled ½" plate glass.

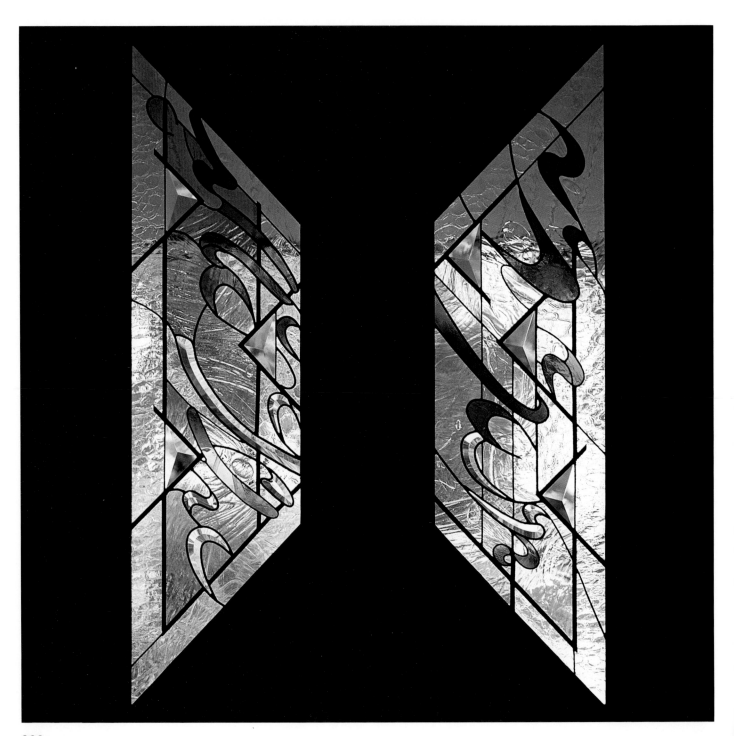

Virginia Hoffman

Glasslite, Inc.
P.O. Box 2313
Sarasota, FL 33578
(813) 365-7450

Virginia Hoffman also creates one-of-a-kind decor pieces which can be both ornamental and functional. Shown here are two fireplace screens, one a folding leaded glass screen created from handblown stained glass, commercial pressed glass and custom beveled glass. The other is a single standing screen made of ½" carved plate glass in a lacquered wood base. These items make an artistic statement, while hiding a fireplace opening when not in use. Ms. Hoffman's studio also creates large format folding screens which can be used as room dividers, as seen on page 10 of the GUILD 1986.

Shown also is a grouping of sculptural pieces influenced by architectural design. Some pieces contain interior lighting elements. Most of Ms. Hoffman's work in this medium is done by commission and each work is of a unique design. However, she often has ready-made sculpture pieces available for immediate purchase. Pricing is available through direct or mail inquiry.

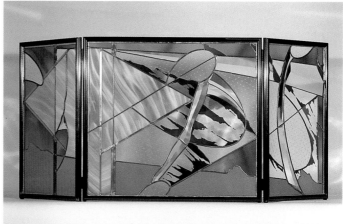

Participation by Design

We live in a designed environment. We have always lived in a designed environment. What we have been living in since the dawn of the industrial age is a mass produced designed environment.

The role of the consumer or the designer or architect who acts as the consumer's intermediary in a mass produced designed environment is one of selection. They pick from among things that have been designed and mass produced by others.

In the affluent economy, there is much to choose among, and the selection process is at least complicated and possibly even difficult. There is a bewildering array of merchandise from which to choose.

So who needs commissioned craft work to add to this cornucopia, and why? More and more people do. They want it and are actively seeking it.

The reason is so they can participate in the process of designing their own environment.

The customer or the customer's intermediary who commissions a specific work for a specific space or purpose gets into the selection process one step earlier.

The customer is still choosing more than creating, but instead of choosing something made, among things that exist, the customer gets to choose a maker, a style, an idea, a concept. The new customer does not want to be shown an array of finished products. The new customer wants to be shown a creative style and some design options to choose among. The new customer is more design conscious. The new customer is more self-assured about his own taste. The new customer is looking for distinctiveness in a mass produced world.

There is some considerable satisfaction in having something unique, something made especially for you, for your home, for your office, for your environment. But something more is going on than a hankering for exclusivity.

What is propelling the commissioning of crafts by designers and architects with the involvement of their clients for their clients' spaces is an urge to participate. Participation means having a considerable say in the kind of artistic and design statement that is being made in your place and on your behalf.

And it is an entirely praiseworthy and exhilarating thing.

We live in a designed environment. It is high time that we became more active in the design of that environment.

Bill Kraus
Chairman of the Board
Kraus Sikes Inc.
New York, New York

Thomas Holzer

Glass Designer
P.O. Box 2278
Boulder, CO 80306-2278
(303) 449-2085

During the last few years I have developed and perfected new techniques in the art glass field. These techniques include an architectural style of design which uses lead lines in an expressive, as opposed to a structural or mechanical manner. Rather than merely framing the design, this technique uses the lead as brush strokes in a painting or pencil lines in a drawing. The result is a dramatically expressive image.

Other innovations include the use of acrylic glass and specially fabricated glass objects in the design and construction of my pieces.

In choosing the glass, I use large areas of neutral and soft pastels or primary colors in bold shapes to support details of vivid color. Free-floating in the design, these images enhance the viewer's illusion of a three-dimensional character.

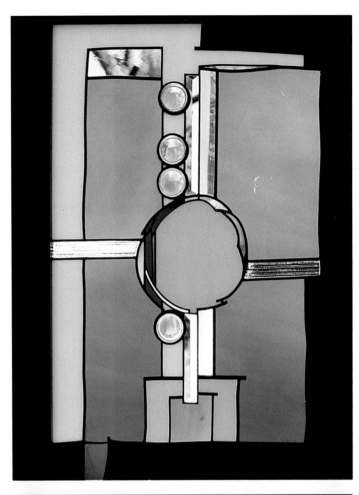

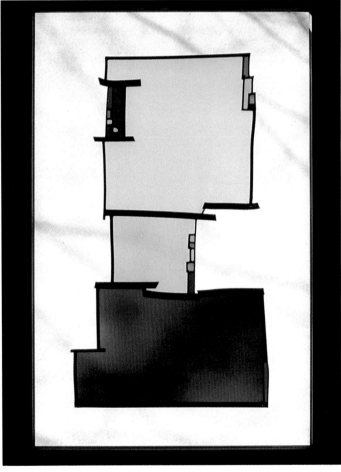

Lyn Hovey

Stained Glass Artist
Lyn Hovey Studio, Inc.
266 Concord Avenue
Cambridge, MA 02138
(617) 492-6566

Commissioned works in stained glass created by Lyn Hovey can be found in homes and public and private buildings around the world. The Lyn Hovey Studio, Inc. emphasizes design integrity within architectural space. A staff of 12 artisans covering the full range of technical expertise, both ancient and modern, provides a wealth of resource to the prospective client. Working closely with cabinetmakers and metalsmiths, the Lyn Hovey Studio, Inc. has expanded the dimensions of expression in stained glass.

(top left) Bent glass lampshade and original design bronze lamp base.
(top right) Art Nouveau mirror and sink. Overall design: Lyn Hovey; Stained Glass: Lyn Hovey Studio, Inc.; Woodwork: Jamie Robertson.
(bottom) Landscape style three-lancet stairway window.

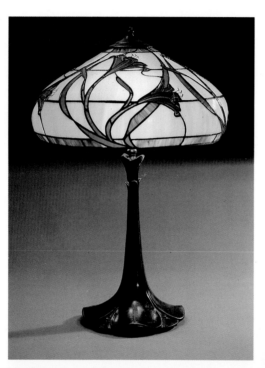

Lyn Hovey

Stained Glass Artist
Lyn Hovey Studio, Inc.
266 Concord Avenue
Cambridge, MA 02138
(617) 492-6566

Ecclesiastical commissions in stained glass created by Lyn Hovey combine beauty, inspiration and meaning. Lyn and his talented staff research theological, historical, and architectural details for soundness and accuracy of conception. Expertise in the full range of stained glass techniques, both ancient and modern, affords the studio great design versatility. By working in concert with religious institutions, their clergy, and their committees we are able to achieve religious works of enduring value.

The Lyn Hovey Studio, Inc. also offers service in the areas of stained glass restoration and conservation, wood or sash consolidation and restoration, and protective glazing.

(left) Brigham and Women's Hospital Chapel Window—(interdenominational) Wd. 2', Ht. 6'
(right) Sainte Anne's Church Resurrection Window—Wd. 7', Ht. 14'

Harriet Hyams

P.O. Box 178
Palisades, NY 10964
(914) 359-0061

Hyams, an artist who has worked in stained glass for more than nineteen years, designs windows, skylights, and glass murals (artificially lit). She has worked with the country's leading architectural firms, such as Gruzen Samton Steinglass Architects, Planners; The Eggers Group; The Ventura Partnership and Eleanore Pettersen.

A few select commissions are: the Hallmark Building, Houston, Texas; Maple Knoll Chapel, Springdale, Ohio; New Dorp High School, Staten Island, NY; Sts. Vartanantz Armenian Apostolic Church, Ridgefield, NJ Harcourt Brace Jovanovich, Inc., Orlando, Florida.

She assumes complete responsibility for her projects right through the installation, doesn't go beyond the specified budget, and completes work on time.

(top) Residence in Saddle River, NJ. 48 ⅝" × 45"
(bottom left) the Chairman's Office, Harcourt Brace Jovanovich, Inc. 10 1/2' × 9'

308

Michael Kennedy

Michael Kennedy Studios
P.O. Box 22226
Seattle, WA 98122
(206) 441-3737

Michael Kennedy Studios specializes in architectural glass applications ranging from progressive leaded glass panels to glass sculpture, custom designed lighting and a wide variety of new technologies. Our services include consultation on architectural glass projects, design, fabrication and on-site installation. Previous projects include glass work for:

Marriott Corporation
Westin Hotels
Red Lion/Thunderbird Inns
Over 25 Art in Public Places and percent for
Art Projects
Corporate Collections

Brochure and additional literature available upon request.

(bottom left) Plate Glass Lighting Fixture - Residence, Seattle, WA, Project Architect: John Savo

(top) Cabinet Door Fronts - Optical Glass Rods/Colored Glass Lamination - Residence, Seattle, WA. Interior Design: Judy Hamilton

(bottom right) Etched Glass Windows/Optical Jewels - Residence, Bellingham, WA Interior Design: Marilyn Master

Mary and Bob Krauski

Krauski Art Glass
W302 N9493 Highway E
Hartland, WI 53029
(414) 966-7500

For twenty years, Krauski studio has been producing originally designed glass art works and executing commissions for private and public buildings. Krauski's expertise in leaded, copperfoiled, etched, stained, painted, faceted, neon, beveled, and carved glass offers a multitude of design possibilities to each individual situation; innovative combinations of these skills produce art works of memorable quality. The studio's network of artists and craftpersons provide a flexible work force capable of transforming client wishes into tangible beauty.

Featured is Mary Krauski, known for her use of natural imagery, pattern and exacting detail.
(top) Art panel, features copper foil fabrication, ornithologically correct heron, opaque images on transparent background. 30"H × 20"W $600.00
(bottom) Art panel features copper foil fabrication, Loon, free form bevels with deep carved fish images, English and German mouth blown glass. 50"H × 72"W $7,500.00
Beveling provided by Kelly Smith/Green Bay Wisconsin.

Duncan I.T. Laurie

29-14 40th Avenue
Long Island City, NY 11101
(718) 482-7407
(718) 392-6821

Specialty: Treatments in glass, including carving, laminating, coloring, leafing, illuminating, fabrication of walls, skylights, tables, lamps, room dividers, doors, fountains, environmental sculpture.

Clients include: Walker Group CNI; Juan Montoya; Plexibility, Inc.; Machinists Associates; R.J. Reynolds III; Louise Nevelson; Gordon Construction Company; Ravin Designs; Ron Seff; Robert Duvall; Jamal Houssain; Butterick, White & Burtis; Dakota Jackson; Macy's, New York City; Tansuya; Beaston & Patterson, Inc.

(top right) "Pre Columbian Head", 36" × 60", sandblasted with gold leaf; Island Gallery, Long Island City, New York © 1986
(bottom right) "Seepapu", 24" × 32", laminated and shattered glass; Island Gallery, Long Island City, New York © 1986
(left) Detail, standing lamp, 12" × 12" × 60"; Island Gallery, Long Island City, New York © 1986

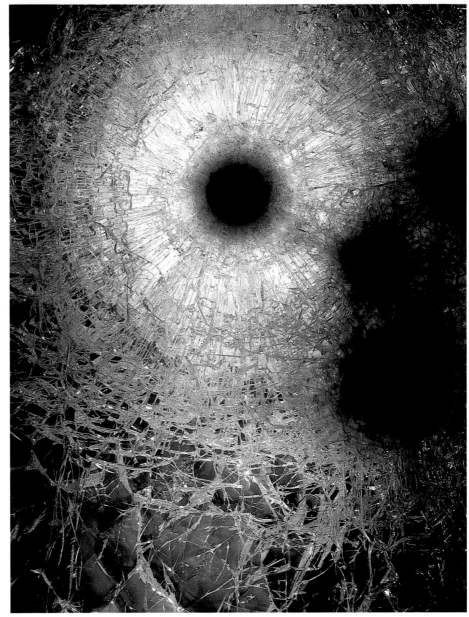

Ellen Mandelbaum

Ellen Mandelbaum Stained Glass
39-49 46 Street
Long Island City, New York, NY 11104
(718) 361-8154

Ellen Mandelbaum, A.I.A. affiliate, is a skillful designer of leaded glass who enriches her work by painting directly on the glass surface. The painted glass is fired for color permanence and all panels are reinforced for strength. Her care with all aspects of design, color and glass selection assures that the quality of light in the finished panel is appropriate to the specific site.

While Mandelbaum's work is currently incorporated into architecture, many of her pieces have been commissioned as art objects in their own right. Clients can count on her close cooperation and attention to detail every step of the way whether their commission involves an extensive architectural design or a more modest project.

Inquiries are invited.

Removable Window Panel. 47" × 38". Professor Laurie Nisonoff Residence, Amherst, Mass.
Hallway Doors 56" × 64". Adina Taylor, Architect, New York, N.Y.

C. Robert Markert

232 West Esplanade Avenue
Louisville, KY 40214
(502) 363-0952

Markert, a glass artist since 1963, has a wide range of experience in all glass media - leaded, faceted, sand-carved, and copper foil. As founder of Fenestra Studios, Inc., in 1969, Bob has designed, fabricated, and installed commissions in every state in the South, Mid-East, and Mid-West. Combining his reputation as a liturgical designer with his glass experience, Bob has designed tapestries, wall hangings, and chancel furniture for both Christian and Jewish communities. His is presently the Second Vice-President of the Stained Glass Association of America. A few select commissions are Temple Adath Israel/B'rith Shalom, Louisville, Kentucky; St. Vincent de Paul, Shelbyville, Indiana; Georgetown, Kentucky. Information sent upon request.

(top) Detail, leaded window, 44 ft. by 11 ft. Trinity United Methodist, New Albany, Indiana. (bottom) Detail, faceted gals window, 25 ft. by 5 ft. Temple Adath Israel/B'rith Shalom, Louisville, Kentucky

Carol Mason

Glassmason Studio
P.O. Box 966
Gambier, OH 43022
(614) 427-2314

Carol Mason has been building designs in contemporary stained glass for residential, public and ecclesiastical window installations since 1977. Most recently her work has been utilized by the corporate market for commissions of large-scale, wall-mounted glass panels. Her training includes four years of fine arts study at the University of Cincinnati and Kent State University, a two-year apprenticeship with a West German craftsman and three months traveling and researching in West Germany, during which she documented the contemporary stained-glass development of that country. Collections include: Honda Corporation, Tokyo Japan; Kreber Graphics Corporation, Columbus, Ohio; Capital University, Columbus, Ohio; Paul Newman and Joanne Woodward, Connecticut; and Kenyon College, Gambier, Ohio.

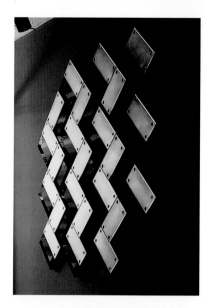

below: Wall mounted piece - 6' × 6'

Edward McIlvane

Artist and Designer in Glass
235 Promenade Street
Providence, RI 02908
(401) 274-6909

New York representative:
Daniel Reiser (718) 643-0516

I specialize in the design and production of architectural stained glass. I have been working professionally in this field since 1969, and am knowledgeable and experienced in both traditional and innovative methods of design and fabrication.

The style of my work is eclectic, and is determined by a consideration of the architectural context, the interior decoration, and the point of view and taste of my clients. I enjoy collaborating with design professionals. A representative portfolio and resumé is available on request.

(left) Temple Beth-El, Providence, Rhode Island; Refractory glass, steel, lead, 4.5' × 30', 1982
(top right) Bank of Boston, reception area, Executive offices; Leaded glass, steel, 9' × 28', 1985
(lower right) Mensch Commission (with James Harmone); Blown and leaded glass, oak, 3.5' × 7', 1981

Thomas Meyers

Artist/Designer
Thomas Meyers Studio
26 RR#1 Old Hancock Road
Antrim, NH 03440
(603) 588-2596

Design in architectural stained glass. Traditional leaded and contemporary fabricating techniques. Fine Art works of a unique style of paper collage.

(top) One of two windows in opposite gable peaks, whose design is a result of collage ideas and architectural glass criteria.
76″ × 38″

(bottom) Glass enclosure: six foot round bath enclosed halfway around by six panels of tempered glass with two inch squares of antique glass applied to the exterior. Design concept by Jasinski Architects, Inc.

Richard Millard

Environmental Glass
RD 3
Hopewell Junctions, NY 12533
(914) 226-6614

Richard Millard has been designing stained glass for thirty five years. Trained as a stained glass painter he has performed extensive restorations of the works of La Farge, Tiffany and Maitlant Armstrong. His primary thrust in stained glass has been to the greater secular utilization of stained glass in corporate environments rather than its confinement to ecclesiastical and Victorian applications.

Commissions have included the Ambassador Dobrynin residence in Moscow and a 4' × 6' applique on plate portrait of Pia Zadora.

(top) Doorway entry 27' × 10'6"
(bottom) Divider 18" × 54"

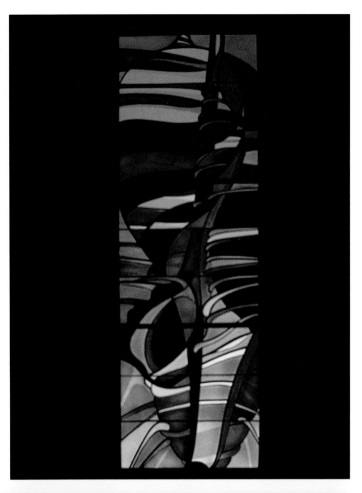

Jean Myers

Architectural Glass
P.O. Box AG
South Lake Tahoe, CA 95705
(916) 541-7878

Jean Myers, founder and owner of Jean Myers Architectural Glass, pursues the rare and demanding art of stained glass. Today the craft and art of working in architectural glass is complex. The concerns of the client, the objectives of the architect, the properties of the glass must be carefully interwoven in a manner which assures clarity, strength and insight. It is essential to have both the knowledge and resources to follow a project from the first drawings to involvement with the final installation.

Since 1975, her firm has served clients across the country, in ecclesiastical, residential, health care and business settings.

(top left) San Damiano Retreat Detail, Danville, CA
(top right) Gloria's Flute Detail, Lake Tahoe, CA
(bottom) Jordan House Entry, Wilmington, NC

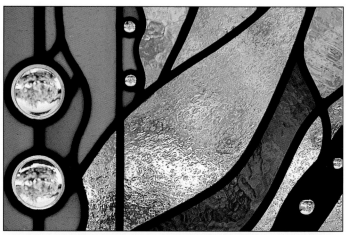

Jean Myers

Architectural Glass
P.O. Box AG
South Lake Tahoe, CA 95705
(916) 541-7878

(top left) Blue Plane, San Francisco, CA
(top right) Fuschia Detail, Lake Tahoe, CA
(bottom) Hallway in Fuqua Industries, Inc.,
Atlanta, GA

Architect as a Collective Noun

We must accept that rebellion in the arts is eternal. Certainly this is true in the art of architecture. Today we are witnessing the clumsy and sometimes silly efforts of the "post modernists" to reject the austerity of Mies and his followers. They in turn—standing on the shoulders of Wright and Sullivan—poured scorn on the copybook classicism of McKim, Mead and White. McKim had to assert his way out of Richardson's Romanesque shadow—and so on back into the recesses of time.

These cycles of fashion are utterly important to the market for crafts—in fact, they govern it. The producer of classic sculpture had a lonesome life in the '60s and '70s. An artist in Romanesque doorways did badly during McKim's reign, whereas the artists in graphics, textiles and furniture are enjoying kingly positions in today's world (1950-1986).

This is probably good. Individual creativity does not flourish in a static world. A changing demand keeps us on our toes to respond. We do not need an Academy to suppress whatever the modern equivalent of the impressionists may be. The market will judge ultimately and wisely. We do not want the Doric formality of Ictinus' Greece or the equally dogmatic formalism of Mies. Predictability palls.

In the first years of this century, a few prophetic architects were predicting design made possible by the machine. Handcrafted ornament was no longer needed—they said. "Correctly" detailed elements could be repeated endlessly. The resulting building would rise with grace, speed and no lost motion. Well—they got their wish. By the end of World War II, mechanized boxes were routine.

It did not happen all at once. The hopeful entrepreneurs of prefabrication had first to fail while they learned that steel panels were not cheap and people did not warm to antiseptic "machines for living." They had to learn to respect the great intelligence that had been poured into conventional building for many centuries. They had to appreciate that the vaunted assembly line for cars was not greatly better organized than any of the great skyscrapers that rose in the '20s. The precise delivering of materials and the equally precise placing of mechanics to receive them was, and is, a marvel of scheduling.

So the patronizing statement that building was the "last handicraft industry" became less and less true. It became a more and more mechanized industry of increasing prefabrication, culminating in "less is more."

The resulting period in architecture and the arts was as inevitable as today's reaction to it. Sir Isaac Newton has been proved right again, that "to every action there is an equal and opposite reaction." We have that reaction in post-modernism and a dozen other aimless efforts, all looking for a principle. If there is any common denominator to the current mood in the arts, crafts and architecture, it is a hunger for interest and richness.

The price of interest and richness is sharing. On any work of consequence, no one mind can be expert in all the trades, crafts and skills needed to accomplish it. Just as the conductor of an orchestra need not be the best oboe, or yet, trombone player in order for the orchestra to function, so the architect or central figure in an artistic production need not be the best weaver or glass blower. What he does need is the perception to appreciate and elicit musicianship in one case and craftsmanship in the other, to produce a whole greater than the sum of its parts.

For that whole to be great, or even good, it must have an aim higher than the display of anyone's ego. Michelangelo and Phidias did not achieve immortality by dredging their own insides. Their work was in the service of ideas larger than themselves, and depended on an army of artists-craftsmen. Self expression was a trivial byproduct.

Where does all this lead? Hopefully, on the part of architects, to an awareness of the rich minds and skills all about them—eager to contribute to lengthen each others' arms. Again, hopefully, the enlightened self interest to share credit generously for the enhancement of their own achievements.

Lawrence B. Perkins
Founding Partner, Perkins & Will
Chicago, Illinois

Lenn Neff

Contemporary Leaded Glass
and Architectural Arts
P.O. Box 1931
Saint Petersburg, FL 33731
(813) 823-3919

The main thrust of Lenn's works in glass is contemporary and site related, reflecting a building's materials, form, structure and orientation to light.

Architectural ornamentation ranges from unique gates and doors to lamps or wall graphics—all in multiple media.

Creativity and imagination sensitively combine in these designs to answer an array of visual challenges. Careful attention to detail and structural integrity is a mark of Lenn's work.

Objects and installations completed for private homes, restaurants, banks, corporate offices, universities and churches.

Commissions may be initiated for architectural contexts of any scale. Write or call to discuss your project.

(top) Kitchen window, cabinet panels, and sconces for a home at Saint Petersburg, Florida. Leaded glass, touch switches.
(bottom) Panel of leaded lucite and glass 33" × 36".

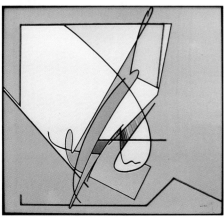

Brigitte Pasternak

Stained Glass
301 River Road
Grandview, NY 10960
(914) 359-2884

We design leaded-glass windows, doors, murals, sky-lights of any size, and build them with old-world devotion to detail and durability.

We pay close attention to light and context, to the client's preference and the builder's requirements.

We keep our work free of surface treatment to insure a sleek and bright finish, elegance beyond passing fashions, and also to hold costs down.

Large projects are fabricated in multiple panels, to be assembled on site into built-in armatures.

Major commissions: First Presbyterian Church, Taipei Taiwan, 18'/5'; General Class International, New Rochelle, New York, 9'/10'; First Presbyterian Church, Katonah, New York, 7'/5'; Valley Cottage Library, Valley Cottage, NY, autonomous panels.

Preston Studios

Artistry in Stained Glass
552 Magnolia Avenue
Melbourne, FL 32935
(305) 259-0044

Formed in 1976 by Jerry D. Preston and John C. Emery with the intent of creating unique and collectible art, the studio has established a reputation in three area—custom work, limited edition panels, and fine original lamps.

The limited edition panels by Preston Studios were featured on page 255 of The Guild 1986. Here, the custom designed commercial work of the studio is exemplified.

Aside from other major commissions throughout the Southeast, Preston Studios art-glass provides the thematic reference for AQUARINA, a world-class development near Sebastian inlet on the East Coast of Florida.

(top) Thomson' Restaurant in Winter Park, Florida; 5 ft. by 5 ft., one of two different installations.
(bottom) The AQUARINA Oceanclub in Melbourne Beach, Florida; 4 ft. by 6 ft., one of many installations in the development.

Narcissus Quagliata

1535 5th Street
Oakland, CA 94607
(415) 626-5976

Narcissus Quagliata specializes in the design and fabrication of stained glass work for residential and commercial buildings. He has developed innovative aesthetic and structural techniques which have freed him from the traditional restraints of his craft.

In collaboration with architects and designers he creates works that range from the bold and colorful to the subtle and elegant while addressing the varied practical and aesthetic requirements of the space and of the client.

His studio is capable of producing any size stained glass work and delivering it for installation anywhere in the United States or abroad.

(top) Lobby of 2101 Webster St., Oakland, California. Headquarters of Blue Cross. 51' × 12' 1985
(bottom) Detail

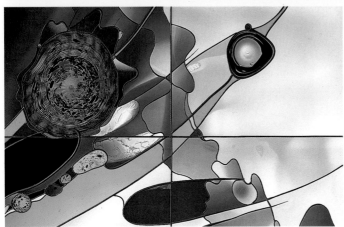

Narcissus Quagliata

1535 5th Street
Oakland, CA 94607
(415) 626-5976

Born in Italy where he began his fine art studies, Narcissus Quagliata came to the west coast in the early 60's where he received his BFA and MFA in painting from The San Francisco Art Institute. He has worked in glass for the last 17 years, is the author of Stained Glass From Mind To Light, and each year lectures and teaches on stained glass art. His work is in the permanent collection of The Metropolitan Museum of Art in New York and in corporate and private collections throughout the country. He received a 1977 and 1986 grant from The National Endowments for the Arts.

(left) Model for proposed environment in white, crystal and blown glass 1985
(right) Detail of dome
(bottom) Reception area of Screen Actors Guild Business Arts Plaza Building, Burbank, California. 7½' × 15½' 1986

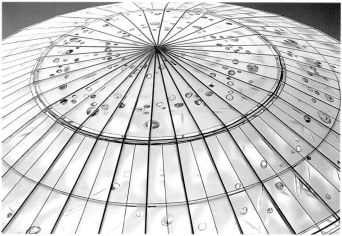

Maya Radoczy

Maya Radoczy Designs
P. O. Box 31422
Seattle, WA 98103
(206) 547-7114

The studios of Maya Radoczy are prepared to serve the architect or designer, from initial concept to final installation. The artist employs a unique combination of glass leading, blowing, etching and fusing techniques to create an original effect for each site. Her experience in glass art is extensive, including study with noted European glass designer Ludwig Schraffrath and work with the West German glass firm, Bleidorn & Maurer.

Maya Radoczy's work was published in Interior Design Magazine, February 1985 and in The New York Times on November 28, 1985. Her exhibitions and private commissions span the country - from New York where she designed for the Trump Plaza Apartments and Habitat Inc. to the Vashon Public Library in Washington State. She will be featured in a forthcoming book on architectural design.

(top) Pocket doors 6' × 7' Seattle, WA (bottom) Free standing conference room, 400 square feet, Habitat Inc. New York, NY.

Sheila Ritz

Leaded Glass
149-151 Grand Street
Brooklyn, NY 11211
(718) 387-3286

Principal Commissions: Art-in-Public Places, Washington State Commission on the Arts, Wapato, WA; Hultgren & Samperton Associates, Vineyards, Healdsburg, CA; Scheuer Tapestry Studio, NYC

Grant: New York Foundation for the Arts, 1986

Publications: New Work , Modern Style , New Glass , Corning Museum, Women in Design International

Review: "Sheila Ritz's elegant linear designs, seemingly devised by some mathematical system, are without question works of abstract art." The New York Times

"Structure XII", 1986 8' 10" × 11' 4"

Rohlf's Studio, Inc.

783 South Third Avenue
Mount Vernon, NY 10550
(914) 699-4848 (212) 823-4545

When designing within the confines of an Architectural Structure it is our intent to work cooperatively with the client to achieve the desired results and to compliment the area for which it was intended.

Rohlf's Studio works with many independent artists along with our own in-house designers on a national scale. Our installation can be viewed throughout the United States, South America, Africa, and the Middle East.

Specializing in all phases of Ecclesiastical, Commercial, Residential, and Restoration Commissions, Rohlf's creates in Stained, Leaded, Faceted and Beveled Glass.

Rohlf's is also a Regional Distributor for Beveled Glass Designs.

Jean Jacques Duval
Christ the King Church
Olmsted, Ohio
2,000 square feet, faceted glass

Hank Prussing
575 5th Ave, NYC
Atrium Ceiling, 30' × 56'

Toland Sand

R.F.D. 2, Box 422
Tilton, NH 03276
(603) 286-4589

Toland Sand has been designing and working with glass professionally since 1977 and now specializes in sculptural pieces and installations. Competent in most aspects of glasswork, he has shown stained glass, blown glass and sandblasted sculptural glass in major shows and galleries and now concentrates on commissioned work. Design elements are geometric with an emphasis on bringing out all the qualities of glass: clarity, opacity, color, reflectivity, refractivity, suspension, and depth. Toland also does the structural work for a piece: welding, painting, construction, and installation and enjoys working with others to find design solutions. A representative portfolio and brochure is available upon request.

(top left) 13″ × 38″
(top right) 14″ × 82″
(bottom) 36′ × 7′ installed sculpture.

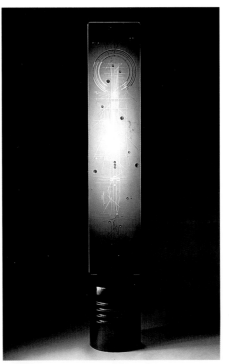
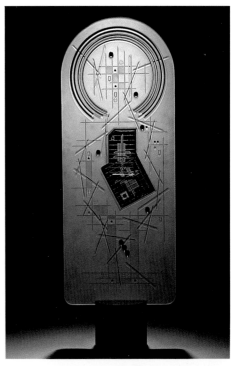

The Triumph of Personal Style

The most consistent and heartfelt message *Metropolitan Home* readers send to the editors is that they want a home that reflects their individuality. And for the past decade, as we've watched the kids of the Sixties mature, they've become quite discriminating about furnishing their homes.

Certainly, some of them have stumbled from black-light posters and lava lamps through austere, no-clutter lofts to arrive at the very warmly personal rooms we see now. In the process, they learned to pick and choose through the marketplace, looking for art and handcrafted pieces that matter to them.

The emotionless, pre-packaged interiors their parents bought off showroom floors don't attract the current generation of home-buyers as they feather their very stylish nests. The museum-like period decor and the antique-laden castles that dominate interior design literature aren't relevant for them either. They're resistant to any arbitrary list of valuables.

To the generation that challenged the status symbols and authority figures of its youth, the notion of spending lots of money for rooms full of "today's hot decorator objet" (read *stale visual cliches*) is anti-style. Our readers' very smart response to the suite mentality of decorating is to choose their own array of collectibles and create their own mix.

How do these people gather the special things in their rooms? The most astute of our readers, the ones who put time, intelligence and effort into their homes, are using their knowledge and interest in crafts. We see remarkable collections and virtuoso pieces in their homes. We hear of their acquisition adventures: the stories of how they tracked down the craftsman for a piece of work because of something seen in a friend's home or found in a show they chanced by on a business side-trip. The serendipity of finding good crafts work becomes a topic of discussion when we interview homeowners or as we analyze the professionally designed rooms appearing in the magazine.

The network of designers, artists and readers is slowly beginning to form in many parts of the country, but the number of people who are actively interested and ready to learn more about craftwork is expanding rapidly.

Providing professionals and consumers across the country with easy access to pockets of regional talent and treasures is a very timely effort. For example, when we're in the midst of the *Met Home of the Year* contest, judging nearly 25,000 photographs of our readers' interior design, we see their very strong urge to fill their homes with personally significant things. At times we also see the need for broader exposure to quality work; but imperfect or not, the impulse to express their style with original handmade work is there.

Fortunately, using *The Guild* as a link between artist and reader (aka *budding collector*) can improve anyone's chances of success. When these readers' homes succeed and the prized handcrafted pieces sit easily with the stuff of their daily lives, it's the result of an educated eye, a connected, well-traveled judge of craftsmanship. It's The Triumph of Personal Style.

Dorothy Kalins

Dorothy Kalins
Editor, Metropolitan Home

Karen Sepanski

2827 John R
Detroit, MI 48201
(313) 832-4941

The professional accomplishments of Karen Sepanski cover a wide area as designer and maker of distinctive glass. Her personal style is present in every project, be it architectural installations, decorative objects and vessels, or sculpture.

The focus of her work has been architectural, creating bas-relief panels using a variety of techniques suited to the special requirements of location and client. Slump-casting, fusing, and etching are some of the processes involved in the production of a single work. Design considerations are geometric/organic and can be produced as multiples or a single image divided into sections for modular presentation.

Her work has been shown in many galleries in the U.S. and Canada and has been commissioned for public, corporate, and private concerns.

Major commissions: "Microcosm", skylight; Ingham County Correctional Facility, Mason, Michigan.
"Peripheral Vision", light fixture; National Steel Corporate Headquarters, Pittsburgh, Pennsylvania.

(top) Platter; 20" diameter
(bottom) French Doors; 80" × 60" × 2" glass, oak

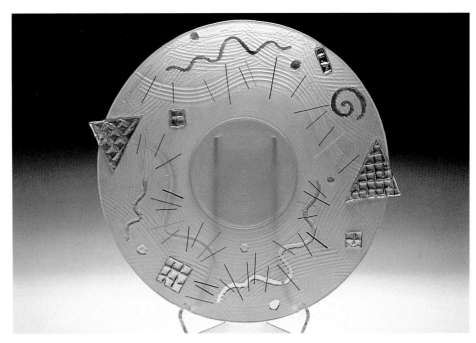

Arthur Stern

Arthur Stern Studios/Architectural Glass
1221 8th Avenue
Oakland, Ca 94606
(415) 835-5162

Arthur Stern Studios produces custom glass and wood detailing for architecture and interior design. We collaborate with other design professionals and clients to create unique, "site-specific art" for residentials, commercial, and public building projects. We have done installations all over the country with each project we undertake receiving the same thorough attention to detail and fine craftsmanship.

We specialize in custom leaded glass windows, window frames, hardwood doors with leaded glass, light fixtures, and limited edition room divider screens. Brochures available upon request.

Arthur Stern was awarded for "Excellence in Design and Craftsmanship" by the California Council of the American Institute of Architects.

(top) Frozen Music/Opus in Yellow, Architectural Screen, 8' wide × 6'6" high
(bottom) Stair landing window with custom frame, 6' wide × 10' high

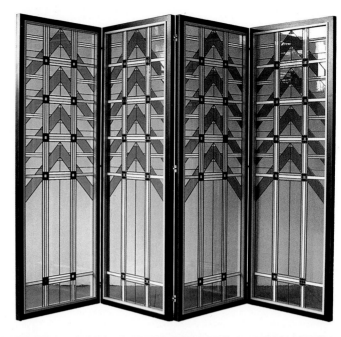

Susan Stinsmuehlen

Artist/Designer
Renaissance Glass Co.
1003 W. 34th Street.
Austin, TX 78705
(512) 451-3971

Susan Stinsmuehlen has been designing leaded and etched glass for commercial and residential commissions since 1972. She is a recipient of a National Endowment Fellowship and an Art in Architecture commission in Dallas, Texas. Past President of the Glass Art Society, Stinsmuehlen is active as teacher and promoter of the glass arts. Her work is widely exhibited, collected and published.

(top) "Ongoing Dialogue of Dots and Dashes", 84"W × 77"H, leaded glass screen with aluminum frame, etched and painted glass, textured clear and opaque glasses with carved lead.
(bottom) Grensted Entrance, William Barbee, Architect, Linda Grensted, Interior Designer, 72"W × 80"H, clear-textured and opaque glasses, bevels, hand blown roundel and varying lead sizes.

Thomas Swift

Pin Oak Design
Route 1 Box 122B
Paw Paw, WV 25434
(304) 947-7109

Architectural leaded glass for residential and commercial spaces.

Featured here are two of the eight large panels designed for the restaurant New Heights in Washington DC. For this commission Mr. Swift also designed and made tables, railings and other interior furnishings.

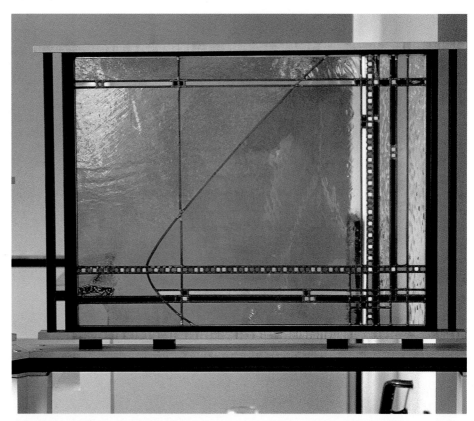

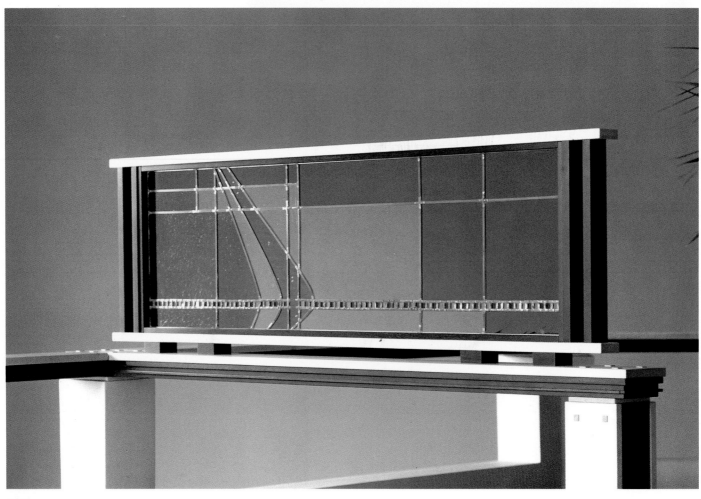

Angelika Traylor

100 Poinciana Drive
Indian Harbour Beach, FL 32937
(305) 773-7640

Specializing in one of a kind autonomous panels, lamps and architectural designs, Angelika Traylor makes an important contribution to the newly revived art of stained glass with her exquisite pieces of fine art.

In addition to numerous regional awards, Traylor was selected a winner in the Prestigious International "Fragile Art 82" competition in California, awarded 2nd place non-figurative composition in the "Vitraux des USA" exhibit at Chartres, France in 1985 and also declared a winner in "The Best Stained Glass 1986," during the international competition held in New York by the editors of Professional Stained Glass

All items pictured are from private collections.

Patricia Tyser

Architectural Glass Designs
87 Clinton Avenue North
Rochester, NY 14604
(716) 232-4620

Patricia Tyser has been designing and fabricating contemporary leaded glass since 1974. As an architectural consultant and the director of Architectural Glass Designs, she specializes in all types of glass work, including custom designed stained, leaded and bevelled glass for both residential and commercial applications.

Her work has been exhibited at the "New American Glass" national invitational exhibition at Huntington Galleries in West Virginia and the Glassmaster's Guild in New York; and appeared in the publications Glass Art Magazine, Interior Design Market and American Art Glass Quarterly.

She is currently creating a full line of room dividers, screens and fireplace screens.

Brochure available upon request.

Suzanne VanGalder

4850 Brown Deer Lane
Janesville, WI 53545
(608) 754-9396

Suzanne VanGalder specializes in custom-designed contemporary stained glass art for homes and commercial buildings of distinctive character.

Working closely with architects and designers for 9 years, she has created original, one-of-a-kind glass windows, doors, room dividers, and ceiling panels. Involving the client to the extent they wish in design development, Suzanne creates her glasswork with the finest European blown glass, American machine made glass, bevels, and faceted jewels.

Brochures available upon request.

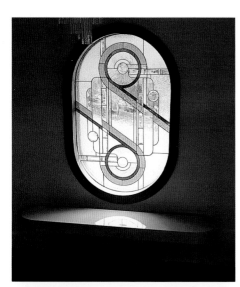

Clark Waterman

Glass Images
6748 Hwy 18 & 151
Verona (Madison), WI 53593
(608) 845-7509

Whether your foremost consideration is aesthetics or function, each custom work of leaded stained glass from Glass Images is designed to enrich your architectural setting. The uniqueness of your site provides the inspiration for our creative solution.

(top) This window, designed for the consultation room of a custom jewelry store in Elkhart, IN, utilizes beveled glass both for its transparency and its jewel-like quality.
46" × 38"
(bottom) "Windows: View for a Library" is owned by the Highsmith Co., Inc. a national distributor of library supplies, located in Fort Atkinson, WI. This window was commissioned for the cover of their 1987 catalog.
36" × 54"

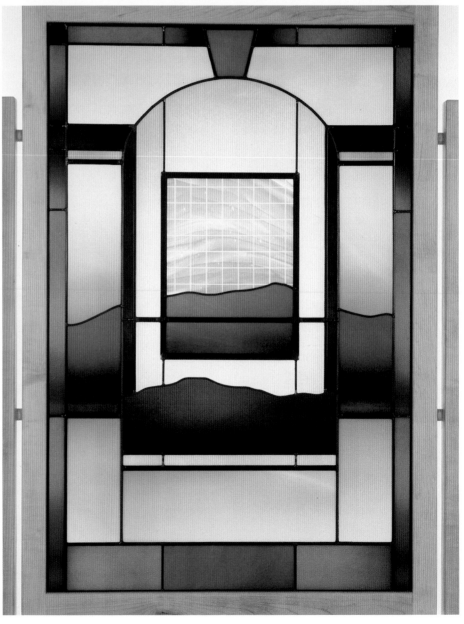

David Wilson

David Wilson Design
RD2 Box 121A
South New Berlin, NY 13843
(607) 334-3015

David Wilson Design offers consultation through design, fabrication and installation on projects that integrate art with architecture.

Besides windows, the studio will undertake murals, sculpture, furniture and space planning. Materials include glass, porcelain enamels, ceramics, paint, metal and wood.

Site specific design in collaboration with client and architect is a part of the design process.

David Wilson has been designing projects for public, private and religious environments since 1963.

(top) Interior view of a leaded glass window for North West Regional Center, Torrington, CT 5'H x 12'W. 1985
(bottom) Exterior view of same installation. A percent for art project for the State of Connecticut.

Larry Zgoda

Larry Zgoda Stained Glass
3447 N. Pulaski Rd.
Chicago, IL 60641
(312) 463-1874

Larry Zgoda has been designing and fabricating stained leaded glass in Chicago since 1973. Vigorous design coupled with imaginative application of materials distinguish these unique compositions.

(left) Stainless Glass, colorless glass with beveled, beaded and engraved glass, 40" × 52"

(right) Untitled pair of vertical panels, pastel glass with colorless glass, cut-facet jewels, beveled wire glass and printed circuits, 33" × 66"

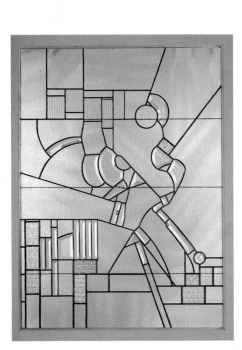

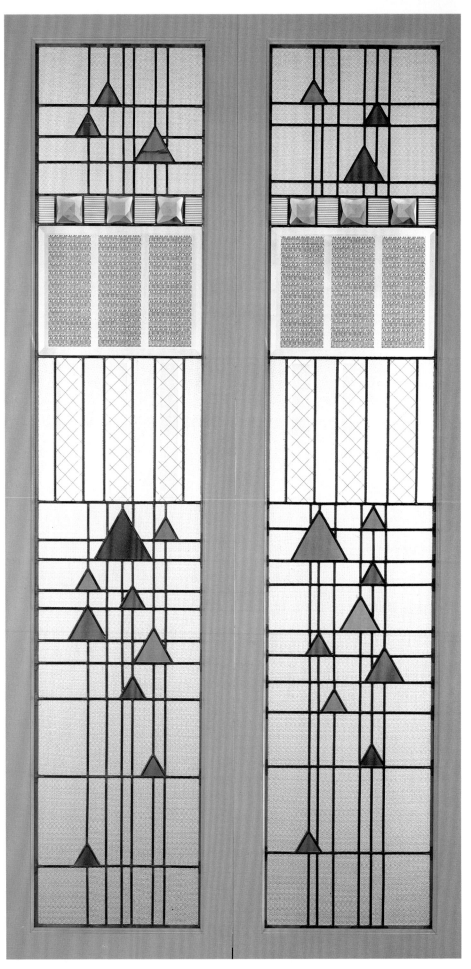

Larry Zgoda

Larry Zgoda Stained Glass
3447 N. Pulaski Rd.
Chicago, IL 60641
(312) 463-1874

Designs in stained glass by Larry Zgoda embrace many design styles and are applicable to a variety of architectural modes. Entirely colorless, or understatedly colored, stained glass compositions by Larry Zgoda compliment the way we live today.

(top) Untitled geometric composition, white, red, black and colorless glass, 34" × 35"

(bottom) Sailing, black, white, peach and colorless glass with beveled, embossed and faceted glass, 66" × 44"

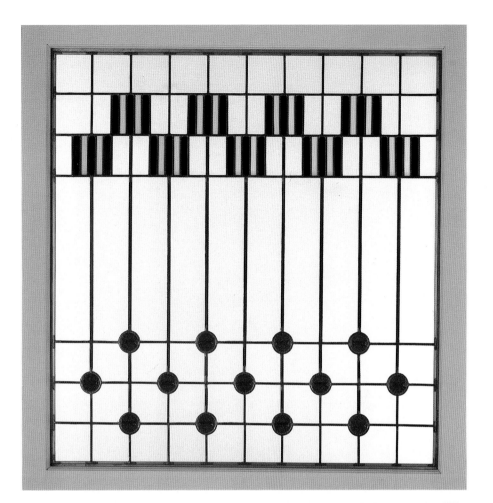

ARCHITECTURAL WOOD WORK

Don & Melva Beeler

Hearthside Heritage
R.R. 1 Box 92
Irving, IL 62051
(217) 594-2208

Our family business is founded on years of training and experience in methods of design, construction, cabinetmaking, and wood carving. We use the finest materials available and traditional methods to construct furniture and architectural components, which at once are both functional and decorative.

Each piece of furniture is individually constructed, hand-carved, painted, and given several coats of lacquer. The final product is durable and easily maintained.

Commissions are accepted. A brochure of our standard pieces is available upon request.

(top) Detail
Table top is 64" × 34" and has wheat designs carved at each end.
(bottom) When the top is tilted back, it reveals carvings and paintings on the underside. A 42" × 16" storage bench can be used for seating.

Jon Berg

38 Plochman Lane
Woodstock, NY 12498
(914) 679-8985

John Berg was Alexander Archipenko's final apprentice and worked on Archipenko's retrospective which opened the Smithsonian's sculpture gallery. He later was invited to become a student of Alfeo Faggi, whose work includes the doors of the Chicago Art Institute and is in most of the major collections of the world, including the Vatican.

John has exhibited at the ACA Gallery - New York City; Maxwell Gallery - San Francisco; Rudolph Gallery - Miami and Woodstock; and numerous other galleries and private collections. His wood reliefs are carved from beautiful rare woods. John's subtle drawings and dramatic use of light combine to make his sculpture as suitable for entire walls as they are for small panels. His years of experience as an industrial designer and unique mastery of carved relief provides the basis for a productive relationship with architects, designers and artists.

Thomas J. Duffy

1 Commerce Street
Ogdensburg, New York 13669
(315) 393-1484

The depth of Tom Duffy's facility is suggested by the two works shown here.

(top) A bench made of Holly veneer (white), English Harewood veneer (gray stripes), Purpleheart legs, dyed wood inlays and gold leaf; 17" × 14" × 34½". This piece was commissioned by the Boston Museum of Fine Arts and is part of their permanent collection.

(bottom) A curved door done in Butternut; 1⅜" × 36" × 80". Duffy designed and built the entire layout of this home which includes three curved doors on a cylindrical wall.

Other commissions include a curved pocket door (motor driven), a hand bookbinding press, and yacht interiors. From furniture making to architectural woodworking of first quality, Tom takes particular interest in circumstances that demand thoughtful solutions. All considerations (i.e., price, time frame, etc.) are quoted upon completion of the design phase.

James M. Jolman

4537 Spruce Street B-2
Philadelphia, PA 19139
(215) 386-7206

James M. Jolman studied marquetry in Germany under a master cabinet-maker. He uses the traditional techniques of marquetry, selecting the finest veneers from a wide variety of exotic and domestic woods and hand cutting them to create images with an emphasis on the specific characteristics of each veneer.

His designs combine the integrity of the grain and the drama of the hue to create exquisite imagery.

Designs may be commissioned. Portfolio available upon request.

below: MAX ATTACK
Marquetry Wall Hanging
30" × 32"
Veneers include: purpleheart, ebony, birds eye maple, Brazilian rosewood, lacewood, mahogany, holly, fiddleback olive ash, maple burl.

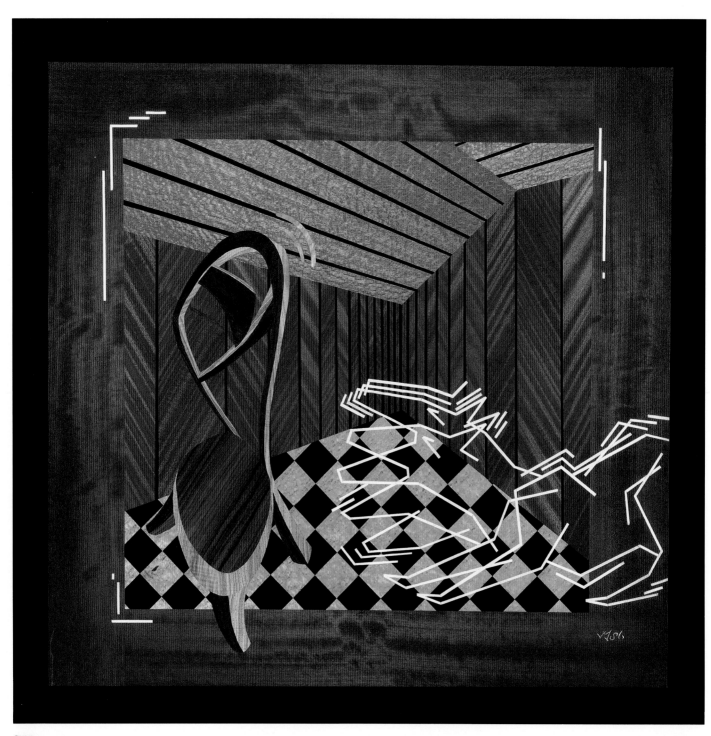

William Keyser

6543 Rush-Lima Road
Honeoye Falls, NY 14472
(716) 533-1041

Keyser produces wooden architectural embellishments, sculpture and furniture for indoor and outdoor use in public, corporate, religious and private environments. The one-of-a-kind pieces address the unique parameters of each particular commission and frequently involve collaboration with either an architect or building committee. Techniques include steambending, laminating, veneering and boatbuilding techniques such as lapstraking and cold molding.

". . .Keyser . . . has the unusual ability to design for a specific problem and then execute the work with superb craftsmanship and originality." (Jonathan Fairbanks, curator, Museum of Fine Arts, Boston, American Furniture, Marek, 1981). Internationally exhibited, Keyser is professor and chairman at the School for American Craftsmen, Rochester Institute of Technology.

(top) Bench, 3' × 6' × 20', Artpark, Lewiston, New York, cold molded veneer
(bottom right) Music stand, ash and rosewood
(bottom left) Subway bench, (one of two), 4' × 7' x 30', Massachusetts Bay Transportation Authority: Featured in New York Times

Robert Mason

343 Serpentine Drive
Del Mar, CA 92014
(619) 755-9150

Robert Mason concentrates on designing and executing sculpture for public, corporate and residential settings.

Mason brings years of experience as a product, interior and exhibit designer to contribute to planning, presentation and installation stages.

Having learned bronze and marble sculpture in Italy, he now works mainly in wood in both contemporary and traditional modes.

(top) One of four bas-reliefs in a corporate center in Solana Beach, California. Undulating shapes were carved in redwood and turned to face two traffic areas.
(bottom) Ten foot, laminated oak figure in Mercy Hospital, San Diego. The project began as a challenge to design a focal point in the long corridor of a new entrance and to satisfy several levels of opinion regarding the sensitive subject. Dedication was celebrated a year later.

Amy Pact

Pact Woodcarving
317 Cumberland Avenue
Portland, ME 04101
(207) 772-6137

Fantasy, myth and whimsy spark the designs in master woodcarver Amy Pact's museum-quality, hand-carved sculptures. The art of Sweden and ancient Egypt also influence the imagery in Pact's work. After earning a degree in three-dimensional product design from the University of Gothenberg, Sweden, Pact studied traditional woodcarving with the late Swiss master Werner Amacher and sculpture with Jan Steen of Sweden, among other noted artists.

One of Pact's specialties lies in utilizing her expert technical skills and extensive working knowledge of a wide variety of woods in the challenge of translating client needs, whether functional, ornamental or restorative, into finished pieces to suit various environments (architectural, ecclesiastical, corporate or residential) on time and within budget.

Member, National Woodcarvers Association and the American Crafts Council.
Screen, "Midsummer Daydream". American Black Walnut 60"H × 63"W × 2"D.

Contemporary Solutions
to Design Challenges

Interior design is a dynamic profession, one in which the techniques of the past are respected equally with the technology of the future.

Although today's practitioners are justifiably committed to integrating the latest technologies in the workplace and at home, interior designers rely on the decorative arts and crafts of the past to humanize modern spaces. At the same time that our highly automated world has grown sophisticated and complex, it has become increasingly vital that we preserve the precious techniques of artisans which have been passed down through the centuries.

Designers are recruiting the skills and talents of artists, sculptors, ceramists, woodworkers—craftsmen of all kinds—to help them create the look they want to achieve. Whether it's Americana, contemporary, or sleek and futuristic, the work of craft artists is a valuable part of the interior design process.

From sculptured doors to hand-painted fabrics to avant garde wall hangings, crafts inject beauty and dignity into a merely functional space, transforming it into a warm and welcoming world. For designers, handmade art objects open the door to artistic freedom, allowing them to not only shape, plan and light a space, but to furnish and adorn it in myriad styles.

Today's residential design client is no longer just the stereotypical upper-income, older person. Studies indicate that young upwardly mobile professionals in increasing numbers are enlisting the aid of designers in planning their environments. The design solutions for these clients need to be as unique and diverse as the clients themselves. Designers regard the crafts as important vehicles of self-expression for clients.

These decorative objects also lend a personal touch to a design in a way that mass-produced goods cannot. More and more, interior designers are taking advantage of the exciting options available to them through the creative use of crafts.

It is perhaps ironic that contemporary solutions to current design challenges lie with something as basic and as rooted in the American spirit as crafts. The appreciation of fine craftsmanship, which has always represented the traditional values of hard work, individualism and pride, is undergoing an important rebirth.

Crafts market centers and the opening of The American Craft Museum in New York testify to its success. With such a wide range of high-quality domestic goods produced today, the trend to purchase American items should continue to grow. After years of seeing many time-honored skills become obsolete, it's satisfying to witness their renaissance.

Joy Adcock

Joy Adcock, FASID
National President
American Society of Interior Designers

Rodger Reid

Wood Interiors by Rodger Reid
Marbledale, CT 06777
(203) 868-7706

Rodger Reid of Wood Interiors creates a timeless elegance with his panelled rooms and libraries for the home and office.

Mr. Reid works in the tradition of the master craftsmen of centuries ago. All the work is done by hand. The natural finishes are hand-rubbed with oil, then waxed to bring out a beauty that gathers warmth through the years.

Committed to the highest quality standards, Mr. Reid hand selects only the world's finest solid hardwoods.

Mr. Reid founded Wood Interiors nearly 20 years ago. He has worked with architects, designers, antique dealers and home owners in the U.S. and Canada. The beauty and design of a Wood Interiors room creates a distinctive setting for your fine furnishings.

Larry Wood

Magus Design
63 Tiffany Place
Brooklyn, NY 11231
(718) 935-9678

Wood's Studio provides a resource for designers requiring the finest work developing pieces that demand unusal proficiency in many fields of expertise. His understanding of design, coupled with his experience with contemporary materials technology, facilitates producing his own work as well as the work of other designers within time and cost restraints set up by most custom furnishings clients. The precision and attention to detail apparent in his work shown here is reflected throughout the entirety of each piece he builds, regardless of the scale, providing the smoothest possible vehicle to carry the full impact of each design. Wood acts as a liaison between designer and materials technology to produce effects in custom and prototype work that might otherwise be impractical.

(top right) Cocktail Table, 68" × 31"
First in a series called "Machinery in Motion"
(center) DETAIL: Room Screen. Brazilian rosewood inlaid with abalone and curly maple.
(bottom) Wall Hangings, 25" × 31" each.

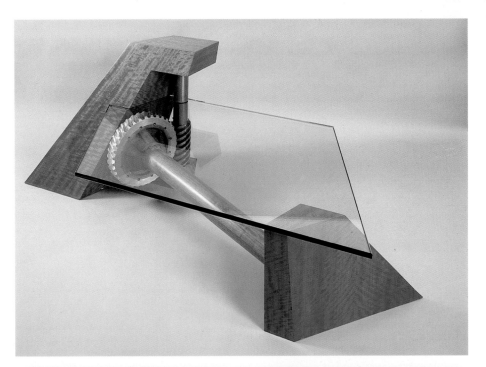

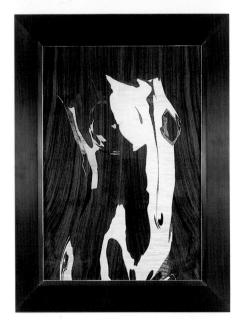

ARCHITECTURAL METAL WORK

Mark E. Bokenkamp

Bokenkamps' Forge
10132 Liberty Road
Powel, OH 43065
(614) 889-0819

Mark Bokenkamp has completed over 400 Decorative Arts commissions since 1974. Whether traditional or contemporary, his designs exhibit a subtle elegance which will enhance their surroundings. Most work is executed in mild steel and given a clear finish which accentuates the unique character of forged metal. For additional emphasis, however, some pieces incorporate copper, brass, bronze, aluminum, stainless steel or areas of translucent color.

From the finest European or Early American styles to the most avant-garde architectural and sculptural metalwork, Bokenkamp designs each piece specifically for his clients' needs. To insure a quality job he frequently travels to survey the site and has shipped works throughout the country.

"Tempest II", cast bronze, 27" × 16" × 22" ©1982, one of sixteen pieces available.

Bob and Jim Foust

Bob's Ornamental Iron Studio, Inc.
734 Southwest Boulevard
Kansas City, KS 66103
(913) 236-4444

Custom metal work in iron, aluminum or bronze, suitable for interior or exterior use; involving all phases of the metal working art.

National and international architectural metal work since 1953 includes reproduction and restoration of hand crafted hardware such as latches, knobs, levers and hinges.

Winner of seventeen national awards for design and fabrication of driveway gates, walk gates, balconies, fence, window grills, entry doors and gazebos.

Each item individually crafted to exacting standards, either from your designer or designed by Bob. A variety of finishes are available for residential and commercial settings.

Winners of the prestigious Gold Art Award by the National Ornamental Metals Manufacturers Association for 1985 and 1986. Members of the Artists and Blacksmiths Association of North America and the National Ornamental Metal Manufacturers Association.

Chris Hughes

Landmark Restoration, Inc.
RR#2, Box 8036
Milford, PA 18337
(717) 296-8354

Mr. Hughes represents a studio of craftsmen with a broad range of capabilities in wrought (hand-forged) and cast iron, as well as bronze and other non-ferrous metals. Specializing in decorative metalwork, the studio accepts commissions for restorations, original designs, fabrication from specification, or one-of-a-kind sculptural objects.

Work by Mr. Hughes has graced such national monuments as Dumbarton Oaks in Washington, DC, the Statue of Liberty and DuPont's pleasure garden in southeast Pennsylvania.

Hughes and company understand the important of on-time delivery and in-progress flexibility.
Brochure available upon request.

(top) An original console table designed and built for Dr. and Mrs. Henry Kissinger of New York City.
(bottom) Railings re-creation commissioned by Willard D. Skolnik Associates, Architects, New York City, for a landmark restoration project on Manhattan's West 11th Street.

Daneil Hurwitz

Brownswill, MD 21715
(301) 432-2154
(301) 293-1168

Mainly working on gates, grand foyer railings, and elegant lamps. Done with the love for historical design and ornament. Product's integrity is guided by iron's better and finer period. The methods used are those of the blacksmith's craft. Consultations are welcome. Art and design capabilities.

John Burgee, noted New York architect—Penthouse stairway

The White House—Restored Fine Interior Gates and Lamps

Senator John D. Rockefeller IV—Estate, Wrought Iron Entry Gate

Statue of Liberty—Bronze Arrival Gates

Call or send for our brochure

(top) Original Iron Peacock Gates
(bottom left) Original Iron Stair Railing
(bottom right) Original Iron Stair Railing

Ned James

Ned James—Wrought Metals
65 Canal Street
Turners Falls, MA 01376
(413) 863-8388

Ned James has been producing fine hand-wrought metalwork for over ten years. He works with a variety of metals including iron, copper, brass, and bronze, and in a variety of styles, traditional and contemporary. The capabilities of his well equipped shop range from forging and fabricating to metal spinning and small castings. He currently specializes in custom work for architects and designers and is comfortable working with blueprints. His products include lanterns and chandeliers, iron furniture, grilles, gates, and fencework. Graceful form, subtle detail, and careful execution mark his work.

Alex and Jack Klahm

Klahm and Sons Inc.
2151 Old Jacksonville Road
Ocala, Fl 32670
(904)622-6565

Third generation ornamental metalsmiths specializing in original and creative architectural design using both traditional and progressive metalworking techniques.

Designs incorporate forged, cast and fabricated work in copper, brass, bronze, stainless steel and iron.

Scope of work includes gates, railings, staircases, signs, decorative grills, furniture and restoration.

Major commissions include:
Restoration of all ironwork—Iolani Palace and Royal Mausoleum, Honolulu, Hawaii.
Original entry gates—Hulihee Palace, Kailua-Kona, Hawaii.
Royal Burial Crypt—Honolulu.
Bronze entry gate—Claire Booth Luce residence, Honolulu.

(top left) Royal Burial Chapel Gate, Honolulu.
(top right) Detail, Forged Copper Entry Doors, private residence.
(bottom right) Entry Gate, private residence.
(bottom left) Entry Door, Klahm and Sons studio.

We invite the opportunity to serve your creative metal needs.

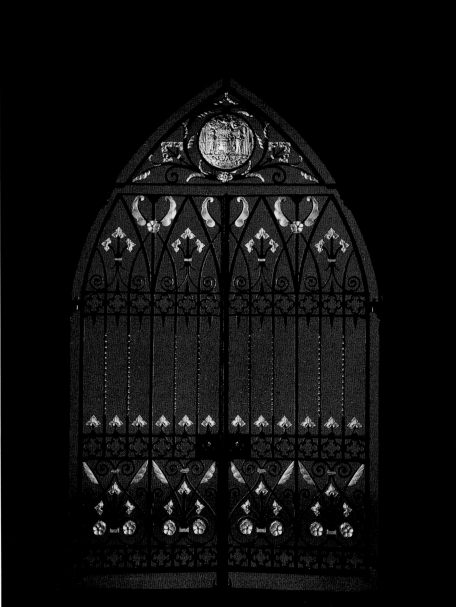

Greg Leavitt

Upper Bank Forge
476 Valleybrook Road
Wawa, PA 19063
(215) 358-1766

Greg Leavitt specializes in a broad range of forged and constructed works, both functional and sculptural. Working in ferrous and non-ferrous metals, Leavitt's work crosses a design spectrum from traditional to Art Nouveau and contemporary styles. Commissions are designed especially for each client, in close cooperation with architects and designers, by the design team of Leavitt and his wife, Lydia. Designs are executed with the attention to process and detail of a master smith, finished and installed with care and consideration for longevity.

Major commissions include numerous public sculptures in compliance with The Philadelphia Redevelopment Authority and Department of Parks and Recreation's 1% resolution. Private works include highly decorative gates and grillwork integrating sculpture and security, as well as free standing sculpture and fountains.

Leavitt's work has been exhibited at The Hudson River Museum, The University of Texas at Austin, The Philadelphia Flower Show, and The Philadelphia Museum of Art.

Representative photos available on request.

Robert E. Lepper

Mountain Ironworks and Gallery
201 Main Street, Box 460
Minturn, CO 81645
(303) 827-4226

Robert Lepper creates functional and non-functional sculpture. Each piece is original, and designed for a specific environment. His style often moves from the traditional image of ironwork into fanciful, organic shapes, integrating bronze, brass and copper with iron. He also works geometrically, sometimes including beveled and stained glass in the finished piece.

His work covers a wide range: tables, chandeliers, gates, grills, doors, railings, headboards, fireplace doors and accessories, as well as non-functional sculpture.

Robert is familiar with interfacing with architects and builders and often ships and installs his work out of the area. His iron-working studio and gallery is located eight miles from the Vail ski area in the Colorado Rockies.

(top) Driveway and person gate, forged iron, over-all width 15'6".
(bottom left) Entrance doors, glass, iron and bronze, door opening 3'6" x 7'.
(bottom right) Stairway railing, hand forged of bronze and iron.

Eric Moebius

Moebius Ironworks
421 South 2nd Street
Milwaukee, WI 53204
(414) 347-0545

Eric Moebius has been designing and producing hand-forged ironwork professionally for fifteen years. Recognized as a leader in the current Renaissance of the blacksmith's art, Moebius was chosen to represent the United States as a lecturer/demonstrator at two world blacksmithing conferences in Hereford, England.

Moebius Ironworks specializes in the design and production of architectural and residential furnishings in both contemporary and historical interpretations. Combining various materials (wood, glass, stone, etc.) with forged metalwork, Moebius has expanded the possibilities and conception of traditional ironwork.

A limited production line of tables, benches, and lighting fixtures are offered along with large commission capabilities.

A representative portfolio is available upon serious inquiry.

(top) Copper grape detail.
(bottom) Hanging kitchen pot rack
Forged copper and steel, Height 20" Width 40"

Architectural Ornamentation

Architectural ornamentation historically was an integral system of application visually detailing the structural integrity inherent in building design and architectural space.

Ornament was not considered a secondary concern of surface decoration, but rather a system of structural symbolism adding accent and focus.

The column capitals of the classical order were not simply a textural passage between the column and the lintel, but were instead an expression and direct focus of this critical, structural union. The capitals' ornamental detailing visually records and manifests this point of contact—the swelling bands and the convoluted detailing create an arena of visual dialog that literally explains the structural forces of tension and compression.

Architectural metalwork responds in kind to this symbolic role. The gate, balustrade, window grill or decorative hardware are not merely security necessities, but create a symbolic dimension of human interaction within the architectural space. Human scale, movement and gesture ultimately are the canons and foundation of formal architectural concepts.

The main function of ornament is to solicit emotional response. Emotion is engaged directly through the senses, personalizing the architectural experience with an intimacy and thus empathy, a condition that pure reason can never solicit. This personalization and humanistic dimension of ornament's role in the urban environment should not be underestimated.

Current architectural theory is redefining ornament's role within the architectural context, awakening the concerns, attitudes and spirit that have lain dormant during the years of the modernist movement.

In this Post Modern era, hopefully the lesson learned from the excessive eclecticism and debasement of ornament during the Victorian era will not be forgotten. Now the vital challenge of architects and designers is to create an ornamental vernacular that reflects our humanity and cultural sensibilities.

The danger during this period of transition, with all its ambiguities, would be to grasp the convenient shroud of historicism to drape our buildings—this would indeed stifle the spirit and quest for a new vision.

Albert Paley
Master Metalworker
Rochester, New York

Albert Paley

Paley Studios, Ltd.
11 Prince Street
Rochester, NY 14607
(716) 461-5087

Founded in metalworking disciplines, the studios produce large-scale sculpture and a wide range of architectural ornamentation—fences, gates, fountains, archways, window grills, door pulls, etc. Other related objects within the decorative arts lineage include tables, lecterns, mirrors, plant stands, fireplace units, etc. All work is designed and produced by Paley Studios.

(bottom) Window Screen, forged and fabricated mild steel and bronze; 82"W × 63"H (Private Commission)

David A. Ponsler

Wonderland Products, Inc.
5772 Lenox Avenue
P.O. Box 6074
Jacksonville, FL 32205
(904) 786-0144

The forged railing with bronze embellishment represents one of many styles of ironwork we design and fabricate. Our work encompasses architectural pieces, furniture and sculpture of traditional and modern styles.

Wonderland Products Incorporated, founded in 1950, is the recipient of numerous national awards and has international trade affiliations.

We welcome inquiries and will be pleased to provide references.

Nol Putnam

White Oak Forge, Ltd.
P.O. Box 341
The Plains, VA 22171
(703) 253-5269

The White Oak Forge produces one-of-a-kind commissioned work designed for those who appreciate finely wrought iron. All the work is heated, shaped over the anvil and joined in the traditional ways of the craft. We are happy to design work for a given space, to work from architectural drawings, or in concert with client and architect. Past projects have ranged from furniture, house hardware, balconies and stair railings, to garden and entrance gates.

We also are happy to assist in restorations of earlier ironwork. This may range from simple consultation to actually doing the work ourselves.

If you want truly hand-forged and embellished ironwork, we urge you to contact the White Oak Forge. We would be happy to send a brochure upon request.

Lee Sauder

Woods Creek Forge
223 McLaughlin Street
Lexington, VA 24450
(703) 463-6632

Lee Sauder has devoted fourteen years to forging iron. His sculptural as well as his functional pieces are designed as expressions of, and focal points for, their environment.

Joel A. Schwartz

Schwartz's Forge & Metalworks
P.O. Box 205, Forge Hollow Road
Deansboro, NY 13328
(315) 841-4477

Schwartz's Forge & Metalworks designs and produces works that complement and enhance their environment. All projects are treated in a manner deserving of the blacksmith's art. In the tradition of past masters, careful attention is given to every detail during the design, fabrication and installation phases. The work has been recognized by numerous contemporary and restoration architects and designers for its high quality of design and craftsmanship. All pieces are individually designed and created. Care is taken to preserve the architect's and designer's conceptual and visual intent. A representative portfolio is available upon request.

GALLERIES AND RESOURCE PEOPLE

California

del Mano Gallery
11981 San Vicente Blvd.
Los Angeles, CA 90049
(213) 476-8508
Ray Leier
Jan Peters
A showcase for the finest
contemporary crafts in all media.

Nancy Epstein Gallery
9301 Wilshire Boulevard
Suite 614
Beverly Hills, CA 90210
(213) 859-0567
Nancy Epstein, Partner
Jane Wyler, Partner
Carla Tulchin, Partner
The finest handcrafted and signed
ceramics, handblown glassware,
tableware and other objets d'art.

Wita Gardiner Gallery
535 4th Avenue
San Diego, CA 92101
(619) 231-2366
Wita Gardiner, Ph.D.
Contemporary arts gallery of
sculptural ceramics, glass,
jewelry and fiber.

International Gallery
643 G Street
San Diego, CA 92101
(619) 235-8255
Stephen Ross
Collector quality works including
contemporary crafts, textiles,
folk, primitive and naive art.

Dan Jacobs Fine Art
P.O. Box 1491
Alpine, CA 92001
(619) 445-5370
By appointment only. Important
contemporary American crafts.
All media.

Colorado

Joan Robey Gallery
939 Broadway
Denver, CO 80206
(303) 355-7741
Mixed media, sculpture, glass,
clay and paper.

Connecticut

Artsource
152 Kings Highway North
Westport, CT 06880
(203) 222-9264
Ellen Schiffman
Serving designers, architects,
corporations, developers to
enhance environments through art.

Company of Craftsmen
43 West Main Street
Mystic, CT 06355
(203) 536-4189
Gallery representing contemporary
American craftsmen working in
all media.

Latitudes, Ltd.
68 Greenwich Avenue
Greenwich, CT 06830
(203) 661-0841
Mark Fox
American ceramics, glass, fiber.
Individual/corporate commissions,
decorative or architectural.

District of Columbia

**Saindon and Seligmann
Fine Art Services, Inc.**
1020 19th Street, NW
Washington, DC 20036
(202) 223-4121
Art consultants to corporations;
commissioned works of fiber,
glass, etc.

Florida

Art Sources, Inc.
1253 Southshore Drive
Orange Park, FL 32073
(904) 269-2014
Jacqueline M. Holmes, President
Development of corporate art
programs; major interest in fine
art applications of craft media.

Gallery Five
363 Tequesta Drive
Tequesta, FL 33469
(305) 747-5555
Paul W. Coben
Fine crafts and wearable art by
over 150 American artists.

Pepper's Revival
1006 West Highway 434
Longwood, FL 32750
(305) 260-0547
Pepper Danowitz, Owner
A mixture of contemporary and
country handcrafts (25 miles
north of Disney).

Georgia

Swanston Fine Arts
177 Harris Street NW
Atlanta, GA 30303
(404) 524-4066
Thomas R. Swanston Jr., President
Paul R. Chojnowski, Director
The total art source for
architecture, design and
corporate communities.

Idaho

The Hissing Goose Gallery
620 Sunvalley Road
P.O. Box 597
Ketchum, ID 83340
(208) 726-3036
Three-dimensional art, including
sculpture, furniture, wearable
art, jewelry, fiber and
contemporary folk art.

Maryland

AMERICAN CRAFT SHOWROOM
Suite 200 Mill Centre
3000 Chestnut Avenue
Baltimore, MD 21211
(301) 889-2933
Susan Graves
Decorative accessories by
American artisans. Discounts
to the trade. Also at SFMC in
High Point, NC/Space D-408.

Massachusetts

**BUYERS MARKET
of American Crafts/Boston**
Suite 300 Mill Centre
3000 Chestnut Avenue
Baltimore, MD 21211
(301) 889-2933
Karen Levin
June 21-24, 1987, June 20-23, 1988/
900 exhibits/
Bayside Expo Center/Boston, MA.

**Pinch Pottery and
the Clay Gallery**
150 Main Street
Northhampton, MA 01060
(413) 586-4509
Leslie Ferrin, Owner
Mara Superior, Owner
Representing over 200 clay
artists and potters featuring
annual teapot exhibitions.

Santa Fe Expo
Tisbury Marketplace
Vineyard Haven, MA 02568
(617) 693-3144
Gail Lofberg
Fine American crafts—
consultants for corporate and
residential interiors.

Society of Arts and Crafts
175 Newbury Street
Boston, MA 02116
(617) 266-1810
Contemporary Crafts Gallery,
est. 1897. All media, special
emphasis on furniture.

Michigan

The Yaw Gallery
550 North Woodward
Birmingham, MI 48011
(313) 647-5470
Nancy Yaw
Lillian Zonars
Gallery of 19th and 20th century
decorative arts; textiles,
metalsmithing, ceramics.

Missouri

Craft Alliance Gallery
6640 Delmar
St. Louis, MO 63130
(314) 725-1151
Barbara Jedda
The gallery exhibits and has for
sale contemporary American crafts.

New Jersey

Dexterity Ltd.
26 Church Street
Montclair, NJ 07042
(201) 746-5370
Shirley Zafirau, Owner
Jay Easton, Manager
Providing a wide variety of
services for the trade.

Santa Fe Expo
2 Blue Sky Lane
Montvale, NJ 07645
(201) 391-3336
Gail Lofberg
Consultants in art and fine
crafts for corporate and
residential interiors.

New York

Craft Company No. 6
785 University Avenue
Rochester, NY 14607
(716) 473-3413
Lynn Allinger, Owner/Director
Specializing in wood, clay,
galss, metal and jewelry. Also,
decorative accessories.

The Gallery at Workbench
470 Park Avenue South
New York, NY 10016
(212) 481-5454
Vanessa S. Lynn, Director
Bernice Wollman, Director
Contemporary handmade
furniture on exhibition
and by commission.

National Craft Showroom
11 E. 26th Street, 3rd floor
New York, NY 10010
212/689-0010
Norbert N. Nelson, Director
Quality American crafts at
wholesale prices year round.

Opus II Accessories
979 Third Avenue
New York, NY 10022
(212) 980-1990
Irv Frank
The foremost contemporary
accessory source exclusively for
interior designers.

North Carolina

Mountain Magic
Green Mansions Village
Hwy. 105, Rt. 1, Box 275
Banner Elk, NC 28604
(704) 963-6629
Bill Fitch
Judy Fitch
Gallery of contemporary crafts
featuring pottery, basketry,
jewelry and fantasy.

Ohio

**A Show of Hands by Ohio
Designer Craftsmen**
Convention Place Mall
Fifth and Elm Street
Cincinnati, OH 45202
(513) 421-7119
Diane Stafford, Manager

**A Show of Hands by Ohio
Designer Craftsmen**
Lane Avenue Shopping Center
1677 West Lane Avenue
Columbus, OH 43221
(614) 486-7154
Ann Adams, Manager

**A Show of Hands by Ohio
Designer Craftsmen**
The Ohio Center
400 N. High Street
Columbus, OH 43215
(614) 224-7119
Ann Adams, Manager

**Ohio Designer Craftsmen
Gallery**
2164 Riverside Drive
Columbus, OH 43221
(614) 486-7119
Hal Stevens, Manager

**Sylvia Ullman
American Crafts Gallery**
13010 Woodland Avenue
Cleveland, OH 44120
(216) 231-2008
Sylvia Ullman, Partner
Marilyn B. Bialosky, Partner
Representing American
craftspeople in working with
architects and designers.

Oklahoma

Gallery 26 East
3509 South Peoria Avenue
Tulsa, OK 74105
(918) 749-7596
Sally Bachman, Director
A gallery of contemporary crafts
representing local, regional and
national artists.

Oregon

American Tapestry Alliance
HC 63 Box 570-D
Chiloquin, OR 97624
(503) 783-2507
Jim Brown, Director
Complete source of professional
flat tapestry weavers in
U.S and Canada.

Pennsylvania

BUYERS MARKET
of American Crafts/Valley Forge
Suite 300 Mill Centre
3000 Chestnut Avenue
Baltimore, MD 21211
(301) 889-2933
Karen Levin
February 13-16, 1988/800 exhibits in
the Valley Forge Convention Center.

Gallery 500
Church and Old York Roads
Elkins Park, PA 19117
(215) 572-1203
Gary Pelkey, Director
Contemporary American paintings,
art, crafts, all media. Corporate
art consulting.

Society for Art in Crafts
2100 Smallman Street
Pittsburgh, PA 15222
(412) 828-6121
Linda Metropulos, Ex. Dir.
Non-profit for contemporary craft
artists: exhibitions; education;
marketing outlet.

The Studio in Swarthmore
14 Park Avenue
Swarthmore, PA 19081
(215) 543-5779
Lee Gilbert
Contemporary craft/art: original
watercolors, prints, pottery,
glass, fiber, metal, wood.

South Carolina

Carol Saunders Gallery
927 Gervais Street
Columbia, SC 29201
(803) 256-3046
Carol Saunders

Texas

Hanson Galleries
800 West Belt G 137
Town & Country Center
Houston, TX 77024
(713) 984-1242
Larry Williams
Donna Milstein
Three dimensional American
handcrafted ceramics, wood, and
blown glass.

Virginia

Gallery 3
213 Market Street
Roanoke, VA 24011
(703) 343-9698
Andy Williams
Maronda Williams
A fine arts and crafts gallery
celebrating the spirit of
American craftsmen.

The Stanley Gallery
333 West 21st Street
Norfolk, VA 23517
(804) 623-9121
Nancy Moore Stanley
Contemporary fine art and crafts,
by national and international artists.

Wisconsin

Katie Gingrass Gallery
714 North Milwaukee Street
Milwaukee, WI 53202
(414) 289-0855
Katie Gingrass, Owner
Referral service for designers
and architects; national and
international glass artists.

NATIONAL CRAFT ORGANIZATIONS

American Association of Woodturners
P.O.Box 982
San Marcos, TX 78667
512/396-8689
Robert Rubel, Administrator

American Craft Council
40 West 53rd Street
New York, NY 10019
212/956-3535
Norton L. Berman, Executive Director

American Tapestry Alliance
HC 63, Box 570-D
Chiloquin, OR 97624
503/783-2507
Jim Brown, Director

Artists-Blacksmiths' Association of North America (ABANA)
Box 303
Cedarburg, WI 53012
414/375-0278
Ruth Cook, Executive Secretary

Embroiderers Guild of America
200 Fourth Avenue
Louisville, KY 40202
502/589-6956
Cynthia Triblehorn, President

Glass Art Society
P.O. Box 1364
Corning Museum
Corning, NY 14830
607/937-5371
Louise Volpe, Secretary to Public Programs

Handweavers Guild of America
65 La Salle Road
West Hartford, CT 06107
203/233-5124
Karen Louise Johnson, Executive Director

National Council on Education for the Ceramic Arts (NCECA)
P.O. Box 1677
Bandon, OR 97411
503/347-4394
Regina Brown, Executive Secretary

National Wood Carvers Association
7424 Miami Avenue
Cincinnati, OH 45243
513/561-9051
Edward Gallenstein, President

Society of Furniture Artists
P.O. Box 416, Kendall Square
Cambridge, MA 02142
617/636-5918
Alphonse Mattia, President

Society of North American Goldsmiths (SNAG)
P.O. Box 13028
Charlotte, NC 28211
704/365-5507
Bob Mitchell, Business Manager

Surface Design Association
311 E. Washington Street
Fayetteville, TN 37334
615/433-6804
Stephen Blumrich, Managing Editor

Woodworking Association of North America
Box 706, Route 3
Plymouth, NH 03264
604/536-3876
Brian Murphy, Managing Director

INDEX

CRAFT ARTISTS BY STATE

PHOTO CREDITS

13 Martin Doyle
16 Sundra Photog.
17 Edward Claycomb
18 Bill Wasserman
23 Steve Budman
26 Robert Arruda
34 Jerry Grayson
47 Ray Bugelsky
55 Jim & Sue Foster
56 Rick Sisciliano
57 Rick Sisciliano
60 Lee Fatherree
62 Frank Poole
64 Tommy Elder
65 Paulina Eccless
72 Mark Rice
74 (bronze) Image Farm
   (glass) Sherman Howe
84 Mel Schockner
99 Sidney Sander
102 Artist
104 Woody Packard
113 Gary McKinnis
117 Timothy Savardi
119 (top) Dick Busher
   (bottom) Roger Schreiber
126 Bobby Hanson
138 Allen Bragdon
141 Steve Budman
145 Rob Karosis
147 William Thuss
156 Dennis Geaney
157 Tom Cooper
160 Barry Halkin
162 Freelance Photographers Limited
175 (top left) Paul Avis
   (bottom) Paul Avis
   (top right) Jack Bingham
177 Bill Bachhuber
182 Rick Echelmeyer
184 Peter Braune
185 Peter Braune
192 Jerry Anthony
   (bottom) Artist
194 (left) Edward Claycomb
   (top right) Bobby Hanson
   (bottom right) David Haas
195 Jim Kuska
   U.W. Photo Media

201 Tom Long
206 Gary Bogue
226 Stephen Diehl, Vici Zaremba
228 Ken Wagner
234 Melville McLean
244 Peter Turo
263 James Lemkin
273 Brendan Poh
275 Tony Walsh
285 Reis Birdwhistell
287 Mark Rice
291 Kenneth E. Fields
294 James Mejuto
300 Robert Clink
   G. Newyear & Co.
306 Alan Oransky
307 (left) Bill Grant
   (right) Alan Oransky
309 (top right) Steve Kaminoff
   (bottom left) Steve Kaminoff
   (bottom right) Roger Schreiber
311 Tim Lee
312 (top) Artist
   Leland Cook
314 Geoff Kilmer
321 Frank Baptie
324 Lee Fatherree
325 Lee Fatherree
326 Art Walker
   Interior Design Magazine
331 Dennis Schobot
338 (top) Artist
   (bottom) Gary Gramley
339 Richard Walker
347 (top) Museum of Fine Arts, Boston
   (bottom) Steve Diehl, Vicki Zoremba
349 (top) James P. McCoy
   (bottom right) David J. Leveille
   (bottom left) Robert Andrusziewicz
359 Phillip Swetz
361 Tommy Elder
362 Jim Jernigan
364 Dann Coffey